NOW IS THE DAY OF SALVATION

Now Is the Day OF SALVATION

An Audience-Oriented Study
of 2 Corinthians 5:16—6:2

Timothy Milinovich

☙PICKWICK *Publications* • Eugene, Oregon

NOW IS THE DAY OF SALVATION
An Audience-Oriented Study of 2 Corinthians 5:16—6:2

Copyright © 2011 Timothy Milinovich. All rights reserved. Except for brief quotations in critical publications or reviews, no part of this book may be reproduced in any manner without prior written permission from the publisher. Write: Permissions, Wipf and Stock Publishers, 199 W. 8th Ave., Suite 3, Eugene, OR 97401.

BWHEBB, BWHEBL, BWTRANSH [Hebrew]; BWGRKL, BWGRKN, and BWGRKI [Greek] Postscript® Type 1 and TrueTypeT fonts Copyright © 1994–2009 BibleWorks, LLC. All rights reserved. These Biblical Greek and Hebrew fonts are used with permission and are from BibleWorks, software for Biblical exegesis and research.

Pickwick Publications
An Imprint of Wipf and Stock Publishers
199 W. 8th Ave., Suite 3
Eugene, OR 97401

www.wipfandstock.com

ISBN 13: 978-1-60899-764-0

Cataloging-in-Publication data:

Milinovich, Timothy

Now is the day of salvation : an audience-oriented study of 2 Corinthians 5:16—6:2 / by Timothy Milinovich.

xvi + 174 p. ; 23 cm. Includes bibliographical references.

ISBN 13: 978-1-60899-764-0

1. Bible. N.T. Corinthians, 2nd, V, 16–VI, 2—Criticism, interpretation, etc. I. Title.

BS2675.52 M55 2011

Manufactured in the U.S.A.

Dedicated to my children,

Thomas and Margaret

Contents

Preface • ix
Acknowledgments • xi
List of Abbreviations • xiii

Introduction • 1
1 Method and Perspective • 13
2 Chiastic Structure in 2 Corinthians 1:1—6:2 • 24
3 Audience Response to 1:1—2:13 • 58
4 Audience Response to 2:14—4:14 • 79
5 Audience Response to 4:15—5:15 • 99
6 Audience Response to 5:16—6:2 • 129
7 Summary and Conclusions • 145

Bibliography • 165

Preface

This study is a revised version of my doctoral dissertation, entitled "Paul's Ministry and God's New Creation: An Audience-Oriented Study of 2 Corinthians 5:16—6:2," written under the direction of John Paul Heil at The Catholic University of America (Washington, DC). Frank Matera and Frank Gignac served as readers. The dissertation was defended October 23, 2009.

The topic for this particular study came about during a conversation with Fr. Heil after the completion of my comprehensive exams. The audience-oriented method intrigued me, and a book-length study with the method had yet to be used on 2 Corinthians. This letter seemed to lend itself well to the method, since its apparent focus is to repair the relationship with the audience. The call to exhortation in 5:20 was the initial entry point for the study, and the research went on from there.

I did not intend to find chiasms. The authorial audience was always the focus of this study. The structures presented in this text came about—or rather, were made apparent—as I translated the letter and analyzed its structure and content to get to the climactic call to reconciliation in 5:16—6:2. An auditory learner, reading the text aloud in the midst of my research brought to light the lexical connections that then became one of the more pronounced contributions of the study as a whole. Spreading pieces of the text on the dining room floor of our house helped to confirm these and bring to light other connections, much to my wife's dismay.

Several libraries took part in this production: Mullen Library at The Catholic University of America (Washington, DC); Latimer Family Library of St. Vincent College (Latrobe, PA); Eberly Library of Waynesburg University (Waynesburg, PA); Whitefish Bay Public Library

(Milwaukee, WI); Rolfing Library at Trinity International University (Deerfield, IL); Raynor Memorial Libraries at Marquette University (Milwaukee, WI); Coates Library at Trinity University (San Antonio, TX); D. E. O'Shaughnessy Library at Oblate School of Theology (San Antonio, TX); and Maybee Library at the University of the Incarnate Word (San Antonio, TX). I am grateful for the support and aid that I received from the staff members and librarians at each campus.

This book went through minor revisions and reformatting between the deposit and its final submission to the editor. For better accessibility, the chapters have been divided and footnotes regarding textual and translation issues have been modified.

San Antonio, TX
June 23, 2010

Acknowledgments

The journey preceding this study began well over a decade ago, and I am grateful to my parents, Tom and Debbie; my grandparents, Anne Marie, Marion ("Jab"), and Hilda; and my sister, Karen, for all of their encouragement through the years.

I am greatly indebted to John Paul Heil, my dissertation advisor, for his counsel, criticism, and incredible response time to questions and chapters alike. The remainder of the New Testament faculty at The Catholic University of America, Frank Matera and Frank Gignac, served as my readers, and I am thankful for their challenging questions and relentless encouragement.

A large portion of this work was written during the Jubilee Year of St. Paul the Apostle (June 28, 2008 to June 29, 2009), during which time I served as Director of Religious Education at St. Ann Parish, Waynesburg, PA. This community gave me considerable support and understanding regarding the realities of pastoral care.

Special thanks are warranted for the Benedictines, faculty, and students of St. Vincent College, where I served first as student and then as instructor; and to my colleagues and students at Waynesburg University and the University of the Incarnate Word, for their inspiration, patience, and exuberance. I am also grateful to my father-in-law, Prof. Samir Massouh, and to my colleagues, T. J. Rogers, Chuck Bieter, and Aron Maghsoudi, for their insightful comments on particular sections. I also greatly appreciate the work of my editor, D. Christopher Spinks, and the editorial staff at Pickwick Publications in producing this text.

Lastly, three very special people need mention. I am grateful to my wife, Leila, for her understanding, love, encouragement, and advice. Her sense of humor and positive outlook on the one hand, and sobering criticism on the other hand, served as the perfect complement to either my dashed dreams or overly intense convictions. My children, Thomas and Margaret, serve as the bookends to this work—in a very real way. Thomas's ultrasound photos emboldened me as I wrote the proposal and first chapter, and Margaret's photos did the same as I was preparing this text for publication. It is to these two that I dedicate this book.

Abbreviations

AB	Anchor Bible
ABD	*Anchor Bible Dictionary*, ed. D. N. Freedman et al., 6 vols. (New York, 1992)
AGSU	Arbeiten zur Geschichte des Spätjudentums und Urchristentums
AnBib	Analecta biblica
ASV	American Standard Version
BAGD	Bauer, W., W. F. Arndt, F. W. Gingrich, and F. W. Danker, *Greek-English Lexicon of the New Testament*, 3rd ed.
BETL	Bibliotheca ephemeridum theologicarum lovaniensium
BFCT	Beträge zur Förderung christlicher Theologie
Bib	*Biblica*
BN	*Biblische Notizen*
BSac	*Bibliotheca sacra*
BTB	*Biblical Theoloy Bulletin*
CBQ	*Catholic Biblical Quarterly*
CBQMS	Catholic Biblical Quarterly Monograph Series
DPL	*Dictionary of Paul and his Letters*, eds. G. F. Hawthorn and R. P. Martin (Downers Grove, IL, 1993)
Ebib	Etudes bibliques
Ep.	*Epistle*, Pliny
ESV	English Standard Version
ETL	*Ephemerides theologicae lovanienses*
EvQ	*Evangelical Quarterly*
ExpTim	*Expository Times*
FRLANT	Forschungen zur Religion und Literatur des Alten und Neuen Testament
GNV	Geneva Bible
Greg	*Gregorianum*
HB	Hebrew Bible

HNTC	Harper's New Testament Commentaries	
ICC	International Critical Commentary	
IDB	*The Interpreter's Dictionary of the Bible*, ed. G. A. Buttrick, 4 vols. (Nashville, 1962)	
Int	*Interpretation*	
INTCS	InterVarsity New Testament Commentary Series	
JB	Jerusalem Bible	
JBL	*Journal of Biblical Literature*	
JBQ	*Jewish Bible Quarterly*	
JSNT	*Journal for the Study of the New Testament*	
JSNTSup	Journal for the Study of the New Testament Supplement Series	
JSOTSup	Journal for the Study of the Old Testament: Supplement Series	
JTS	*Journal of Theological Studies*	
KJV	King James Version	
LEC	Library of Early Christianity	
LSJ	Liddell, H. G., R. Scott, and H. S. Jones, *A Greek-English Lexicon*, 9th ed. (Oxford, 1996)	
LXX	Septuagint	
NA27	Nestle-Aland, 27th ed.	
NAB	New American Bible	
NASB	New American Standard Version	
NEB	New English Bible	
NICNT	New International Commentary on the New Testament	
NIGTC	New International Greek Testament Commentary	
NIV	New International Version	
NJB	New Jerusalem Bible	
NKJV	New King James Version	
NovT	*Novum Testamentum*	
NRSV	New Revised Standard Version	
NTC	New Testament in Context	
NTG	New Testament Guides	
NTL	New Testament Library	
NTS	*New Testament Studies*	
NTT	New Testament Theology	
OBT	Overtures to Biblical Theology	
Od.	*Odyssey*, Homer	
P.Oxy.	Oxyronchus Papyri	
Pss. Sol.	*Psalms of Solomon*	
RB	*Revue Biblique*	
REB	Revised English Bible	

RSV	Revised Standard Version
Quinct.	*Pro Quintcio*, Cicero
ResQ	*Restoration Quarterly*
RevExp	*Review and Expositor*
RSV	Revised Standard Version
SBEC	Studies in the Bible and Early Christianity
SBLSBS	Society of Biblical Literature Sources for Biblical Study
SBLStBl	Society of Biblical Literature Studies in Biblical Literature
SBLSymS	Society of Biblical Literature Symposium Series
Sib. Or.	*Sibylline Oracles*
SNTSMS	Society for New Testament Studies Monograph Series
SP	Sacra pagina
TCGNT	*A Textual Commentary on the Greek New Testament*, B. M. Metzger
TDNT	*Theological Dictionary of the New Testament*, eds. G. Kittel and G. Friedrich, trans. G. W. Bromiley, 10 vols. (Grand Rapids, 1964–76)
TNTC	Tyndale New Testament Commentaries
T. Dan	*Testament of Dan*
T. Gad	*Testament of Gad*
T. Reu.	*Testament of Reuben*
T. Sim.	*Testament of Simeon*
TynBul	*Tyndale Bulletin*
VT	*Vetus Testamentum*
WBC	Word Biblical Commentary
WTJ	*Westminster Theological Journal*
WUNT	Wissenschaftliche Untersuchungen zum Neuen Testament
ZNW	*Zeitschrift für die neutestamentliche Wissenschaft und die Kunde der älteren Kirche*

Introduction

Second Corinthians 5:16—6:2 rests within one of the most magisterial and problematic sections in Paul's letters. Paul's ministry was in danger at Corinth. Tension grew between Paul and his community after the rough reception of 1 Corinthians and the painful visit. To make matters worse, opponents infiltrated the community there and undermined Paul's authority by questioning his apostolic commission (2 Cor 10–11). Dissension ensued when some Corinthian believers sided with the opponents against him (11:1–6). In 5:16—6:2 Paul explicitly calls on the community to accept and be reconciled to his ministry.[1]

The description of God's new creation and reconciliation in Christ serves as a catalyst for Paul's call for the Corinthian audience to be reconciled to his ministry. Paul sets forth his gospel before the community as proof of his divine commission to preach new creation and reconciliation in Christ (5:16—6:2). Since the sinless Christ has died on the cross for humanity (see 5:14–15), humanity's sins are no longer credited against them (5:19), and thus those who are in Christ and heed his ambassadors (5:20) are now a new creation (5:17).

Numerous previous studies have varied on how to delimit the section and how to understand the call to reconciliation in 5:18–20 within Paul's theology. These studies have focused on the perspective of the

---

1. *Pace* Matera (*II Corinthians*, 156–58), 6:11—7:4 does not reflect an "explicit" call to reconciliation from Paul to the community, per se. The content certainly implies an attempt to assuage current tension in their relationship (e.g., 7:2), but 5:16—6:2 contains an explicit call to reconciliation since the passage makes repeated use of the noun καταλλαγή ("reconciliation") and the verb καταλλάσσω ("to reconcile"). The section 6:11—7:4 contains no mention of these terms. The content of the section may well echo themes of explicit reconciliation, but it does so in a complementary and secondary manner compared to 5:16—6:2.

author Paul, often comparing 2 Cor 5:18–20 with Rom 5:1–10 (among other texts), or attempting to understand the origin of the concept of reconciliation within his theological matrix.[2] This study proposes a new interpretation of Paul's call to reconciliation in 5:16—6:2 by focusing on how the authorial audience (i.e., the "textual" or "implied" audience) responds to the microchiastic structure of 5:16—6:2 and the macrochiastic structure of 4:15—6:2. [3]

The audience-oriented method adopted for this study is "text-centered" in that it analyzes how the authorial audience responds to the oral presentation of a text. This method demonstrates for modern readers what the audience experiences within the text's performance, that is, this method *shows* what the audience *hears*. Within this method the exegete "listens" carefully to repeated terms, themes, and structures.

The present study represents the first audience-oriented study of 2 Cor 5:16—6:2 (and 1:1—6:2 as a whole) and demonstrates it to be a chiastic unit with an A (5:16–17)–B (5:18)–B´ (5:19–20)–A´ (5:21—6:2) structure that is grounded objectively on grammatical and lexical criteria. Furthermore, this study demonstrates 5:16—6:2 to be the closing A´ unit to a six-part macrochiastic unit in 4:15—6:2, and thus presents lexical parallels with the A unit, 4:15–18. As a chiastic unit, 5:16—6:2 has paralleling elements that develop Paul's exhortation as it progresses through the unit's structure. In addition to being the conclusion of the macrochiasm 4:15—6:2, the unit 5:16—6:2 is also shown to be the climactic exhortation of 1:1—6:2, which consists of three macrochiastic arguments (1:8—2:13; 2:14—4:14; 4:15—6:2) and emphasizes the symbiotic relationship that Paul and the audience share in Christ.

History of Interpretation

Delimitations of the Text

The passage considered in this study, 2 Cor 5:16—6:2, has been studied under various delimitations that can be grouped into two major categories: 5:11–21 and 5:11—6:2. This section will survey the major positions

---

2. See, e.g., Matera, *II Corinthians*, 126–27; Fitzmyer, "Reconciliation," 169; Harris, *Second Epistle*, 454–55; Martin, *Reconciliation*, passim.

3. The term "authorial audience" and the audience-oriented method will be discussed in greater detail in the next chapter.

regarding the textual delimitation and demonstrate why this study prefers 5:16—6:2 as the proper delimitation.

Several influential commentaries and biblical translations delimit the text as 5:11–21 for thematic and grammatical reasons.[4] Jan Lambrecht, for instance, argues that "a different line of thought [breaks] through" in 5:11: the future destination of believers in 4:16—5:10 is replaced by the present situation of salvation in 5:11.[5] Furthermore, he alleges, the grammatical connector οὖν in v. 20 concludes the paragraph of 5:11–21.

Other scholars who agree with the terminus at v. 21 see v. 14 as the proper genesis of the passage. Reimand Bieringer delimits the section as 5:14–21 based on the different theological content in 5:11–13 and 5:14–21.[6] Along with Bieringer, Henrick Boer contends that the subject ἡμᾶς has different referents in vv. 11–13 (Paul alone) and vv. 14–21 (Paul and his audience). In addition, Boer alleges there are no thematic links between Paul's defense of his ministry and the discussion of reconciliation.[7]

Despite the large number who prefer v. 21 as the terminus, several scholars consider the terminus at v. 21 to be artificial and argue that 6:2 is the proper endpoint. Richard Mead, e.g., claims the division at v. 21 originates from the "tyranny [sic] of chapter divisions."[8] Mead contends that Paul commonly cites OT Scripture at the climax of an argument.[9] The OT quotation in 6:1–2 then necessitates that 6:2 be the terminus

---

4. Lambrecht ("Reconcile," 161–209) exemplifies the scholars who delimit the text as 5:11–21. Other scholars who follow this delimitation include Barrett (*Second Epistle*, 161–62), Martin (*2 Corinthians*, 115–69), Martyn ("Epistemology," 89–110), and Matera (*II Corinthians*, 127–28), among others. Bible translations with this delimitation include RSV, REB, NIV, and NAB.

5. Lambrecht ("Reconcile," 170) constructs this section concentrically: (a) 5:11–13, "self-defense"; (b) 5:14–21, "emissary of Christ"; (a′) 6:1–10, "self-defense." This tripartite structure seems to contradict his delimitation of 5:11–21 as an independent section.

6. Bieringer, "Versöhnung," 432.

7. Boer, "2 Corinthians 5:14—6:2," 529–30. Against Boer, the different referents of ἡμᾶς do not warrant a prominent break at v. 14; theological themes in vv. 11–13, (such as internal/external and seen/unseen contrasts) are seen in 5:16 and 5:17.

8. Mead, "2 Corinthians 5:14–21." Despite the title of his article, Mead argues that the correct delimitations are 5:14—6:2. The chapter divisions are traditionally believed to be introduced into the biblical text by Stephen Langton, ca. 1200 CE.

9. Mead ("2 Corinthians 5:14–21," 144–45) lists a considerable number of examples of Paul's climactic use of OT citations. See also Heil, *Rhetorical Role*, 10–15.

of the section since a break at 5:21 defuses the poignant statements in 6:1–2. Paul Barnett adds that Paul's ambassadorial actions in 6:1–2 stand in thematic unity with the defense of his ministry in 5:11–21.[10]

Despite the arguments stated above, this study will treat 5:16—6:2 as a section. This position is grounded on grammatical data since ὥστε in v. 16 presents a logical consequence of the activities of Christ in vv. 14–15, and the terminus of the section is denoted by the abrupt shift from appeal in 6:2 to a recitation of Paul's hardships in 6:3.[11]

In addition, the chiastic A-B-B′-A′ structure in 5:16—6:2 presented in this study affirms the grammatical delimitations. The words "now" (νῦν), "behold" (ἰδού), "to know" (γινώσκω), and "to become" (γίνομαι) establish the A (5:16–17) and A′ (5:21—6:2) sections of the chiasm. The B (5:18) and B′ (5:19–20) sections are marked by the repeated use of the terms "reconciliation/reconcile" (καταλλάσσω/καταλλαγή) and "us" (ἡμῖν).

> A 5:16 As a result, *now* [νῦν] we regard no one in a worldly manner; even if we once *knew* [ἐγνώκαμεν] Christ in a worldly way, we do not *know* [γινώσκομεν] him so *now* [νῦν]. 17 As a result, whoever is in Christ is a new creation. The old things pass away; *behold* [ἰδού]: new things *have come* [γέγονεν]!
>
>> B 18 And everything is from God, who has *reconciled* [καταλλάξαντος] us to himself through Christ and given *us* [ἡμῖν] the ministry of *reconciliation* [καταλλαγῆς],
>>
>> B′ 19 such that God was *reconciling* [καταλλάσσων] the world to himself through Christ, not holding them accountable for their sins, and placed on *us* [ἡμῖν] the message of *reconciliation* [καταλλαγῆς]. 20 So we are ambassadors on Christ's behalf, as though God were pleading through us. We implore on Christ's behalf: be *reconciled* [καταλλάγητε] to God.
>
> A′ 21 He made the one who did not *know* [γνόντα] sin to be sin for us so that we might *become* [γενώμεθα] the righteousness of God in him. 6:1 Working in unison then, we plead with you not to receive

---

10. Barnett, *Second Epistle*, 299, 315. Witherington (*Conflict*, 199–201) argues on rhetorical grounds that 5:11—6:2 is a well-conceived argument that climaxes with the proclamations at 5:19–20 and 6:1–2. Boer ("2 Corinthians 5:14—6:2," 530) agrees that the paraenetic appeals in 5:19–20 and 6:1–2 establish semantic continuity.

11. Harris, *Second Epistle*, 424–26.

the grace of God in vain. 2 For it says: "At the acceptable time I heard you, and on the day of salvation I helped you." *Behold* [ἰδού]: *now* [νῦν] is the acceptable time! *Behold* [ἰδοῦ]: *now* [νῦν] is the day of salvation!

This structure, as well as the chiastic structures that precede in 1:1—5:15, will be discussed in further detail in chapter 2.

Occasion for the Letter

This section will provide further foundation for studying the authorial audience of 2 Corinthians by addressing the situations that precede, are mentioned in, and thus likely influenced the composition of the letter. These issues involve the inception of the community, problems that led to 1 Corinthians, and the events that occurred between the composition of 1 and 2 Corinthians.

Events between 1 and 2 Corinthians

Paul likely chose Corinth for his ministry because of the size of the city, the popularity of the Isthmian games, and the trade that occurred there.[12] According to Acts 18:5–11, Paul spent eighteen months in the city when he founded the community. Within this time period, Paul likely set the foundation for the community's theological understanding of Christ and the Parousia.

Problems ensued in Corinth shortly after Paul left. It is difficult to determine the exact number of parties that fractured the community (if there were in fact multiple parties).[13] What is apparent is that an indeterminable but considerable portion of the community, for one reason or another, began to doubt Paul's apostolic integrity. The community had sent a letter to Paul to request clarification of his teachings on sexuality and food customs (1 Cor 7:1; 8:1). Possible slogans contained in the Corinthians' letter to Paul indicate a combative attitude among some of the members (1 Cor 6:12–13; 7:1; 8:4; 10:23, 26). In addition to the Corinthians' direct correspondence with Paul, Chloe's associates brought word of discord and immorality in the community (1 Cor 1:10). Paul responded to these issues in 1 Corinthians, and it is

12. Thistleton, *First Epistle*, 17.
13. Fee, *First Epistle*, 47–51.

apparent from the letter that he thought his apostolic integrity was being questioned by some in the community (1 Cor 1:10—4:21; 9:1–10). Paul also showed great emotion and rhetorical strategy in responding to matters of immorality (1 Cor 5:1–13; 6:12–20), lawsuits (6:1–11), the Lord's Supper (11:17–34), conduct in worship (11:2–15; 14:1–34), and the resurrection (15:1–58).

It is difficult to determine whether or not 1 Corinthians had initial success with the community. A change in travel plans may have resulted from a negative response to the letter.[14] Regardless of how 1 Corinthians was initially received, problems ensued between the writing of 1 and 2 Corinthians that created more tension for Paul's ministry in the city. A study of the situations that occasioned 2 Corinthians, however, is complicated by the sparse details regarding Paul's visits and correspondence with the community at Corinth between 1 and 2 Corinthians.

In regards to events that took place between 1 and 2 Corinthians, debate focuses around five major topics: (1) Paul changed his travel itinerary and arrived at Corinth earlier than he had planned (1 Cor 16:5–6; 2 Cor 1:15–16). (2) A "painful visit" ensued (2 Cor 2:1). (3) Paul did not return through Corinth as he had planned (2 Cor 1:23) but replied with a "tearful letter" (2 Cor 2:4). Next, (4) Paul suffered a type of malady (2 Cor 1:3–11; 2:10–13), whether an illness or imprisonment; it appears some Corinthians considered him too "weak" to be an apostle of the glorious Lord Jesus. In addition, (5) a group of "false apostles" had infiltrated the community and stirred up mistrust against Paul (2 Cor 2:17; 3:1; 10:1—13:10).[15]

> (1) The change in travel plans caused some within the Corinthian community to question Paul's authority. The difference in itineraries listed in 1 Cor 16:5–6 and 2 Cor 1:15–16 betrays a change in Paul's plans to visit the community in Corinth between 1 and 2 Corinthians. The itinerary in 1 Cor 16:5–9 shows that the journey is to begin in Ephesus, proceed to Macedonia, and conclude

---

14. Barrett, *First Epistle*, 5; Barnett, *Second Epistle*, 15–17.

15. For matters of brevity and relevance, this study will not engage the issue of the integrity of 2 Cor at length. It suffices to say that this study agrees with the majority who view the contents of 2 Cor 1–7 as immediately following the tearful letter, which is lost and is not represented in the present section 2 Cor 10–13. In this way, the findings of this study are compatible with nearly all unity and composite theories regarding the letter.

in Corinth. The modified itinerary in 2 Cor 1:15–16 shows two stops in Corinth: one on the way from Ephesus to Macedonia and a second visit on the return from Macedonia to Ephesus. Although such a change could have occurred for many reasons (bad weather, etc.), the community appears to have viewed the change as instability or weakness in Paul's character. Some scholars argue that Paul changed his itinerary in response to growing problems in Corinth.[16] Whatever the cause, the change required an explanation and defense of his travel plans in 2 Cor 1:15–17.

(2) A "painful visit" immediately followed the first change in itinerary (2 Cor 2:1–11). Two questions arise in regard to the painful visit: when did this visit occur and what transpired during this visit? As to the first question, the extant evidence in Paul's letters and Acts describe three trips to Corinth. The painful visit was not likely the initial founding of the community and cannot be the impending third visit (2 Cor 13:1). Thus the painful visit has traditionally been associated with the second visit that Paul made after 1 Corinthians and prior to 2 Corinthians, and this view remains the preferred position today.

Some scholars speculate in detail about what transpired during the painful visit.[17] Other scholars suggest that what can be known is that "the offender" played a major role in the frustration that Paul encountered during the visit and that this affected Paul's next travel itinerary and two further letters.[18]

Debate regarding the offender centers around his identity and the time and content of the offense. The offender is discussed in 2 Cor 2:5–11 and 7:12.[19] This figure was traditionally identified with the incestuous man of 1 Cor 5,[20] but this identification has

---

16. The discrepancy in the itinerary inspires speculation among some scholars. Barnett (*Second Epistle*, 28) believes Paul came earlier to deal with immorality that continued even after his warnings in 1 Cor. See also Murphy-O'Connor, *Theology*, 11.

17. Murphy-O'Connor, *Theology*, 15; Barnett, *Second Epistle*, 7; Lambrecht, *2 Corinthians*, 5–6; Barrett, *Second Epistle*, 7.

18. Matera, *II Corinthians*, 17.

19. The term "offender" comes from τοῦ ἀδικήσαντος in 7:12.

20. This traditional view was prominent from the time of Tertullian to the nineteenth century. Some modern scholars, e.g., Kruse (*Second Epistle*, 42–45; idem, "Offender") prefer this theory. Cf. Harris, *Second Epistle*, 226.

been rejected by most modern scholars. Lexical connections between 1 Cor 5 and 2 Cor 2:5–11 are negligible or nonexistent, and the tearful letter is no longer viewed as 1 Corinthians, as it once was. Alternative theories vary in details but present the offender either as one from within[21] or from without the Corinthian community.[22] The view that the offender is an outsider is not compatible with the text. If the man had come from without, in what manner would the community punish him, and why would they accept him back after the punishment (2 Cor 2:4–9)?

The majority of scholars place the time of the offense during the painful visit. Paul speaks of the offense within the context of defending his change of travel plans (1:15—2:4), and the term "pain" (λύπη) is used in reference both to the painful visit (2:1) and to the offense (2:5).

This study agrees with those scholars who see the offender as a member of the community but not as the incestuous man of 1 Cor 5. The offender likely rebuked Paul publicly to the extent that Paul recalled the event as "painful," amended his travel plans, and wrote a letter in great distress shortly thereafter.

(3) In response to the painful visit and the offender, Paul wrote a "severe" or "tearful" letter prior to 2 Corinthians. According to 2 Cor 1:23—2:11; 7:5–16, the tearful letter emphasized Paul's love for the community and admonished them to punish the offender who had rebuked him. Some scholars identify this letter with 1 Corinthians or a letter preserved in 2 Cor 10–13 that preceded 2 Cor 1–9.[23] The most widely held position today, however, views the tearful letter as a letter written between the painful visit and 2 Corinthians and as no longer extant.

(4) There is no present consensus on the nature of Paul's affliction in Ephesus. Several offer that this affliction was an imprisonment and possible death sentence (as intoned in 2 Cor 1:9, τὸ ἀπόκριμα

---

21. Moffatt, *Introduction*, 122; Watson, "Paul's Painful Visit"; Barnett, *Second Epistle*, 17; Lambrecht, *2 Corinthians*, 5–6. In particular, see Thrall ("Offender") for a list of proposed criteria regarding the offender and the offense.

22. Barrett, *Second Epistle*, 7; idem, "HO ADIKĒSAS."

23. Kennedy, *Second and Third*, 81–85, cited in Fulton, "Rhetorical Analysis," 28–30; Batey, "Interaction," 139–46.

τοῦ θανάτου). This position has possible merits. Acts of the Apostles 19 recounts a tense episode in which Paul was accosted and tried by a mob, then imprisoned. Another option is that Paul had a recurrent illness that relapsed during periods of immense stress, such as the time that followed the painful visit. This view is supported by the use of the verb βαρεῖν, which commonly meant to suffer an illness,[24] and by the other mentions of Paul's illness (Gal 4:13). Although the illness is not easily diagnosed, it is thought to be a type of malaria.[25] This view also coincides with his departure from Troas (2 Cor 2:10–13). The tension with the Corinthians exasperated his health to the point that his recurrent illness reemerged, and this physical setback caused his status in Corinth to decline further. Whatever the nature of his illness, the Corinthians found it objectionable enough to question his qualification to be an apostle.

The Opponents

(5) In addition to the problems mentioned above, certain Christian missionaries who undermined Paul's authority arrived at Corinth. The identity of these "superapostles" (2 Cor 11:5; 12:15), as Paul calls them, is strongly debated. What Paul knew of these opponents and when he learned of them is unclear from the content of the letter. Evidence in the letter that the opposing Christian missionaries were Jewish (e.g., 11:22–23) leads many to believe the opponents may have been similar to the Judaizing intruders of Galatia and Philippi.[26] Barrett argues that Paul inspired animosity among conservative Jewish Christians. The opponents who knew Jesus personally in Palestine were recommended and funded by the church in Jerusalem. The theology of these Christian missionaries emphasized along with faith in Christ a righteousness based on the law.[27]

24. Harvey, *Renewal*, 9; BDAG, s.v.

25. Harris, *Second Epistle*, 172.

26. Baur (*Paul*, 288) proposes that the opponents acted under the auspices of the Jerusalem church. See also Gunther, *Opponents*, 314.

27. Scholars differ on the influence James had on this group of opponents. Baur (*Paul*, 277) reads "superapostles" (2 Cor 11:5; 12:15) to mean the opponents were

The Judaizer position has many flaws. First, there is no debate over law, food customs, or circumcision in 2 Corinthians. Barrett retorts that Judaizers had a different agenda for every city,[28] but Judaizers without a concern for the law or circumcision in any city would be decidedly ineffective Judaizers. The term Ἑβραῖος (11:22) does not denote Palestinian origin with any degree of certainty since Paul uses the same term for himself (11:22) but is a native of Tarsus. The opponents may well be Jewish Christian missionaries, but there is no evidence that they were from Palestine or under the auspices of the Jerusalem community.

An alternative to the Judaizer position views the opponents as Gnostics.[29] This position, in principle, considers the opponents in 2 Corinthians to be related to the Gnostic problems that Paul encounters in 1 Corinthians. While many scholars have accepted that some content of 1 Corinthians deals with Gnostic-like tendencies, the view that the opponents of 2 Corinthians are Gnostics has not won wide approval. It is difficult to define what characterizes a "Gnostic" in 55 CE. In addition, the qualities that some scholars see as Gnostic, such as dualism and "gnosis," were widely held in various forms throughout the Hellenistic world, including Hellenistic Judaism.[30]

Because of the lack of Judaizing terms or evidence for Gnostic tendencies, this study agrees with those scholars who view the opponents as Hellenistic Jewish Christian missionaries with a background similar to that of Paul. These opponents see their abilities and credentials as superior to Paul's, particularly in terms of spiritual gifts. There is no explicit reference to Jerusalem to argue for the Palestinian origin for the opponents, and the "Gnostic" attributes mentioned by Bultmann and

---

prominent apostles from Jerusalem. However, more recent proponents of the Judaizer position argue that the opponents overstated their affiliation with Jerusalem or used their letters of recommendation without Jerusalem's complete compliance. Barrett ("Opponents"; idem, *Paul*, 35) understands the opponents to be under the auspices of Jerusalem in coming to investigate Paul's work in Corinth, but they go too far in infiltrating the community. See also Martin, "Opponents," 286; Thrall, "Super Apostles"; idem, *II Corinthians*, 576–89; Harris, *Second Epistle*, 70–80; Lüdemann, *Opposition*, 90–97.

28. Barrett, *Paul*, 35.

29. Lütgert, *Freiheitspredigt*, cited in Harris, *Second Epistle*, 79; Bultmann, *Second Letter*, 203; Schmithals, *Gnostics*, 26–36; idem, *Gnosis*, 173–77.

30. Schnelle, *History*, 88.

Schmithals do not distinguish the opponents as Gnostics because those attributes were common throughout the Hellenistic Jewish Diaspora.[31]

The text of the letter tells us little about the identity or the origin of the opponents. Paul prefers to present them as shadowy figures rather than outline their positions (a strategy that was common in ancient letters).[32] From a rhetorical angle, he is more interested in addressing what he believes the opponents have said or done, particularly in regards to him and his ministry.

It is probable that the opponents:

- were Jewish Christian missionaries (10:7; 11:6, 22, 23a)
- carried letters of recommendation to demonstrate credibility (3:1)
- boasted in "worldly" things (5:11–13; 11:18)
- accepted payment for their ministry (2:17; 4:1–2)
- had ecstatic experiences, oratorical skills, and performed wonders (4:7–11; 11:20–24)
- overstepped their bounds in their ministry at Corinth, according to Paul's missionary protocol (10:13–14).

It is likely that the opponents accused Paul of the following:

- he lacked credibility because he had no letters of recommendation (3:1)
- he acted in a worldly fashion (implying a weak nature; 10:2)
- his letters were strong but his presence was weak (10:10–11)
- he was an untrained speaker (5:11–13; 11:6)
- he refused money for himself but took a collection allegedly for the poor in Jerusalem (12:17).[33]

This represents a general description of the opponents that is based on the evidence provided by the letter itself. The list speaks more to what the opponents said about Paul than to their identity, origin, or specific

---

31. Georgi, *Opponents*, 9–14, 248; Friedrich, "Die Gegner"; Schnelle, *History*, 108; Furnish, *II Corinthians*, 53; Witherington, *Conflict*, 247.

32. Du Toit, "Vilification."

33. For a similar methodology and list of attributes see Furnish (*II Corinthians*, 47–54) and Matera (*II Corinthians*, 20–24). A discussion of methodology can be found in Witherington (*Conflict*, 345–50) and Harris (*Second Epistle*, 67–87).

theology. This list is sufficient, however, for the close reading of the text that will follow.

In summary, the following may describe a likely scenario for the events that immediately preceded the composition of 2 Corinthians. Paul intended to visit Corinth on his trip from Ephesus to Macedonia at the time of writing 1 Corinthians (1 Cor 16:1–5). For reasons we no longer know, he changed his travel plans to arrive in Corinth earlier and hoped to pass through Corinth again on his return to Ephesus (2 Cor 1:15–16). A painful visit ensued, during which the offender openly rebuked Paul in front of the community (2 Cor 2:4–9). Paul did not pass through Corinth on his return to Ephesus as he intended—leading to another change in travel plans (1:23—2:3). Instead he sent Titus with a "tearful letter" to address the painful visit and measures to be taken against the offender (2:4, 9). Paul journeyed to Troas but, despite the promise of a productive ministry, left due to his illness and to find Titus in Macedonia to learn how his letter was received in Corinth. Titus gave Paul a fairly positive, yet mixed, report. The Corinthians had sided with Paul and punished the offender appropriately (7:5–16), but intruders in the community posed a new threat to the relationship. In light of these events Paul was now being forced to defend both his sincerity as a minister to the community and his qualification to be an apostle of Christ.

1

Method and Perspective

Method

This study will examine how the authorial (i.e., the "implied" or "textual") audience responds to the chiastically structured arguments in 2 Cor 1:1—6:2, and particularly how they respond to the climactic call to reconciliation in 2 Cor 5:16—6:2. This examination is based on the authorial audience's (i.e., the Corinthian community's)[1] prior knowledge and recollection, which would include 1 Corinthians, the events that transpired between the letters, and the content of 2 Cor 1:1—6:2. The audience-oriented method of this investigation will treat 5:16—6:2 as a climax within its immediate contextual argument, which begins in 4:15.

Audience Oriented

The methodology of this proposed study will employ the tools of audience-response criticism. This method focuses on how the "authorial audience" responds to Paul's rhetorical argument in the text as the letter progresses. Within the scope of the audience-oriented method, the "authorial audience" is understood to be a historical group of addressees of whom the author is cognizant as he/she writes.[2] This is not a group

---

1. To avoid cumbersome repetition, the authorial audience in this study may also be referred to as "the Corinthians," "the Corinthian community," and "the Christian community in Corinth."

2. Carter and Heil, *Matthew's Parables*, 12–13.

that is historically reconstructed or created by the reader; rather, the authorial audience is understood as the group of addressees implied within the text, and thus may be referred to as the "implied," "textual," "intended," or "ideal" audience.³

In employing the audience-oriented method, this study follows the work of Peter Rabinowitz and its developments by Warren Carter and John Paul Heil. The "authorial audience," as Rabinowitz explains, is "the hearers or readers the author has 'in mind' in creating the text," that is, "the hypothetical [audience] who the author hoped or expected would" experience the text.⁴ This audience is deduced from the text itself and is not "created" in the mind of the reader as the text progresses, as some reading theorists propose.⁵ The author "assumes this audience possesses the socio-cultural knowledge and interpretive skills necessary to actualize the text's meaning."⁶

Pace Wolfgang Iser, this study agrees with Carter's and Heil's adoption of Rabinowitz's terminology of audience as opposed to "reader."⁷ As Carter and Heil explain, "the term 'reader' suggests interaction with the text through reading of one's own copy."⁸ "Reader" then is anachronistic

---

3. "Intended/ideal audience" here is to be taken as synonymous with the "implied," "authorial," and "textual" audience since within audience theory all five of these terms are dependent on the author's understanding of the audience as he/she addresses them in the text. This is distinct from reading theories that differentiate the above categories in the following manner: the intended audience is the addressees to whom the author intended to write; the implied audience is constructed by the reader in the process of reading; and the ideal audience is the group that would understand all of the author's rhetorical allusions and strategies. Audience theory, however, equalizes all of these categories under the auspices of "authorial" or "textual" audience. Since the "implied/intended" audience is the group of addressees that the author imagines as he/she writes, this group is ipso facto "ideal" in the sense that the author intends for them to be able to understand his/her allusions and rhetorical strategies within the text as the letter is composed.

4. Rabinowitz, "Whirl without End," 85.

5. See, e.g., Moloney, *Belief*, 9–10; Byrne, *Romans*, 3–4; Osborne, "Hermeneutics," 285. In reading theory, the reader molds the text and identity of the implied author and implied reader(s) like clay. However, in audience theory, the identities of the implied author and implied audience are more static since they are defined within the text by the author. For this reason, the "implied" audience in audience theory may be referred to as the "authorial" or "ideal" audience. This is not a "real" audience that is presently reading, nor a historical construct, but is based on how the author describes the audience within the text.

6. Rabinowitz, "Whirl," 85.

7. Iser, "Indeterminacy," 29.

8. Carter and Heil, *Matthew's Parables*, 15.

for the life setting of an ancient letter since the author did not imagine individuals reading his/her letter privately, but rather imagined his/her surrogate delivering the letter in an oral, public performance before the intended audience. Furthermore, "hearing a text means interacting with it not as a printed object but more as a process and event."[9]

In addition, this study is "rhetorical" (in the broad sense of the term) in that it utilizes a "text-centered" approach that focuses not on classical rhetorical forms but on listening carefully to the repeated terms, themes, and chiastic structures in the text of the letter to determine and evaluate Paul's rhetorical strategy.[10] Paul's focus on his ministry and the call to reconciliation dominate the first half of the letter. This study evaluates the climactic section, 5:16—6:2, of Paul's apologia and call for the community to be reconciled to him.

The Authorial Audience in Corinth

The audience-oriented method explicates how the audience implied by the text is expected to respond based on what is stated in the text. In this case, the authorial audience is the Christian community at Corinth whom Paul founded, preached to, and visited. The letter 2 Corinthians serves to convey Paul's presence and stands as one event among many in the relationship between the apostle and the community.[11] The method of this study presumes that the letter was written in such a manner as to be understood by the authorial audience and thus conveys terms, positions, and phrases that would be readily understood when heard by the Corinthian community.[12]

---

9. Ibid., 16.

10. For a similar approach to rhetorical study, see Heil, *Ephesians*, 9.

11. In efforts to defend the letter's integrity, or to explain away the shift in tone at 2 Cor 10, some scholars (e.g., Belleville, *2 Corinthians*, 28) have argued that the letter has different intended audiences. For example, 2 Cor 1–7 is written for the pro-Pauline contingent in Corinth, 2 Cor 10–13 is written for the anti-Pauline contingent and the opponents, and 2 Cor 8–9 is intended for both the Corinthians and the churches in Achaia. These positions, however, are unsupported by the textual evidence. The Corinthians and their relationship to Paul are addressed throughout the letter, including 2 Cor 10–13 (esp. 10:12–18; 12:14–21). Furthermore, why would Paul say that he loves the opponents (11:11)? From a text-centered perspective, the "audience" is the group of addressees listed in 2 Cor 1:1–2, and the letter they are intended to receive is 2 Corinthians in its present canonical form (with textual variants to be considered).

12. Heil, *Rhetorical Role*, 6–8.

One system of terms and phrases that Paul presumes his audience to understand is Scripture. During his initial visit, Paul likely preached the gospel with OT support. This fact is important to an audience-oriented reading since the community was likely comprised of Jews and Gentile "God-fearers" from the synagogue, as well as Greek and Roman pagan converts (1 Cor 1:22–24; 7:18; 9:20-21; 12:13). Given the number of OT allusions and citations in 1 and 2 Corinthians, it is likely that Paul presumed that the Corinthians were familiar enough with Israel's Scriptures to understand their use in his rhetorical argument.[13]

This study follows the unanimous position of scholarship that the author of 2 Corinthians is the historical apostle Paul, the author of the uncontested Pauline letters. The historical Paul wrote 2 Corinthians within a timeline of events in his relationship with the Corinthian community. The letter was likely written eight months to a year after 1 Corinthians and shortly after Paul found Titus in Macedonia (2 Cor 7:5), thus placing the writing of the letter in Macedonia around the fall of 55 CE.[14]

It is at this point that Paul would have imagined his authorial audience as he composed 2 Corinthians. The history between Paul and the Corinthians—seen particularly in the tone of 1 Corinthians and 2 Cor 1:8—2:13—made necessary Paul's rhetorical strategy in which he defends his previous actions, and his ministry, against internal dissidents and external opponents. For this reason, the authorial audience is also to be understood as a mixture of pro- and anti-Pauline factions. The proportions of these groups are disputed with little consensus. For the present study it is sufficient to recognize the community as a complex entity that includes both receptive and resistant contingencies. The letter as a whole, however, is addressed to all members of the Corinthian community. The on-again, off-again relationship between Paul and this complex group, now complicated by the opponents' arrival, made the apologia for his ministry of central importance in the letter.

The Rhetorical and Heuristic Aspects of the Letter

The authorial audience Paul has in mind as he writes is aware of all of the events mentioned above. They have come close to reconciling with Paul following the tearful letter (7:5–17), but the opponents represent

---

13. Ibid., 9–10; Meeks, *First*, 73.
14. Schnelle, *History*, 79–88.

a new threat (3:1; 4:2; 10:1—12:12). In his apologia, Paul sets forth the content of his gospel—new creation and reconciliation in Christ—as evidence of his apostolic integrity. God has sent him to proclaim reconciliation and new creation in Christ (5:18-20). The opponents, in causing dissension, were frustrating God's plans of salvation for his chosen elect in the community (6:1).

This study anticipates that determining and analyzing the responses of the authorial audience will explicate the theological meaning of new creation and reconciliation within the rhetorical context of Paul's apology for his ministry, in that this method will study how the themes of new creation and reconciliation progress within the chiastic unit and how they are received by the authorial audience in light of what is said in 1 Corinthians and 2 Cor 1:1—5:15. It will follow closely the rhetorical argument of the letter and examine the chiastic structures within the immediate context of 5:16—6:2 and the macrochiastic structure found in 4:15—6:2. The identity of the chiasms and their respective structures will be dealt with in the next chapter.

The Oral Culture and Setting of Paul's Correspondence

Paul and his communities lived within a culture that emphasized oral communication. Letters were dictated and performed aloud to the addressee(s). The oral milieu was so prevalent that "no writing occurred that was not vocalized."[15] The emphasis on sound patterns in NT studies gained wide attention with Paul Achtemeier's presidential address at the 1989 Annual SBL meeting.[16] Achtemeier claims that the NT texts were composed and intended to be performed audibly within the oral culture of late Western antiquity. These texts are, in every sense, "oral to the core," and so should be studied with sensitivity to how the texts sound. Sound patterns, such as repetition, inclusion, parallels, anaphora, and alliteration (among others) help to delimit borders, structures, and otherwise unheard meaning of the texts.[17]

Common formulae within an oral culture's literature included parallelism (the pairing of synonymous or antithetical terms or themes)

---

15. Achtemeier, "*Omne*," 15–16; see also Harvey, *Listening*, 40–42.
16. Achtemeier, "*Omne*," 18.
17. Ibid., 19-21.

and the chiasm. In its most general structure, a chiasm consists of "inverted parallelism—a passage in which the second part is inverted and balanced against the first."[18] An example may be found in 2 Cor 1:5:

> 5a Because just as *overflow* [περισσεύει]
> 5b the sufferings of *Christ* [τοῦ Χριστοῦ]
> 5c to us,
> 5d so too, through *Christ* [τοῦ Χριστοῦ],
> 5e *overflows* [περισσεύει] our consolation.

Since Greco-Roman literature and correspondence had limited line-breaks and punctuation, chiasms served as the oral equivalent of a paragraph. The chiasm's structure helped to frame the author's argument and distinguish his/her main point, which lay in the final element of the structure.[19] The closure of a chiasm (the connection of the final A′ unit with the beginning A unit) also alerted the audience that the present section had concluded and a new section would follow.

Chiasmus in Ancient Rhetoric and Literature

Extent Ugaritic, Sumero-Akkadian, Greek, and Latin examples demonstrate the ubiquity of this oral literary form both temporally and geographically.[20] Examples, such as the one given here from Amos 5:4–6, are numerous throughout the Hebrew Bible:

> **Seek** me and you shall **live**:
> But do not seek **Beth el**
> nor enter into **Gilgal**
> and do not pass to Beer-sheba;
> for **Gilgal** shall surely go into exile
> and **Beth-el** shall come to nought:
> **Seek** the Lord, and **live**.[21]

---

18. Stock, "Chiastic Awareness," 23; see also Bailey and Vander Broek, *Literary Forms*, 49–50.

19. Stock, "Chiastic Awareness," 23.

20. Smith, "Sumero-Akkadian"; Welch, "Ancient Greek and Latin"; Douglas, *Thinking in Circles*, 112–15.

21. Translation from Klaus, *Pivot Patterns*, 227; emphasis his. See also, e.g., Muilenberg, "Form Criticism"; Boadt, "A:B:B:A Chiasm"; Fredericks, "Qoheleth 5:9—6:9."

Aramaic and Haggadic examples add evidence of the form in religious, political, and domestic spheres.[22] Cognizance of the form and its use in textual interpretation is seen in rabbinic comments on Lev 6:16; Josh 24:4; Ruth 1:5.[23]

The term chiasmus comes from the Greek verb χιάζω. Although this verb is only first seen in rhetorical handbooks in Dio-Hermogenes (fourth c. CE), the Homeric commentator Aristarchus notes the inverted structure of the discussion between Odysseus and his mother (*Od.* 11:170–74).[24] These inverted patterns in Homer, sometimes referred to as *hysteron proteron*, were also noted by Crates and the Stoics of Pergamum as essential to the analysis of the text.[25] Other examples may be found in Isocrates, Demosthenes, Aristotle, Cicero, Dio-Chrysostom, and the Cynics.[26] Along with larger texts, chiasms are also found in both public and private letters of antiquity.[27]

Chiastic structures were likely perpetuated in Greco-Roman literature by the culture's method of education. At the age of seven, young men began to memorize the alphabet *alpha* to *omega*, then *omega* to *alpha*. Once this was mastered, the student was required to learn and recite the alphabet in successive concentric groups: *beta* to *psi* (and *psi* to *beta*), *gamma* to *chi* (and *chi* to *gamma*), up to *mu-nu* (and *nu-mu*).[28] In secondary stages of education, texts were read aloud repeatedly and memorized, meaning that young students would be reading and memorizing arguments framed in a chiastic structure. In rhetorical training the students were taught to begin and end a speech with similar material.[29] They were also often encouraged to arrange the content of their argument in three- or five-part groups of concentric patterns in order to emphasize a central point.[30]

---

22. Porten, "Aramaic Contracts and Letters"; Frankel, "Talmudic-Aggadic Narrative"; Klaus, *Pivot Patterns*, 15–18.

23. Klaus, *Pivot Patterns*, 15.

24. Welch, "Greek and Latin," 254.

25. Ibid., 256.

26. Harvey, *Listening*, 71–82; Douglas, *Thinking*, 110–18; Stephen Nimis, "Cycles."

27. Heil, "Philemon"; Stowers, *Letter Writing*, 73.

28. Stock, "Awareness," 24.

29. Ibid., 25.

30. Wuellner, "Arrangement," 78–79.

The consistent indoctrination of reading aloud and writing in chiasms over a period of seven to fourteen years would produce writers who listened for, analyzed, and composed texts in chiasms. Based on the prevalence of the form in Hebrew, Aramaic, Greek, and Latin texts, the awareness and utilization of the form in ancient textual analysis, and its occurrence at all levels of public education, it is plausible that Paul and his audience in Corinth were exposed to, and aware of, chiastic and inverted patterns within correspondence and literature.

That said, this study does not see cognitive awareness as a necessity in the audience's reception. As Heil explains, "Chiastic patterns serve to organize the content to be heard and . . . lead an audience through introductory elements to a central point." Due to the ubiquity of inverted and chiastic patterns in late Western antiquity "the original ancient audience may and need not necessarily have been consciously identifying or reflecting upon any of these chiastic structures in themselves," but rather "experienced the chiastic phenomenon, which had an unconscious effect on how they perceived the content." A study of how an intended audience experiences these structures is useful because it demonstrates to the modern reader what the text originally conveyed in its aural structure to its intended ancient audience.[31]

As this section closes, it is reasonable to note that not all corresponding elements within a chiasm are of equal value. In some cases, a pair of elements will share more superficial, rather than substantive, connections. In such cases, however, the weakness of two elements does not necessarily negate the strength of the unit as a whole. First, even if substantive correlation is lacking, so long as there is an aural connection—be it grammatical echo, alliteration, or repetition of sound—the authorial audience still experiences the elements' contributions to the unit's overall structure. Second, these less substantive connections often occur within units where the other elemental connections are significant in both meaning and sound, such that even if one or two elements appear ambiguous, the other elements in that unit and adjacent units suitably manifest the chiastic structure.

Also, it is not necessary for a composition to be made completely of chiasms. In some texts, chiasms are used only occasionally for effect (as in Amos, seen above). In the present work, however, twenty chiastic

---

31. Heil, *Ephesians*, 15–16; see also Nimis, "Cycles," 191.

units do happen to be evident. These structures will be presented with explanation in the next chapter.

Chiasmus and Interpretation

Chiastic structures are prevalent throughout Western literature, geographically and temporally. Literary scholars have found chiastic structures in the works of William Shakespeare, Nathanial Hawthorne, and even in modern-day literary works.[32] Since chiasms frame particular sections of an author's argument and distinguish the central point, literary scholars for centuries have used chiastic structures for effective textual analysis. For example, scholars in Roman Britain used chiastic analysis in their study of ancient British poetry.[33]

The study of chiastic structures in biblical texts, however, is relatively new. In 1930, Nils Lund became the first to evaluate chiasms in New Testament literature.[34] Since Lund's work, the use of chiasms has aided biblical scholars of both Testaments. The benefits gained from the study of chiasms are manifold: they are able to (1) deduce the literary limits of a section when grammar is inconclusive;[35] (2) determine the proper referent and action where pronouns are unclear;[36] (3) explicate narrative or character development in a story;[37] (4) examine the relationship of poetic cola;[38] and (5) argue for or against the literary integrity of a text.[39] Still, the strongest and most basic benefits from the study of chiasms are the ability to deduce the structure and main point of the author's argument and perceive the development of that argument as it progresses through the chiastic structure.

The analysis of chiastic structures has benefited Pauline studies since the Second World War in several ways.[40] The structure of the

32. Davis, "Secrets"; Ullen, "Hawthorne's Romances."
33. Davis, "Secrets," 238.
34. Lund, "Presence of Chiasmus."
35. Holmgren, "Isaiah LI 1–11"; Parunak, "Transitional Techniques."
36. Holladay, "Chiasmus."
37. Assis, "Biblical Narrative"; Jackson, "Retracing"; Yudkowsky, "Chaos."
38. Willis, "Juxtaposition."
39. Luter and Lee, "Philippians."
40. Lund, *Chiasmus*, 137–225; Jeremias, "Chiasmus"; Collins, "Chiasmus"; Lambrecht, "1 Cor 15:23–28"; Myers, "Chiastic Inversion"; Luter and Lee, "Philippians"; Porter and Reed, "Philippians"; Martin, "Scythian"; Heil, *Ephesians*, 13–45.

chiasm demonstrates a rhetorical strategy that is otherwise unapparent to the modern reader, and the comparison of parallel elements aids the exegesis of any given textual unit.[41] This is made all the more important when a letter's structure is presumed to be unclear. Beyond setting the borders, a chiasm also denotes the center point, or pivot, of a unit. This pivot may operate in one of two ways: as "the interpretive focal point of the passage," or as "an important transition in the movement of thought" of the unit.[42]

Chiasmus in 2 Corinthians

At the present time, the chiastic structures previous scholars have proposed for 2 Corinthians, in my opinion, have not been satisfactory. Some scholars attempt to find "concentric" patterns in 2 Corinthians without using exhaustive criteria. Jan Lambrecht, e.g., proposes a concentric and complicated structure for 2 Cor 2:14—4:6.[43] His execution, however, does not follow a set of criteria, and the pattern he deduces becomes cumbersome. Blomberg follows useful and strict criteria in his proposal of a chiastic structure for 2 Corinthians 1–7, but his analysis produces a synthetic pattern of disjointed units.[44] In addition, the center unit he proposes (5:11–21), although central to Paul's overall theology, seems too late in the letter itself (as Blomberg determines the text) to be the proper center of 2 Cor 1–7. The structures proposed by Peter Ellis are thematically based and asymmetrical in their final form.[45]

The majority of structures scholars propose for 2 Corinthians at this time are subjectively delimited or focus on thematic connections. In the next chapter I will propose chiastic structures for 2 Cor 1:1—6:2 that are grounded objectively in lexical and grammatical criteria and that are aurally apparent to the authorial audience. In particular, by paying close attention to the sound patterns that are inherent within oral literature, these structures *demonstrate* what the authorial audience *hears* within the text. This method of listening closely to the text is in line with Achtemeier's concern that some aspects of oral literature "are

---

41. Baily and Vander Broek, *Literary Forms*, 51.
42. Ibid, 53.
43. Lambrecht, "2 Cor 2:14—7:4."
44. Blomberg, "Structure," 4–8.
45. Ellis, *Seven*, 139–72.

more apparent to the ear than to the eye" and treats the text as it was originally intended, that is, as correspondence that was both written and performed aloud.⁴⁶

Chapter Summary

This study utilizes the audience-oriented method in order to pay close attention to how the authorial audience responds to Paul's rhetorical argument as it progresses within the text. The authorial audience is not a group of flesh-and-blood addressees, but rather is a literary entity that corresponds to the audience the author has in mind as he/she writes the text. The authorial audience then equates to a historical audience but is not in itself the original or historical audience. This method pays close attention to the oral milieu of late Western antiquity and treats the letter as a text that was composed and intended to be performed aloud to its addressees. Like many of its contemporaneous texts, the aural structure inherent in 2 Corinthians consists of oral patterning and, in particular, chiasms. Scholars have utilized chiasms in critical exegesis of Paul's letters for decades. However, many of these past studies have been based on thematic rather than objective lexical criteria. The next chapter will demonstrate chiastic structures that are objectively grounded on lexical and grammatical criteria. These findings lay the groundwork for the remainder of the study.

---

46. Achtemeier, "*Omne*," 19: "To be understood, the NT must be understood as speech."

2

Chiastic Structures in 2 Corinthians 1:1—6:2

Criteria

This study prefers to recognize chiastic structures that are linguistically rather than conceptually or thematically based and thus follows the criteria presented by Craig Blomberg:

- There must be a problem in perceiving the structure of the text in question, which more conventional outlines fail to resolve.
- There must be clear examples of parallelism between the two "halves" of the hypothesized chiasm, to which commentators call attention even when they propose quite different outlines for the text overall.
- Linguistic (or grammatical) parallelism as well as conceptual (or structural) parallelism should characterize most if not all of the corresponding pairs of subdivisions.
- The linguistic parallelism should involve central or dominant imagery or terminology important to the rhetorical strategy of the text.
- Both linguistic and conceptual parallelism should involve words and ideas not regularly found elsewhere within the proposed chiasm.

- Multiple sets of correspondences between passages opposite each other in the chiasm, as well as multiple members of the chiasm itself, are desirable.
- The outline should divide the text at natural breaks that would be agreed upon even by those proposing very different structures to account for the whole.
- The central or pivotal, as well as the final or climactic, elements normally play key roles in the rhetorical strategy of the chiasm.
- Ruptures in the outline should be avoided if at all possible.[1]

I propose that 2 Cor 1:1—6:2 is chiastic in structure and contains twenty separate chiastic units and three macrochiasms. The first two chiasms (1:1–2 and 1:3–7) stand apart as introductory material and are not included under a macrochiasm. The overall structure of 1:1—6:2 would then be:

Introduction: 1:1–7
Macrochiasm I: 1:8—2:13
Macrochiasm II: 2:14—4:14
Macrochiasm III: 4:15—6:2

For the remainder of this chapter I will demonstrate the chiastic structure, grammatical delimitations, and transitional terms for each unit. Transitional terms are words that connect one unit to the unit that immediately precedes it. Such terms are normally found near the end of one unit and at the beginning of the following unit.[2] In each case the transitional terms progress the line of thought from one unit to the next, and thus demonstrate a cohesive progression of the chiastic structures.

Parallel terms of corresponding elements are italicized, in bold, and accompanied with Greek text. The linking terms are underlined (without Greek text, for brevity). Debatable textual issues are placed in brackets.

---

1. Blomberg, "Structure," 4–8. Harvey (*Listening*, 108–9) also prefers these criteria.

2. In some instances, the border elements (either the first or last element in a unit) are too short to allow for common terms. In such instances, however, the transitional terms may be found as close as possible to the endpoint/beginning of the unit, so long as the terms create an aural link from one unit to the next.

Analysis of Structures

Introduction (1:1–7)

The introductory sections consist of a greeting (1:1–2) and blessing (1:3–7). These units stand apart from the three macrochiastic arguments that are comprised in the remaining eighteen units in 1:8—6:2. Both units contain a complex A-B-C-D-C′-B′-A′ pattern.

Greeting (1:1–2)

A   1:1a Paul, an apostle of *Christ Jesus* [Χριστοῦ Ἰησοῦ],
  B   1b by the will of *God* [θεοῦ], and Timothy our brother, to the church of *God* [θεοῦ]
    C   1c *that is* [τῇ οὔσῃ] *in* [ἐν] Corinth
      D   1d with all the holy ones,
    C′   1e *those who are* [τοῖς οὖσιν] *in* [ἐν] all Achaia.
  B′   2a Grace to you and peace from **God** [θεοῦ] our **Father**
A′   2b and the **Lord Jesus Christ** [Ἰησοῦ Χριστοῦ].³

Aside from the chiastic structure, 1:1–2 is distinguished as a formulaic introduction for an ancient letter: sender(s) to addressee(s), greetings.⁴ The alternation of "Christ Jesus" in 1:1 and "Jesus Christ" in 1:2 establishes the A and A′ elements of the chiasm. The triple occurrence of the genitive form θεοῦ—the "will of God" and the "church of God" in 1:1 and the "peace from God" in 1:2—establishes the B and B′ elements of the unit. The preposition ἐν ("in") in 1:1c and 1:1e establishes the C and C′ elements. The unparalleled line in 1:1d is set apart as the pivotal D element of the chiasm.

All of the aforementioned terms are peculiar to their respective elements and are not found elsewhere in the unit. Paul's introduction concerns the defense of his apostleship from Christ and God to those who are in Corinth and Achaia. The center, or pivot, of the introduction focuses on the state of holiness that Paul's apostleship has brought to the community (1 Cor 1:1).

---

3. The translations presented here attempt to demonstrate what the audience hears. Whenever possible, I try to maintain the word order and verbal connections that are apparent in the Greek, which, although wooden at times, serve to demonstrate the aural experience of the authorial audience. The translation mostly follows the NA²⁷; textual differences are noted with brackets and/or footnotes.

4. Harris, *Second Epistle*, 127–28; Aune, *Literary Environment*, 184–86.

Blessing (1:3–7)

A 3 Blessed be the **God and Father** of our **Lord Jesus Christ**, the Father of compassion and God of *consolation*[5] [παρακλήσεως], 4 who consoles us in every affliction, so that we can console others in affliction, through the *consolation* (παρακλήσεως) by which we ourselves are *consoled* [παρακαλούμεθα] by God.

  B 5a Because just as *overflow* [περισσεύει]

    C 5b the sufferings of *Christ* [Χριστοῦ]

      D 5c to us,

    C' 5d so too, through *Christ* [Χριστοῦ],

  B' 5e *overflows* [περισσεύει] our consolation.[6]

A' 6 If we are **afflicted**, it is for your *consolation* [παρακλήσεως] and salvation. If we are *consoled* [παρακαλούμεθα], it is for your *consolation* [παρακλήσεως], which is effected through enduring the same sufferings that we ourselves suffer.[7] 7 And our hope for you is firm, since we know that just as you are sharers of the sufferings, so too are you sharers of the *consolation* [παρακλήσεως].

The second chiasm of the letter immediately follows the greeting. It is debated whether the blessing continues to v. 11 or ends at v. 7. The boundaries of 1:3–7 may be argued on grammatical grounds. The γάρ phrase of v. 8 appears to open a new section and line of thought. Affliction is treated in general terms in vv. 3–7, whereas a specific incident of affliction is addressed in vv. 8–11. The two sections are not unrelated, but they are distinct.[8]

---

5. The verb παρακαλέω may be rendered as "to encourage," "to exhort," "to comfort," or "to console" (BAGD, s.v.). This passage requires that the same term be used in both noun and verbal forms. The last option, "to console, consolation" is preferred in this passage by Matera (*II Corinthians*, 35) and Lambrecht (*Second Corinthians*, 17–19).

6. The term "consolation," as it appears in the B' element (1:5e), may be distinguished from the occurrences found in the A and A' elements. In the Greek, v. 5e has the nominative παράκλησις with the pronoun ἡμῶν; however, the occurrences in the A and A' elements are all in the genitive case, παρακλήσεως.

7. The variants that omit the words καὶ σωτηρίας εἴτε παρακαλούμεθα ὑπὲρ τῆς ὑμῶν παρακλήσεως likely arose because of homoeteleuton and elision. I retain the words, as does NA[27].

8. For a discussion on the relationship and separation of 1:3–7 and 1:8–11, see Lambrecht, *Second Corinthians*, 24–25.

The second unit (1:3–7) is linked to the first unit (1:1–2) by the transitional phrase "Lord Jesus Christ" in 1:2 and 1:3. The line of thought thus progresses from the grace and peace that Paul brings from God and "our Lord Jesus Christ" given to the audience in 1:2 to Paul's exclamation of praise given to God the Father of "our Lord Jesus Christ" in 1:3.

The genitive form of παρακλήσεως ("consolation") and the first plural subjunctive form of παρακαλέω (παρακαλούμεθα, "that we might be consoled") establish the A and A′ elements of the unit. The occurrence of παράκλησις in v. 5 does not negate the structure because it is in the nominative form. The repetition of the verb περισσεύω in 1:5a and 1:5d establishes the B and B′ elements; περισσεύω does not occur elsewhere in the unit. The genitive Χριστοῦ in 1:5b and 1:5c establishes the C and C′ elements. The name Ἰησοῦ Χριστοῦ appears in 1:3, but may be distinguished from the lone title Χριστοῦ with the definite article τοῦ. The unparalleled activity of Christ "in us" stands at the center of Paul's praise to God.

Macrochiasm I (1:8—2:13)

The first macrochiasm contains seven chiastic units with one central unparalleled unit acting as the pivot: (A) 1:8–11; (B) 1:12–14; (C) 1:15–17; (D) 1:18–22; (C′) 1:23—2:3; (B′) 2:4–9; (A′) 2:10–13.

A. Paul's Suffering in Asia (1:8–11)

A 8 For we do not want you to be unaware, brothers and sisters, *of our* **affliction** [ὑπὲρ ἡμῶν] that came about in Asia, in such a way that we were weighed down beyond our power, such that we despaired even of life.

   B 9 Indeed, we have received a *death sentence* [θανάτου] in order that we might trust not in ourselves but in God *who* [τῷ] raises the dead,

   B′ 10 *who* [ὅς] rescued us from *deadly situations*[9] [θανάτων] and will rescue us, in *whom* [ὄν] we hope. And[10] he will rescue us again,

---

9. I read the plural τηλικούτων θανάτων, which, in addition to being read by the earliest Pauline witness (P[46]), is the more difficult reading and coincides with Pauline style (Metzger, *TCGNT*, 506; Furnish, *II Corinthians*, 114).

10. I omit ὅτι, following P[46] B D (also Barrett, *Second Epistle*, 57; Matera, *II Corinthians*, 36).

A′ 11 so long as you, for your part,[11] join in solidarity with *us* [ὑπὲρ ἡμῶν] by your prayer, in order that thanks may be given *on our*[12] *behalf* [ὑπὲρ ἡμῶν] from many for the **gift** given to us by the prayers of many.

Grammatically the unit is distinguished by the γάρ clauses in v. 8 and v. 12 and the fact that vv. 8–11 exist as a single sentence in Greek. Whereas 1:3–7 focuses on consolation in the face of general affliction, 1:8–11 concerns a specific incident. In addition, vv. 12–14 show a change in tone in which Paul expresses his boast and his reasons for writing. The first unit of Macrochiasm I (1:8–11) is linked to the preceding chiastic unit (1:3–7) by the verb θλίβω ("to afflict;" 1:7) and the noun θλῖψις ("affliction;" 1:8). The line of thought thus progresses from the "affliction" that Paul suffers for the audience's consolation and salvation in 1:7 to the "affliction" that Paul endured in Asia in 1:8.

The repetition of the phrase "concerning us" in vv. 8 and 11 establishes the A and A′ elements of the unit. The preposition ὑπέρ and the genitive plural pronoun ἡμῶν do not occur elsewhere in the unit. The double occurrence of ὑπὲρ ἡμῶν in v. 11 strengthens the parallelism.

The noun θάνατος ("death") and the relative pronoun ὅς ("who") in vv. 9 and 10 establish the B and B′ elements of the unit. Neither θάνατος or ὅς is found elsewhere in the unit, and the double occurrence of the relative pronoun in v. 10 strengthens the parallelism. Paul's hope in God acts as the pivot between Paul's affliction and the prayers offered to God by many for the sake of Paul while he is afflicted.

B. Paul's Reason for Writing the Present Letter (1:12–14)

A 12 For our *boast* [καύχησις] is this: the testimony of our conscience, that *by* [ἐν] godly holiness[13] and sincerity—not *by* [ἐν] human

---

11. So Harris, *Second Epistle*, 160.

12. Some texts read ὑμῶν instead of ἡμῶν, which does not fit well in the present context. The problem likely arose when the sounds *hū* and *hē* both shortened to [i].

13. Witnesses differ on whether the text should read ἁγιότητι or ἁπλότητι. Neither reading fully explains the other since ἁγιότητι → ἁπλότητι and ἁπλότητι → ἁγιότητι are equally possible textual progressions. The external evidence favors ἁγιότητι with old and reliable witnesses of wide geographical representation (P⁴⁶ ℵ* A B). In addition, it is more likely that scribes would correct ἁγιότητι to ἁπλότητι to parallel εἰλικρίνεια if they had any doubts regarding the validity of ἁγιότητι.

wisdom, but *by* [ἐν] the **grace** of God—we have conducted ourselves *in* [ἐν] the world—and even more so towards you.

B 13a For we do not write to you anything except what *you can read*[14] [ἀναγινώσκετε] and *understand* [ἐπιγινώσκετε].

B′ 13b And I hope that you will *understand* [ἐπιγνώσεσθε] fully, 14a just as you have *understood* [ἐπέγνωτε] us partially,

A′ 14b that we are your *boast* [καύχημα], just as you are ours, *on* [ἐν] the day of the[15] Lord Jesus.

Verses 12-14 may be distinguished as a section on grammatical and verbal grounds. Grammatically the section begins with the γάρ clause of v. 12 and closes with the ὅτι clause of v. 14b. Whereas vv. 8-11 consist of a single sentence (in the Greek), v. 12 begins a new sentence and line of thought. The ὅτι clause of v. 14 concludes Paul's reasons for writing in vv. 13-14. The unit's distinct vocabulary affirm the grammatical delimitations.

The transitional terms χάρισμα (1:11) and χάριτι (1:12) link the A (1:8-11) and B (1:12-14) units of Macrochiasm I. The line of thought thus progresses from the grace that the audience participates in through prayer on Paul's behalf in 1:11 to the manner in which Paul carries out his ministry.

Two nouns from which the verb καυχάομαι is derived (καύχησις and καύχημα) and the preposition ἐν in 1:12 and 1:14b establish the A and A′ elements of the unit. The terms are not found elsewhere in the unit, and καύχησις and καύχημα are not found elsewhere in Macrochiasm I (1:8—2:13). The quadruple use of the verb γινώσκω establishes the B and B′ elements. The double occurrence of pairs in 1:13a and 1:13b-14 strengthens the parallelism. Paul's reason for writing to the Corinthians, namely that they might know him fully, acts as the pivot between Paul's boast in his positive manner of preaching and his hope that he and the community may mutually share a boast in one another on the day of Christ.

---

14. "Read" translates ἀναγινώσκω, which in the Greek has an alliterative and lexical connection to γινώσκω ("to read, understand").

15. For this translation I follow P[46vid] A C D Ψ M and Ambrosiaster to omit ἡμῶν, which NA[27] places in brackets as doubtful. The pronoun was likely added by scribes to echo the same phrase in 1:3.

C. Decision to Change Travel Plans before the Painful Visit (1:15–17)[16]

A 15a With *this* [ταύτῃ] confidence I formerly *decided* [ἐβουλόμην]

  B 15b to *come to you* [πρὸς ὑμᾶς ἐλθεῖν], so that you might have a double **favor**,

    C 16a and by way of you pass through to *Macedonia* [Μακεδονίαν],

    C′ 16b and again from *Macedonia* [Μακεδονίας],

  B′ 16c *come to you* [ἐλθεῖν πρὸς ὑμᾶς], and by you be sent off to Judea.

A′ 17 So when I made *this* [τοῦτο] *decision* [βουλόμενος], was I flip-flopping? Or did I *decide* [βουλεύομαι] in a worldly way when I made the *decision* [βουλεύομαι], such that from me it is "**yes, yes**," and "**no, no**?"

Verses 15–17 may be distinguished formally as a travelogue. The section stands out from its surrounding context. The second person pronouns in 1:14 and 1:15 act as transitional terms that link the B (1:12–14) and C (1:15–17) units of Macrochiasm I. The line of thought thus progresses from Paul being the boast of "you," the audience, in 1:14 to Paul's plan to come to "you," the audience, in 1:15.

The demonstrative pronoun οὗτος ("this") and the verb βούλομαι ("to decide") in 1:15a and 1:17 establish the A and A′ elements of the unit. These are the only occurrences of βούλομαι in the entire letter. The repetition of the three word phrase ἐλθεῖν πρὸς ὑμᾶς ("to come to you") in 1:15b and 1:16c establish the B and B′ elements, and these terms are not found elsewhere in the unit. The repetition of Macedonia in 1:11a and 1:16b establishes the C and C′ elements. It is not mentioned elsewhere in the unit and only occurs in the letter in 2:13 and 7:5. Macedonia acts as the literal and logistical center of Paul's travel plans, and thus is the pivot between his desire to come to Corinth twice and the activity of his decision making.

---

16. See also Matera (*II Corinthians*, 52) and Furnish (*II Corinthians*, 132). Barrett (*Second Epistle*, 69), Martin (*2 Corinthians*, 22–29), Harris (*Second Epistle*, 190-94), and NAB prefer 1:15-22.

D. All Things are "Yes" in Christ (1:18–22)

A 18 But as God is faithful, *our*[17] [ἡμῶν] message to you is not both "**yes**" and "**no**." 19a For the Son of God, Jesus Christ, who was proclaimed to *you* [ὑμῖν] by *us* [ἡμῶν]—by myself and Silas and Timothy—

  B 19b he is not "yes" and "no," but *in him* [ἐν αὐτῷ] is "yes."

  B′ 20a For as many as are the promises of God, they have their "yes" *in him* [ἐν αὐτῷ].

A′ 20b Therefore, *our* [ἡμῶν] amen is through him to the glory of **God**. 21 The one who established us with you in Christ and anointed *us* [ἡμᾶς] is **God**— 22 he who sealed *us* [ἡμᾶς] with *you* [ὑμῖν] and gave *us* the down payment of the Spirit in *our* [ἡμῶν] hearts.

Grammatically 1:18–22 may be distinguished as a section.[18] The δέ clause of v. 18 shifts from the travelogue in 1:15–17 to a declaration of God's faithfulness. The abrupt shift from the literary first person plural pronouns in vv. 21–22 to a literal first person singular pronoun in v. 23, as well as the call for God to act as witness against Paul's life, mark v. 23 as the start of a new section. The διό clause in vv. 20b–22 acts as the conclusion to the statements of vv. 18–22a and contains the same use of plural pronouns that is seen in vv. 18–19, and thus it should be included with vv. 18–20a.

The transitional terms ναί and οὔ ("yes" and "no") in 1:17 and 1:18 link the D (1:18–22) and C (1:15–17) units of Macrochiasm I. The line of thought thus progresses from the "yes, yes/no, no" that Paul claims he does not express in 1:17 to the fact that God's reliability affirms that Paul's message is not both "yes" and "no" but is only "yes" in 1:18–19.

The first person plural pronouns ("our, for us") and the dative second person plural pronoun ("to you, for your benefit") establish the A and A′ elements of the unit. These pronouns are not found elsewhere in the unit. The repetition of the phrase ἐν αὐτῷ ("in him") in vv. 19b and 20a establishes the B and B′ elements of the unit and does not occur elsewhere in the unit or throughout Macrochiasm I (1:8—2:13). The fact that all things are "yes" in Christ acts as the pivot between Paul's defense of his sincerity and his "resumé" of qualification from God.

---

17. The first-person plural pronouns in this verse are likely not literary plurals but rather refer to the team of Paul, Timothy, and Silas.

18. Fee, *Christology*, 171.

C´. Change in Travel Plans After the Painful Visit (1:23—2:3)

A 1:23 And I call **God** as witness against my life that it was to spare you that I did not come again to Corinth. 24 Not that we lord over your faith; rather we work together for *your joy* [χαρᾶς ὑμῶν]. For you stand firm in the faith.

  B 2:1 For *this reason* [τοῦτο τό] I determined in myself not to come visit you again in *pain* [λύπῃ].

    C 2a For if I *cause you pain* [λυπῶ],

      D 2b who will be the one who gladdens me,

    C´ 2c if not the one *who is pained* [λυπούμενος] by me?

  B´ 3a And I wrote *this very thing* [τοῦτο αὐτό] so that when I do come I might not *be pained* [λύπην] by those from whom I must gain joy;

A´ 3b for I am confident in all of **you** that my joy will be **your** *joy* [χαρὰ ὑμῶν] as well.

Grammatically 1:23—2:3 may be delimited as a section.[19] The abrupt change to first person singular ("I") in v. 23 and Paul's request for God to act as witness against him mark the genesis of the section. Peculiar vocabulary also delimits 1:23—2:3 as a section. The clause in 2:4 opens a new section that addresses Paul's affliction while he wrote the tearful letter.

The transitional term θεός in 1:20-21 and 1:23 links the C´ (1:23—2:13) and D (1:18-22) units of Macrochiasm I. The line of thought thus progresses from the fact that God has confirmed, anointed, sealed, and set the Spirit in the hearts of the audience because of Paul's preaching in 1:21-22 to the fact that God acts as Paul's witness for his testimony to Corinth in 1:23.[20]

The repetition of the phrase χαρὰ ὑμῶν ("your joy") in 1:24 and 2:3b establishes the A and A´ elements of the unit. This phrase is not

---

19. Scholars differ widely on the limits of this section: 1:23—2:2 in Furnish (*II Corinthians*, 132); 1:23—2:13 in Barrett (*Second Epistle*, 82-83); 1:23—2:11 in Martin (*2 Corinthians*, 30-31); 1:23—2:4 in Harris (*Second Epistle*, 211). The variety arises due to the scholars' criteria for delimiting sections, which focuses on the content or themes of the material.

20. The referent for ἡμῶν in 1:21-22 is debated, but I prefer to see the pronoun as inclusive of the audience. The topic of the ambiguous plural pronouns in 2 Corinthians will be addressed in the following chapters.

found elsewhere in the unit or Macrochiasm I (1:8—2:13). The repetition of the demonstrative pronoun οὗτος ("this, this one") and the noun form of λύπη in 2:1a and 2:3a establish the B and B′ elements. Distinguished from the noun form, the repetition of the verb λυπέω in 2:2a and 2:2c establishes the C and C′ elements of the chiasm. The unparalleled D element (2:2b), which is focused on joy, is set apart and serves as the pivot of the unit. Paul's contention that pain should not come from a relationship that is supposed to bring joy acts as the pivot between Paul's double mention of his concern for the community's benefit.

B′. The Letter of Tears and the Offender (2:4–9)

A 4 Because in great distress and with a pained heart I wrote to **you** with many tears, not that **you** be pained, but *so that you might know* [ἵνα γνῶτε] of my love that overflows for **you**.

   B 5 But if anyone has caused pain, he did not cause pain to me, but, in a way—not to exaggerate—to all of you. 6 The penalty for *this one* [τῷ τοιούτῳ] by the majority is sufficient 7a so that you should rather forgive and *encourage* [παρακαλέσαι] him,

   B′ 7b or else *this one* [ὁ τοιοῦτος] may be swallowed up by excessive pain. 8 Therefore, I *encourage* [παρακαλῶ] you to reaffirm your love for him.

A′ 9 It was for this reason that I previously[21] wrote: *that I might know* [ἵνα γνῶ] **your** character, whether **you** are obedient in everything.

Grammatically, 2:4–9 may be delimited as a section.[22] The γάρ clause of v. 4 introduces a new line of thought, namely, the matter of how Paul intends his letter to directly affect the audience. The phrase "for this reason" in v. 9 acts as the conclusion to the section. This point is affirmed by the δέ clause in v. 10 that changes the focus to general forgiveness and Paul's change in travel plans (2:10–13).

The second person pronouns in 2:3 and 2:4 act as transitional terms that link the B′ (2:4–9) and C′ (1:23—2:3) units of Macrochiasm I. The line of thought thus progresses from the fact that Paul does all

---

21. The term "previously" is added to show that I do not consider ἔγραψα in this verse to be an epistolary aorist, but rather to refer to the previous tearful letter. See, e.g., Harris (*Second Epistle*, 178–79) and Thrall (*II Corinthians*, 230–31).

22. Harris (*Second Epistle*, 222–23) and Furnish (*II Corinthians*, 153) delimit the unit as 2:5–11.

things for the benefit of "you" the audience in 2:3 to the fact that Paul wrote to "you" the audience a tearful letter.

The repetition of the conjunction ἵνα ("in order that") and the subjunctive form of the verb γινώσκω ("that you/I may know") in 2:4 and 2:9 establishes the A and A′ elements of the unit. The terms are not found elsewhere in the unit. The repetition of the demonstrative adjective τοιοῦτος ("this one") and the verb παρακαλέω ("I exhort, encourage") in 2:6–8 establishes the B and B′ elements. The adjective τοιοῦτος is not found elsewhere in the letter, and the verb παρακαλέω is not found elsewhere in Macrochiasm I (1:8—2:13). The call for the community to encourage "this one," the offender, acts as the pivot between Paul's hope for mutual knowledge for him and the community: that they might know the extent of his love for them and that he might know the extent of their obedience.

A′. Paul's Anguish in Troas (2:10–13)

A 10a Anyone **you** forgive anything, *I* do also [κἀγώ]. For what *I* [ἐγώ] forgive—if I have forgiven anything—

   B 10b is for **your** sake in the presence *of Christ* [Χριστοῦ],

      C 11 so that we might not be outwitted by Satan—for we are not unaware of his schemes.

   B′ 12a When I went to Troas for the gospel *of Christ* [Χριστοῦ],

A′ 12b and a door was opened to *me* [μοι] by the Lord, 13 I did not have comfort in *my* [μου] spirit because *I* [με] could not find Titus, *my* [μου] brother. Then, I left them and went on to Macedonia.

Grammatically the δέ clause in v. 10 and the subsequent δέ clause in v. 14 establish 2:10–13 as a distinct unit.[23] The δέ clause in v. 10 marks a new section with a general discussion of forgiveness. The δέ clause in v. 14 shifts the focus from Paul's search for Titus to imagery of a

---

23. Some may still find the unit of 2:10–13 to be unconvincing because 2:10–11 and 2:12–13 appear to have different themes. However, this unit presents an excellent example of aural/grammatical dissonance that occurs within modern delimitation of sections in ancient texts. Within this audience-oriented study, I aim to demonstrate not necessarily the thematic or grammatical delimitations alone, but rather to *show* in the passage what the authorial audience *hears*. For this reason, even if some see 2:10–13 as having thematically distinguishable sections, the structure above demonstrates that the authorial audience *hears* 2:10–13 as a chiastic unit that is aurally coherent.

triumphal parade. Although the placement and purpose of vv. 12-13 are debated, the content of 2:12-13 is in fact consonant with 2:10-11. Throughout 1:8—2:11 Paul demonstrates his love for the community in Corinth. In 2:12-13, Paul explains that he was anxious as he waited to hear from Titus how his tearful letter was received in Corinth, such that his health was compromised and he left a promising ministry in Troas to find Titus in Macedonia. For this reason, 2:12-13 are consonant with, and make a fitting conclusion for, Paul's demonstration of his love for the community in 1:8—2:11.

The second person pronouns in 2:9 and 2:10 act as transitional terms that link the A´ (2:10-13) and B´ (2:4-9) units of Macrochiasm I. The line of thought thus progresses from the fact that Paul wrote that he might know the obedience of "you" the audience in 2:9 to the fact that whatever Paul forgives is for the sake of "you" the audience in 2:10.

The repetition of first singular pronouns ἐγώ ("I") and μοι/me ("me") in 2:10a and 2:12b-13 establishes the A and A´ elements of the unit. First singular pronouns are not found elsewhere in the unit. The repetition of Χριστοῦ in 2:10b and 2:12a establishes the B and B´ elements. The name Χριστοῦ is not found elsewhere in the unit. The unparalleled C element (2:11) concerns Satan and his schemes. The acknowledgement of Satan's plans to foil the eschatological rewards of the community acts as the center and pivot between Paul's actions for the sake of the community in terms of forgiveness in v. 10 and Paul's journey from Troas to Macedonia in v. 13 to learn of the community's reaction to his letter.

Overview of Macrochiasm I (1:8—2:13)

A 1:8-11: ἀγνοεῖν (1:8); ἐσχήκαμεν (1:8)
  B 1:12-14: περισσοτέρως (1:12); ἀνα-/ἐπιγινώσκω (1:13)
    C 1:15-17: ταύτῃ, τοῦτο (1:15, 17)
      D 1:18-22
    C´ 1:23—2:3: τοῦτο, τοῦτο (2:1, 3)
  B´ 2:4-9: περισσοτέρως/ᾳ (2:4, 7); γνῶτε, γνῶ (2:4, 9)
A´ 2:10-13: ἀγνοοῦμεν (2:11); ἔσχηκα (2:12)

As with the elements of the individual units, it is also useful to compare the corresponding units of the macrochiasm. The lexical parallels found in the structure show a development in the author's argument and underscore the central and important points of the structure.[24]

A. Paul's Suffering in Asia (1:8–11) // A′. Paul's Anguish in Troas (2:10–13)

That Paul does not want the community to be unaware (οὐκ ἀγνοεῖν) of his affliction in 1:8 parallels his assertion that he and the community are not unaware (οὐκ ἀγνοοῦμεν) of Satan's plans to separate the believers through a lack of forgiveness in 2:11. The verb ἀγνοέω is not found elsewhere in 1:8—2:13. That Paul has (ἐσχήκαμεν) a death sentence in 1:9 parallels the lack (οὐκ ἔσχηκα) of rest in his spirit in 2:13. The verb ἔχω is not found in the perfect tense with the first person suffix elsewhere in 1:8—2:13.

B. Paul's Reason for Writing the Present Letter (B, 1:12–14) // B′. Paul's Reason for Writing the Tearful Letter (2:4–9)

The holiness, sincerity, and grace of God by which Paul conducts himself in the world—and even more so (περισσοτέρως) to the community—in 1:12 parallels Paul's overflowing love (περισσοτέρως) for the community in 2:4. This term does not occur elsewhere within Macrochiasm I (1:8—2:13). That Paul writes so that the Corinthians can read (ἀναγινώσκετε) and understand (ἐπιγινώσκετε) the letter so that they might understand (ἐπιγνώσεσθε) him fully just as they have understood (ἐπέγνωτε) him partially in 1:12–14 parallels Paul's wish that the Corinthians might understand (ἵνα γνῶτε) the extent of his love for them and that he might understand (ἵνα γνῶ) their obedience for him in 2:4, 9. The verb γινώσκω is not found elsewhere in Macrochiasm I.

C. Paul's Travel Change before the Painful Visit (1:15–17) // C′. Paul's Travel Change after the Painful Visit (1:23—2:3)

The double occurrence of οὗτος ("this" confidence by which Paul made his decision to change his travel plans and "this" decision Paul made to change his plans prior to the painful visit) in 1:15 and 1:17 parallels the double occurrence of οὗτος ("this" decision to change his travel plans following the painful visit and "this" tearful letter that he wrote) in 2:1

---

24. Bailey and Vanderbroek, *Literary Forms*, 51, 53.

and 2:3. Although οὗτος also occurs in 1:12 and 2:1, the doublet of the word only occurs in 1:15, 17 and 2:1, 3.

D. All Things are "Yes" in Christ (1:18–22)

The unparalleled unit 1:18–22 acts as the pivot and center of the entire Macrochiasm I in 1:8—2:13.[25] The unit sets the person of Christ as proof of Paul's sincerity and defense of his actions that preceded 2 Corinthians. Since all things are "yes" in Christ, Paul's plans and statements cannot be both "yes" and "no." Thus his changes in travel plans (1:15–17; 1:23—2:3) do not display personal instability in Paul but rather demonstrate to the community that he made his decisions in a manner that was intended only to benefit the community (1:15, 23; 2:3). In addition, Paul writes the present letter (2 Corinthians) so that the community might know him fully and have him as their boast at the Parousia (1:14); and he wrote the previous letter (the tearful letter) so that he might know of their obedience (2:9).

Macrochiasm II (2:14—4:14)

The second macrochiasm contains an A-B-C-B´-A´ structure, consisting of five chiastic units: (A) 2:14—3:6; (B) 3:7–18; (C) 4:1–6; (B´) 4:7–11; (A´) 4:12–14.

A. Paul's Qualifications to be a Minister for God (2:14—3:6)

A 14 But thanks be to God, who, in **Christ**, always leads *us* (ἡμᾶς) in a triumphal parade and makes known through us the fragrance of the knowledge of him in every place. 15 Because *we are* (ἐσμέν) the aroma of **Christ** for God, among those who are being saved and among those who are perishing. 16 For the latter, we are an odor from death to death, and for the former an odor from life to life. And who is *qualified* (ἱκανός) for this? 17 For *we are* (ἐσμέν) not like the many who sell the *word* (λόγον) of God—but as from sincerity, as *from God* (ἐκ θεοῦ)—before God we speak in **Christ**.

---

25. Some have argued that this section is a regression within Paul's larger defense, but this structure demonstrates that 1:18–22 is pivotal and rhetorically placed to emphasize Paul's central point regarding his sincerity within a larger apologia for his recent administrative decisions.

   B 3:1 Are we beginning to commend ourselves again? Or do we need, as some do, *letters* [ἐπιστολῶν] of recommendation to you or from you? 2 You are our *letter* [ἐπιστολή], *written* [ἐγγεγραμμένη] on [your][26] *hearts* [καρδίαις], known and read by all people,

   B′ 3 making clear that you are a *letter* [ἐπιστολή] from Christ, administered by us, *written* [ἐγγεγραμμένη] not with ink but by the Spirit of the living God, not on stone tablets but on fleshy *heart* [καρδίαις] tablets.

A′ 4 Such confidence we have through Christ toward God. 5 Not that *we are qualified* [ἱκανοί ἐσμεν] in ourselves to *take credit* [λογίσασθαἰ for anything that comes from us; rather, our *qualification* [ἱκανότης] comes *from God* [ἐκ τοῦ θεοῦ], 6 who has indeed *qualified us* [ἱκάνωσεν ἡμᾶς] to be **ministers** of a new covenant, not of **letter** but of **Spirit**. For the **letter** kills but the **Spirit** gives life.

   Grammatically 2:14—3:6 may be distinguished as a unit.[27] The δέ clause of 2:14 introduces a shift from first person singular pronouns (seen in 2:10-13) to first person plural pronouns; these plural pronouns continue to 3:6. The conditional clause and δέ conjunction in 3:7 mark a new section. The first person plural pronouns, which are prominent in 2:14—3:6, do not appear again until v. 18.

   The repetition of Χριστός in 2:10b, 12, 14, 15 links the A unit (2:14—3:6) of Macrochiasm II with the A′ unit (2:10-13) of Macrochiasm I, and so Christ acts as the transitional subject between Macrochiasms I and II. The line of thought progresses from the fact that Paul went into Troas for the purpose of the gospel of "Christ" in 2:12 to the fact that in "Christ" God leads Paul in a triumphal parade in 2:14–15.

   The occurrence of the root ἱκανός ("worthy, qualified"), first person plural pronouns ἐσμέν and ἡμᾶς ("we, us"), the noun λόγος ("word") and its corresponding verb λογίζομαι ("I accredit"), and the repetition of the phrase ἐκ θεοῦ ("from God") in 2:14-17 and 3:4-6 establish the A

---

26. Although ἡμῶν has external support in the majority of witnesses, I prefer to read ὑμῶν (along with Barrett [Second Epistle, 96], Martin [2 Corinthians, 51], Thrall [II Corinthians, 223], RSV, and NAB [1970]). I consider ἡμῶν to arise from assimilation to ἐν ταῖς καρδίαις ἡμῶν from 1:21.

27. Lambrecht ("Structure," 153) and Matera (*II Corinthians*, 70) also denote these verses as a unit with parallel sections. Lambrecht prefers however to use the term "concentric pattern" rather than chiasm, and delimits the structure as (A) 2:14-17, (B) 3:1-3, (A′) 3:4-6.

and A´ elements of the unit. The root ἱκανός does not occur elsewhere in the units or in Macrochiasm II (2:14—4:14). The multiple occurrence of this root in 3:5–6 strengthens the parallelism. The term λόγος and its corresponding verbal form λογίζομαι do not occur elsewhere in the unit, or in Macrochiasm II.

The repetition of the noun ἐπιστολή ("letter"), the perfect passive participle ἐγεγραμμένη ("what has been written") and the noun καρδία ("heart") in 3:1–3 establishes the B and B´ elements. Although γράφω was prominent in Macrochiasm I (1:8—2:13), the verb appears only here and in 4:13 in Macrochiasm II (2:14—4:14). The term καρδία is prominent in the earlier part of the letter, but is not found elsewhere in this unit. Paul's rhetorical question regarding his need for letters of recommendation (3:1–2), and his subsequent answer that the audience is his letter (3:3), act as the pivot between Paul's rhetorical question of who is qualified for this ministry (2:16) and his response that he does not find his qualification in himself, but from God, who has qualified him for the ministry of a new covenant (3:5–6).

B. Believers are Gloriously Transformed by Paul's Ministry (3:7–18)

A 7 Now if the **ministry** of death that was engraved in **letters** of stone was so *glorious* [δόξῃ] that the Israelites were not able to look intently on the face of Moses because of the *glory* [δόξαν] of his face that was passing away, 8 much more will the **ministry** of the **Spirit** be *glorious* [δόξῃ]. 9 For if the **ministry** of condemnation was *glorious* [δόξα], much more will the ministry of righteousness overflow with *glory* [δόξῃ]. 10 For that which was *glorified* [δεδοξασμένον] is no longer *glorious* [δεδόξασται] when compared to the surpassing *glory* [δόξης]. 11 For if that which is now passing away was *glorious* [δόξης], much more will that which remains be *glorious* [δόξῃ].

B 12 Since we have this hope, we act with great boldness, 13 and not like *Moses* [Μωϋσῆς], who placed a *veil* [κάλυμμα] over his face so that the Israelites could not see the end of what was passing away. 14a But their senses were dulled. For to *this day* [σήμερον] the *veil* [κάλυμμα] remains whenever the old covenant is read,

C 14b since it is not revealed that in Christ it is passing away.

B′ 15 But to *this very day* [σήμερον], whenever *Moses* [Μωϋσῆς] is read, a *veil* [κάλυμμα] is placed over their hearts. 16 But for whoever turns to the Lord, the *veil* [κάλυμμα] is taken away.

A′ 17 But the Lord is the Spirit, and where the Spirit of the Lord is, there[28] is freedom. 18 **All** of us who look on the *glory* [δόξαν] of the Lord—as though through a mirror—with unveiled face, are being transformed into the same image from *glory* [δόξης] to *glory* [δόξαν], as from the Lord who is the Spirit.

Grammatically 3:7–18 may be distinguished as a section.[29] The conditional clause of v. 7 interrupts the prominent use of first person plural pronouns found in 2:14—3:6. Instead, 3:7 introduces a shift in topic from Paul's qualifications to a midrash on Exod 32:27–35. The phrase διὰ τοῦτο ("for this reason") in 4:1 begins a new line of argument that builds from Paul's preaching comments. The particular vocabulary, namely the terms "glory" and "veil," denote a lexical cohesiveness that affirms the grammatical delimitations for the section.

The transitional terms διάκονος/διακονία ("minister"/"ministry"), πνεῦμα ("Spirit"), and γράμμα ("letter"), which are found in 3:6 and 3:7-8, link the B (3:7-18) and A (2:14—3:6) units of Macrochiasm II. That Paul is qualified by God for the ministry of the new covenant in 3:6 progresses to a discussion on the ministry of the old covenant in 3:7; that this new covenant is not of the letter but of the Spirit in 3:6 progresses to a discussion in 3:7 of the old covenant written in letters on stone and made antithetical to the spiritual covenant, which will be even more glorious.

The multiple occurrences of the term δόξα ("glory") in 3:7-11 and 3:18 delimit the A and A′ elements of the unit. The term δόξα does not occur in 3:12-16 (the midpoints of the unit), and the multiple occurrences of the term (ten times in 3:7-11 and three times in 3:17-18) strengthen the parallelism. The terms σήμερον ("today"), κάλυμμα ("veil"), and the nominative form Μωϋσῆς ("Moses") establish the B and B′ elements. The term σήμερον does not occur elsewhere in the letter. The double occurrence of κάλυμμα in both B and B′ elements strengthens the parallelism. The unparalleled C element (3:14b) concerns the activity of Christ

---

28. Some witnesses from the Western tradition insert ἐκεῖ before ἐλευθερία, which appears to be an amelioration.

29. Matera, *II Corinthians*, 68; Martin, *2 Corinthians*, 56. Others (Harris, *Second Epistle*, 292; NAB) divide the sections 3:7-11, 12-18.

in revealing the true status of the old covenant. That Christ reveals the true status of the old covenant and the glory of the new acts as the pivot between Paul's comparison of the old and new covenants in 3:7–11 and the fact that the new covenant gloriously transform believers in Paul's time in 3:17–18.

C. Paul's Gospel is Unveiled (4:1–6)

A 1 For this reason, since we have this ministry just as we have been shown mercy, we are not discouraged. 2 But we renounce the shameful hidden things, since we do not act with trickery, nor do we falsify the word of God; rather, with honest transparency we commend *ourselves* [ἑαυτούς] before God to **everyone's** conscience.

  B 3a And even if our *gospel* [εὐαγγέλιον] *is* [ἐστίν] veiled, it *is* [ἐστίν] veiled

   C 3b *to* [ἐν] those who are perishing—

   C′ 4a *to* [ἐν] those, the unbelieving, whose minds the god of this age has blinded,

  B′ 4b so that they might not see the light of the *gospel* [εὐαγγελίου] of the glory of Christ, who *is* [ἐστίν] the image of God.

A′ 5 For we do not proclaim *ourselves* [ἑαυτούς] but Jesus Christ as Lord, and *ourselves* [ἑαυτούς] as your servants for the sake of Jesus. 6 For **God** who said, 'From darkness let there be light,' has set in our hearts the light of the knowledge of the glory of **God** on the face of Christ.[30]

Grammatically 4:1–6 may be distinguished as a unit.[31] The phrase "because of this" in 4:1 builds on the preceding comments in 3:7–18. In 4:1–6 Paul's ministry is veiled only to those who are blinded by Satan, but Paul's gospel offers believers the opportunity to look with unveiled face upon Christ. The ὅτι clause that begins 4:6 depends on the content of 4:1–5. The participle ἔχοντες in 4:7 and the shift in imagery from light to earthen vessels affirm the delimitations for 4:1–6.

---

30. Some texts read Ἰησοῦ Χριστοῦ. The shorter reading is to be preferred since pious scribes often added Ἰησοῦ to the original lone Χριστοῦ. Metzger (*TCGNT*, 510) notes that the shorter reading "best explains the origin of the others."

31. This section is commonly delimited as a unit. See Lambrecht, *Second Corinthians*, 64; Best, *Second Corinthians*, 36; Thrall, *II Corinthians*, 297.

The transitional term πᾶς ("all, every") in 3:18 and 4:2 links the C (4:1–6) and B (3:7–18) units of Macrochiasm II. The line of thought thus progresses from the fact that "all" of "us" look with unveiled face on the glory of the Lord in 3:18 to the fact that Paul commends himself to the consciences of "all" people in 4:2.

The repetition of the reflexive pronoun ἑαυτούς ("ourselves") in 4:2 and 4:5 establishes the A and A´ elements of the unit. The term ἑαυτούς does not occur elsewhere in the unit. The noun εὐαγγέλιον ("gospel") and the enclitic ἐστίν ("it is," "to be") establish the B and B´ elements. These terms do not occur elsewhere in the unit. The double occurrence of ἐστίν in 4:3 strengthens the parallel. The preposition ἐν ("in") in 4:3b and 4:4a establishes the C and C´ elements. The idea that Paul's gospel is not veiled but instead reveals to believers the glory of Christ (4:3–4) acts as the pivot between Paul's assertion of confidence that he is not one who sells the word of God but acts in truth (4:2) and his assertion that he proclaims not himself but Christ as Lord (4:4–5).

B´. Paul's Mortality Makes Known the Life of Christ (4:7–11)

A 7 But we hold this treasure *in* [ἐν] jars of clay, so that the surpassing power may be from **God** and not from *us* [ἡμῶν].

   B 8—In every way we are afflicted *but not* [ἀλλ' οὐ] constricted, confused *but not* [ἀλλ' οὐκ] at a loss,

   B´ 9 persecuted *but not* [ἀλλ' οὐκ] abandoned, beaten down *but not* [ἀλλ' οὐκ] destroyed—

A´ 10 always bearing the death of Jesus *in* [ἐν] our body, in order that the life of Jesus may also be manifest *in* [ἐν] *our* [ἡμῶν] body.
   11 For we who live are always being handed over to **death** for the sake of Jesus, so that the life of Jesus may be manifest *in* [ἐν] *our* [ἡμῶν] mortal flesh.

Grammatically 4:7–11 may be distinguished as a section.[32] The ὅτι clause of v. 6 is the logical conclusion that depends on 4:1–5. A new

---

32. Most commentators prefer to delimit the section as 4:7–12 or 4:7–15 (e.g., Barnett, *Second Epistle*, 227; Lambrecht, *Second Corinthians*, 71; RSV), but such delimitations are based on thematic criteria rather than sound patterns. The structure here demonstrates how the authorial audience hears the text as it is performed by marking the parallel repeating terms. These objective criteria denote two chiastic structures in 4:7–11 and 4:12–14.

section is marked by the lack of first person plural pronouns beginning in v. 12. This delimitation is aided by the strong break suggested by the ὥστε clause of v. 12.[33] While the ὥστε clause of v. 12 builds on the concluding image of v. 11, the focus turns from Paul (4:7–11) to the direct impact of Paul's mortality for the life and resurrection of the audience (4:12–14).

The transitional term θέος in 4:6 and 4:7 links the B´ (4:6–11) and C (4:1–5) units of Macrochiasm II. The line of thought thus progresses from the idea that "God" set in believers' hearts a light of the knowledge of the glory of "God" on the face of Christ in 4:6 to the idea that Paul carries "this treasure" in "jars of clay" in order to show that the surpassing power is from "God" and not from human carriers.

The repetition of the preposition ἐν and the pronoun ἡμῶν in 4:6–7 and 4:10–11 establish the A and A´ elements of the unit. Neither term is found elsewhere in the unit. The double occurrence of both terms in the border elements strengthens the parallelism. The repetition of ἀλλ᾽ οὐκ ("but not") in v. 8 and v. 9 establishes the B and B´ elements. The phrase is not found elsewhere in the letter. The double occurrence of the phrase in both elements strengthens the parallelism.

The fact that Paul is afflicted but not destroyed (4:8–9) acts as the pivot between his contention that he carries the knowledge of the glory of God in "jars of clay" to manifest the power of God (4:6–7) and his contention that affliction in his life occurs so that the life of Christ might be apparent in his own mortal body (4:10–11).

A´. Paul Proclaims his Faith for the Life of the Community (4:12–14)

A 12 So **death** is at work in us, but life *in you* [ὑμῖν].

  B 13a Since, then, we have the same Spirit of faith, according to what is written, "I *believed* [ἐπίστευσα], therefore I *spoke* [ἐλάλησα],"

  B´ 13b we too *believe* [πιστεύομεν] and therefore *speak* [λαλοῦμεν].

A´ 14 Because we know that the one who raised Jesus[34] will also raise us with Jesus and set us *with* **you** [ὑμῖν].

---

33. This break at v. 12 is seen in the NAB (1980). The NA[27] also presents a new paragraph beginning at 2 Cor 5:16 with ὥστε.

34. It is easier to explain why some witnesses add κύριος than it is to explain why others omitted it. Thus I prefer the shorter reading Ἰησοῦ.

Grammatically 4:12–14 may be distinguished as a section. The ὥστε clause of v. 12 moves away from Paul's afflictions and speaks of the direct impact on the audience with second person plural pronouns. The γάρ clause of v. 15 builds on the imagery seen in v. 14 but presents new transcendent (the "eternal weight of glory") and dualistic ("the things that are seen" and "the things that are not seen" in 4:18) terminology.

The transitional term θάνατος ("death") in 4:11 and 4:12 links the A´ (4:12–14) and B´ units (4:7–11) of Macrochiasm II. The line of thought thus progresses from the fact that in 4:11 the living are handed over to death so that the life of Christ may be manifest to the fact that in 4:12 death is working in Paul but life in "you" the audience.

The second-person plural pronoun ὑμῖν ("to you, for your benefit") in v. 12 and v. 14 establishes the A and A´ elements of the unit. The pronoun is not found elsewhere in the unit. The repetition of the verbs πιστεύω ("I believe") and λαλέω ("I speak") and the conjunction διό ("so," "therefore") in 4:13a and 4:13b establishes the B and B´ elements of the unit. These terms are not found elsewhere in the unit. The use of the noun πίστεως ("faith") along with the verb πιστεύω in v. 13a strengthens the parallelism.

That Paul believes and therefore speaks, just as it is written in Scripture (4:13), acts as the pivot between his assertion that the afflictions work death in him but bring life for the community (4:12) and the assertion that God will raise him up with Jesus and set him with the community, who are also to be raised (4:14).

Overview: Macrochiasm II (2:14—4:14)

A 2:14–3:6: λαλοῦμεν (2:17); ἐγγεγραμμένη (3:2, 3)
  B 3:7–18: ὑπερβαλλούσης (3:10)
    C 4:1–6
  B´ 4:7–11: ὑπερβολή (4:7)
A´ 4:12–14: λάλησα, λαλοῦμεν (4:13); γεγραμμένον (4:13)

A. Paul's Qualifications to Be a Minister to the Community (2:14—3:6) // A´. Paul Proclaims His Faith for the Life of the Community (4:12–14)

That Paul speaks (λαλοῦμεν) in Christ out of sincerity before God (2:17) parallels the fact that Paul believes and therefore speaks (λαλοῦμεν) his gospel, a characteristic that is affirmed in Scripture (4:13). The double occurrence of λαλέω in 4:13 strengthens the parallelism. That the Corinthians are Paul's letter of recommendation written (ἐγγεγραμμένη) on his heart, not in ink but by the Spirit of the living God (3:2–3), parallels the passage written (ἐγγεγραμμένη) in Scripture that Paul speaks with the same Spirit as the suffering psalmist who spoke on the basis of his faith in God (4:13). The terms λαλέω and γράφω are not found elsewhere in Macrochiasm II (2:14—4:14).

B. Paul's Ministry Makes Known the Glorious New Covenant of Life (3:7–18) // B′. Paul's Participation in Christ's Death Makes Known the Life of Christ (4:7–11)

The glory of the new covenant that surpasses (ὑπερβαλλούσης) even that of the old (3:10) parallels the surpassing (ὑπερβάλλην) power of God that is manifested in Paul's participation with Christ's suffering (4:7). The verb ὑπερβάλλω and its corresponding noun are not found elsewhere in Macrochiasm II (2:14—4:14).

C. Paul's Gospel is Unveiled (4:1–6)

That Paul is confident that he proclaims the word of God with the appearance of truth, that his gospel is veiled only to those who do not believe, but to those who believe his gospel see the light of the glory of Christ and receive the glory of God in their hearts, acts as the center and pivot of Paul's defense of his qualifications to be a minister of Christ and the new covenant.

Macrochiasm III (4:15—6:2)

The third macrochiasm contains an A-B-C-C′-B′-A′ structure with six chiastic units: (A) 4:15–18; (B) 5:1–5; (C) 5:6–10; (C′) 5:11–13; (B′) 5:14–15; (A′) 5:16—6:2.

A. The Benefit of the Audience and the Glory of God (4:15–18)

A 15a For all of *the things* [τὰ πάντα][35] are for your benefit

---

35. Although neuter plurals in Greek are collective (e.g., "everything"), this rendering in English would lose the aural connection between 4:15a and 4:18 since the former would be rendered "everything" and the latter "what is seen/not seen." The translation offered here is preferred for this particular study since retaining the plural *shows* the present reader what the authorial audience *hears*, namely, an aural connection between the phrases τὰ πάντα in 4:15a and τὰ (μὴ) βλεπόμενα in 4:18.

B 15b in order that the grace, which overflows among the growing number of believers,[36] may increase the thanksgiving[37] for the *glory* [δόξαν] of God.

    C 16a So we are not discouraged: *even though* [ἀλλ'] *our* [ἡμῶν] outer self is continually decaying,

    C′ 16b *yet* [ἀλλ'] *our* [ἡμῶν] inner self is being renewed day by day.

B′ 17 For the temporary, light burden of our affliction is working out for us an eternal weight of *glory* [δόξης] out of all proportion,[38]

A′ 18 since we are not concerned with *the things that are seen* [τὰ βλεπόμενα], but with *the things that are not seen* [τὰ μὴ βλεπόμενα]. Because *the things that are seen* [τὰ βλεπόμενα] are temporary, but *the things that are unseen* [τὰ μὴ βλεπόμενα] are eternal.

The A unit of the macrochiasm is determined grammatically by the γάρ clause in 4:15 and the subsequent γάρ clause in 5:1. The ὅτι clause in 4:14 concludes the section 4:11–14; Paul asserts in v. 11 that his affliction occurs so that (ἵνα) the life of Jesus might be manifest in his flesh.[39]

    36. The term οἱ πλείονες has the sense of "majority" in 2 Cor 2:6 and 9:2, but here Paul is speaking of the "ever greater number of believers" (Thrall, *II Corinthians*, 345; Furnish, *II Corinthians*, 260; Martin, *2 Corinthians*, 90–91; cf. Barrett, *Second Epistle*, 144–45). The word "believers" is supplied.

    37. Translation of this passage is complicated because both verbs can have intransitive and transitive meanings. I follow Thrall (*II Corinthians*, 345–46) in reading πλεονάζω as intransitive and περισσεύω as transitive.

    38. So Barrett, *Second Epistle*, 147.

    39. Almost all commentators prefer to place v. 15 with what precedes (4:7–14). The structure presented here is based primarily on the aural patterning of the text that demonstrates a chiastic structure in 4:15–18. As mentioned in chapter 1 above, not all elemental pair correspondence is equally substantive. On some occasions, the connection is due to a repetition of sound rather than terminology. Although the definite article τά with a neuter plural substantive might seem inconsequential, such terms and repeated sounds stand out within an aural performance and thus serve as markers for the authorial audience (see Achtemeier, "Omne," 19–22).

Even if one considers this aural connection weaker than those found in the B–B′ and C–C′ element pairs, the integrity of the unit is not jeopardized. First, the echo the audience hears in the repeated neuter plural with definite article has an equal aural impact to that of lexical connectors seen in other examples in this chapter. Both 4:15a and 4:18 repeat the τὰ -ά sound, with the latter recalling and connecting with the former. Second, regardless of how strong one considers this connection to be, the lexical connectors between the B–B′ and C–C′ pairs, along with the significantly apparent integrity of the units prior (4:12–14) and after (5:1–5), safely establish 4:15–18 as a coherent unit.

The content of 4:14 develops the image of the life of Jesus manifest in Paul in the assertion that God will raise Paul and his coworkers just as he raised Jesus. The γάρ clause in 4:15 presents a shift in subject from Jesus Christ (4:11-14) to the glory of God (4:15-18). The γάρ clause in 5:1 introduces a new analogy to explain the assertion of faith in what is unseen in 4:18, and thus stands as a separate section.

The second person pronouns (4:14, 15) act as transitional terms that link the A unit (4:15-18) of Macrochiasm III with the A′ unit (4:12-14) of Macrochiasm II. Thus "you," the audience, acts as the transitional subject between Macrochiasms II and III. The line of thought progresses from the fact that God will raise Paul with Jesus and set him with "you," the audience, in 4:14 to the fact that all things are for the benefit of "you," the audience, in 4:15.

The only occurrences in this section of the neuter plural with a definite article, in 4:15 and 4:18, establish the A and A′ elements. The terms τὰ πάντα and τὰ (μὴ) βλεπόμενα create an aural connection [ta-a] for the authorial audience that sets the borders for the unit as a whole. The repetition of the sound four times in 4:18 strengthens the parallelism with v. 15. The glory (τὴν δόξαν) of God in 4:15 parallels the eternal weight of glory (δόξης) in 4:17, and these terms determine the B and B′ elements of the unit. Although δόξα is found prior to this section in 3:6—4:14, these are the only instances of the term in this unit and in Macrochiasm III (4:15—6:2) as a whole. In this way, "glory" serves as the marker of the B and B′ elements and further bridges this macrochiasm with Macrochiasm II (2:14—4:14).

The repetition of the conjunction ἀλλά and the pronoun ἡμῶν in 4:16b and 4:16c establish the C and C′ elements. Thus Paul's contrast of "our" inner and outer self acts as the pivot between the things that are for the audience's benefit and the things that are seen or unseen.

B. Waiting and Groaning in this Earthly Dwelling (5:1-5)

A 1 For we know that even if our earthly dwelling, a tent, is *destroyed* [καταλυθῇ], we have a building from *God* [θεοῦ]—an **eternal** building not made by hands—in heaven.

    B 2 For even *in* [ἐν] this *we groan* [στενάζομεν], desiring to put on in addition our heavenly residence,

   C 3 so that[40] when we put it on[41] we will not be found naked.

B´ 4a For while we are *in* [ἐν] this tent, *we groan* [στενάζομεν] anxiously, because[42] we do not wish to be **unclothed** but to be further **clothed**,

A´ 4b so that what is mortal may be *swallowed up* [καταποθῇ] by life.
   5 The one who has *conditioned us* [κατεργασάμενος] for this matter is *God* [θεός], who has given us the down payment of the Spirit.

The B unit (5:1–5) of Macrochiasm III is grammatically distinguished by the conditional clause in 5:1 that separates the context of the unit from what precedes. The γάρ clause in v. 1 introduces new imagery to explain the assertions of faith in what is unseen in 4:18. The peculiar vocabulary—dwelling place, clothed/unclothed, groaning—affirms 5:1–5 as a distinct section.[43] The terminal boundary is marked by the concluding ἵνα clause in vv. 4b–5. The οὖν clause in v. 6 builds on the imagery of 5:1–5, but takes on language of being at home and being away that is distinct from the tent and clothing imagery.

The transitional term "eternal" (4:18 and 5:1) links the B (5:1–5) and the A (4:15–18) units of Macrochiasm III. The line of thought thus progresses from the eternal things that believers look toward in 4:18 to the eternal building in heaven that believers look forward to inheriting in 5:1.

The noun θεός and verbs containing the prefix κατα- establish the A and A´ elements of the unit. The house that is being destroyed (καταλυθῇ) in 5:1 parallels the mortality that may be swallowed up (καταποθῇ) in 5:4. The similar sounds of these verbs (κατα -ῇ) create consonance and accentuate the parallel between the A and A´ elements. Although θεός is prominent throughout the letter, the term is not found

---

40. The phrase εἴ γε καί (NA²⁷; also in Gal 3:4) is read by the majority of manuscripts and is the preferred reading.

41. External evidence favors the reading ἐνδυσάμενοι (RSV, GNV, ASV, NASB, NIV, NJB; Matera, *II Corinthians*, 116). The variant ἐκδυσάμενοι (read by NAB [1980] and NRSV) is preferred with some reservation in the NA²⁷ (Metzger, *TCGNT*, 580). I follow the majority of scholars and translations in favoring ἐνδυσάμενοι.

42. The force of ἐπί here is debated, but the sense is most likely causal, as it is in Rom 5:12; Eph 2:10 (Wallace, *Grammar*, 389).

43. Some scholars prefer to view 5:1–10 as a complete section (e.g., Martin, *2 Corinthians*, 96; Thrall, *II Corinthians*, 356); however, several others agree that 5:1–5 and 5:6–10 should be considered as separate sections (e.g., Barnett, *Second Epistle*, 255).

in the units that precede or follow the present chiasm and it is not found elsewhere in the unit.

The B and B' elements contain the similar sounding phrases ἐν τούτῳ ("in this" 5:2) and ἐν τῷ ("in the [tent]," 5:4) as well as the verb στενάζομεν ("groaning") in 5:2, 4. The verb στενάζω is not found elsewhere in the letter. The parallel between "in this we groan" in 5:2 and "in this tent we groan" in 5:4 creates a near exact repetition of several syllables.

C. Encouraged and Acceptable While Away from the Lord (5:6–10)

A 6 So we are *always* [πάντοτε] courageous—although we know that while we are **at home** in the body we **are away** from the Lord—
7 for we walk by faith, not by sight.

  B 8a But we are courageous,[44] although we prefer *to be away* [ἐκδημῆσαι] from the body

    C 8b and *at home* [ἐνδημῆσαι] with the Lord.

    C' 9a So we aspire, whether we are *at home* [ἐνδημοῦντες]

  B' 9b or whether we *are away* (ἐκδημοῦντες), to be acceptable to him.

A' 10 For we must *all* [πάντας] **appear** before the judgment seat of Christ, so that each one may receive recompense for what one did in the body,[45] whether good or whether evil.[46]

Grammatically the boundaries of the C unit (5:6–10) of Macrochiasm III (4:15—6:2) are defined by the οὖν clause in v. 6 and the corresponding relative clause in v. 10.[47] The image of Christian life in v. 6 is presented as comparable to longing for one's homeland from a distance. The imagery is concluded with the eschatological judgment scene in v. 10, in which all believers have reached their destination before Christ.

---

44. The variant θαρροῦντες likely occurs in a few witnesses (e.g., ℵ 33 Tertullian) by assimilation to the same form in v. 6. I follow the NA²⁷ to prefer θαρροῦμεν.

45. The majority of witnesses read τὰ διὰ τοῦ σώματος πρὸς ἃ ἔπραξεν. A Western tradition in D* F G that replaces τά with ἅ and omits πρός is likely a scribal amelioration.

46. A number of good witnesses (P⁴⁶ B D F G C¹) read κακόν, but since φαῦλον (ℵ C) is the less expected word, it is also more likely original.

47. See Fee, *Christology*, 201; Barnett, *Second Epistle*, 267.

The οὖν clause of v. 11 builds on the previous imagery in 4:15—5:10 but focuses on Paul's rebuke of his opponents.

The verb pairs ἐκδύω/ἐπενδύω (5:2-4) and ἐκδημέω/ἐνδημέω (5:6-8) act as transition terms that link the C (5:6-10) and B (5:1-5) units of Macrochiasm III. The line of thought thus progresses from the fact that believers prefer not to be unclothed but to be clothed in 5:3-4 to the fact that believers would rather be home with the Lord and away from the body in 5:6.

The compound and accusative plural forms of πᾶς, which only occur in 5:6 and 5:10 of this section, establish the A and A´ elements of the unit. The repetition of the verb ἐκδημέω ("to be away from home") in 5:8a and 5:9b establishes the B and B´ elements. The repetition of the verb ἐπενδημέω ("to be at home") in 5:8b and 5:9a establishes the C and C´ elements. That believers aspire to be at home with the Lord acts as the pivot between the fact that Paul is "always" (πάντοτε) courageous (5:6) and that "all" (πάντας) must appear before the judgment seat of Christ (5:10).

C´. An Opportunity for Boasting (5:11-13)

A 11 Therefore, since we know the fear of the Lord, we try to persuade others. We are apparent *to God* [θεῷ], and I hope we are also **apparent** to your consciences.

  B 12a We are not commending ourselves to you again but are giving you an opportunity *of boasting* [καυχήματος] in **us**,[48]

  B´ 12b so that you may have something to say to *those who boast* [καυχωμένους] of external appearance rather than of the heart.

A´ 13 For if we are beside ourselves, it is *for God* [θεῷ]; if we are of sound mind, it is for you.

Grammatically the C´ unit of Macrochiasm III is defined by the use of οὖν in v. 11 and the concluding relative clause in v. 13. The content of v. 11 shifts abruptly away from the eschatological judgment scene in v. 10 (the climax of 5:6-10) and directly confronts the opponents. The emphasis on second person pronouns distinguishes 5:11-13 as a unit.

---

48. Matera, *II Corinthians*, 128: "Some significant manuscripts (P⁴⁶, ℵ, B) read ὑμῶν ("you"), perhaps to deflect attention from Paul, but the context suggests that Paul is providing them with reasons to boast about himself to others."

The γάρ clause in v. 14 introduces a section in which πᾶς is used as a general pronoun in place of the second person pronouns.

The transitional term φανερόω (5:10 and 5:11) links the C′ (5:11–13) and the C (5:6–10) units of Macrochiasm III. The line of thought thus progresses from the fact that all must appear before the judgment seat of Christ in 5:10 to the fact that Paul is apparent to God and the consciences of the community in 5:11.

The parallel dative singular forms of θεῷ in vv. 11 and 13 establish the A and A′ elements of the unit. These are the only occurrences of θεός in the unit, and the dative θεῷ is not found in the units that precede or follow this unit.

The "boast" (καύχημα) that the audience is to have (5:12a) and "those who boast" (καυχημένους) in external appearance (5:12b) establish the B and B′ elements. These are the only occurrences of these terms in Macrochiasm III (4:15—6:2). Boasting in appearances in 5:12 acts as the pivot between Paul being apparent to God in 5:11 and Paul's manner of preaching about God in 5:13.

B′. Christ Died for All So That All Might Live (5:14-15)

A 14 For the love of Christ compels[49] **us**: we are certain that since one *died for*[50] [ἀπέθανεν ὑπέρ] all, therefore all have *died*[51] [ἀπέθανον]. 15a He *died for* [ἀπέθανεν ὑπέρ] all,

  B 15b so that *those who live* [ζῶντες]

  B′ 15c may no longer *live* [ζῶσιν] for themselves,

A′ 15d **but** for him who *for their sake died* [ἀπέθανεν ὑπέρ] and was raised.

---

49. BAGD (s.v.) lists eight different translations for συνέχω: (1) to hold together; (2) to close; (3) to crowd; (4) to guard; (5) to cause distress; (6) to occupy a person's attention; (7) to provide an impulse for activity; urge, impel; and (8) to hold so as to guide. Of these listed, BAGD considers options 7 (as in the NRSV, NIV, NAB, NKJV) and 8 (as in the RSV, REB, KJV, NASB, ESV) to be the most probable meanings for the present verse.

50. Some have proposed that the preposition ὑπέρ here has a substitutionary meaning (BAGD, s.v.; Wallace, *Grammar*, 383, 387), as in Gal 3:13. However, a combined meaning of substitutionary and representative traits is also persuasive (e.g., Hooker, "Interchange," 121; Matera, *II Corinthians*, 149).

51. The term ἀποθνῄσκω is translated as a consummative aorist to emphasize the completed action; see also Mark 5:39 (Wallace, *Grammar*, 560).

Grammatically the B′ unit of Macrochiasm III is defined by the γάρ clause in v. 14 and by the ὥστε clause that begins the next section in v. 16. The γάρ clause of v. 14 moves away from direct comparison with the opponents in 5:11–13 and explains further Paul's confidence in his ministry. The use of πᾶς as a general pronoun also distinguishes the section as a particular unit. The ὥστε clause in v. 16 moves from the activity of Christ's death on the cross to the effect of Christ's death in a new creation.

The first person pronouns in 5:12 and 5:14 act as transitional terms that link the B′ (5:14–15) and C′ (5:10–13) units of Macrochiasm III. The line of thought thus progresses from the fact that the audience has an opportunity to boast of "us" (Paul and his co-workers) in 5:12 to the fact that the love of Christ compels "us" (Paul and his co-workers) to proclaim the gospel of Christ's saving death in 5:14.

The repetition of the verb ἀποθνῇσκω ("I die") and the preposition ὑπέρ ("in place of") establish the A and A′ elements of the unit. That "he died [ἀπέθανεν] for [ὑπέρ] all" in 5:14–15a parallels "him who for [ὑπέρ] them died [ἀπέθανεν] and was raised" in 5:15d. The verb ἀποθνῇ σκω is not found elsewhere in Macrochiasm III.

Those who live (ζῶντες) in 5:15b and those who may no longer live (ζῶσιν) for themselves in 5:14c establish the B and B′ elements of the unit. The verb ζάω is not found elsewhere in Macrochiasm III. "Those who live" (5:15b–15c) act as the pivot between the reiteration that one died (ἀπέθανεν) in place of (ὑπέρ) all (5:14–15a, 15d).

A′. Now Is the Time: Be Reconciled to God (5:16—6:2)

A 16 As a result, from *now* [νῦν] on we regard no one in a worldly manner; even if *we once knew* [ἐγνώκαμεν] Christ in a worldly way, **but** we do not *know* [γινώσκομεν] him so *now* [νῦν]. 17 As a result, whoever is in Christ is a new creation. The old things have passed away; *behold* [ἰδού]: new things *have come* [γέγονεν]!

B 18 And everything is from God, who has *reconciled* [καταλλάξαντος] us to himself through Christ and given *us* [ἡμῖν] the ministry of *reconciliation* [καταλλαγῆς],

B′ 19 to the effect that God was *reconciling* [καταλλάσσων] the world to himself through Christ, not counting their transgressions against them and placing on *us* [ἡμῖν] the message of *reconcilia-*

tion [καταλλαγῆς]. 20 So we are ambassadors on Christ's behalf, as though God were pleading through us. We implore you on Christ's behalf: *be reconciled* [καταλλάγητε] to God.

A′ 21 He made the one who did not *know* [γνόντα] sin to be sin for us so that we *might become* [γενώμεθα] the righteousness of God in him. 6:1 Working in unison then, we plead with you not to receive the grace of God in vain. 2 For it says: "At an acceptable time I heard you, and on a day of salvation I helped you." *Behold* [ἰδού]: *now* [νῦν] is the[52] acceptable time! *Behold* [ἰδού]: *now* [νῦν] is the day of salvation!

Grammatically the A′ unit (5:16—6:2) of Macrochiasm III is defined by the strong conjunctive particle ὥστε at its beginning, and its terminus is defined by the double exclamations in 6:2 as well as the change in tone and content in 6:3. The sacrificial imagery of 5:14-15 is replaced with that of new creation. The strong break at 5:16 moves from the subject of Christ's death to the effect of the cross in a new epistemology and new creation. The appellative tone in 6:1-2 is consonant with the imperatives to be reconciled to God in 5:20. In addition, the section 6:3-10 appears to stand as a separate sentence that moves from the imagery of ambassadors and returns to the subject of Paul's personal affliction.

The conjunction ἀλλά in 5:15 and 5:16 acts as a transition term that links the A′ (5:16—6:2) and B′ (5:14-15) units of Macrochiasm III. The line of thought thus progresses from the fact that believers should no longer live for themselves but rather live for the one who died for them (5:15) to the fact that believers previously may have known Christ in a worldly manner but now they do not know him in such a way (5:16).

The A and A′ elements are established by the repetition of several terms: the triple occurrence of γινώσκω (5:16, 21), the double occurrence of γίνομαι (5:17, 21), the temporal marker νῦν (5:16; 6:2), and the interjection ἰδού (5:17; 6:2). None of these terms are found elsewhere in Macrochiasm III.

The act of knowing (ἐγνώκαμεν, γινώσκομεν) Christ in 5:16 parallels "the one who did not know [γνόντα] sin" in 5:21. The new things

---

52. Definite articles do not appear in the Greek, but the contextual marker "now" determines that the definite article should be included in an English rendering. Hence, by saying "now," Paul is specifying a time that is ipso facto definite, and I include the article to show this emphasis.

that have come (γέγονεν) in 5:17 parallel the believers who may "become [γενώμεθα] the righteousness of God in him" in 5:21. The new way of knowing Christ now (νῦν) in 5:16 parallels the acceptable time now (νῦν) and the day of salvation now (νῦν) in 6:2. Paul's imperative for the audience to "behold" (ἰδού) the new things that have come (5:17) parallels his imperative for the audience "behold" (ἰδού) the acceptable time and the day of salvation that is presently before them (6:2).

The repeated use of the verb καταλλάσσω (5:18, 19, 20, "to reconcile"), the pronoun ἡμῖν (5:18,19), and the noun form of καταλλαγή (5:18, 19, "reconciliation") establish the B and B′ elements of the unit. That God has reconciled (καταλλάξαντος) *us* to himself through Christ (5:18) parallels the fact that God was reconciling (καταλλασσῶν) *the world* to himself through Christ (5:19). The ministry of reconciliation (καταλλαγῆς) given to Paul and his coworkers (ἡμῖν) in 5:18 parallels the message of reconciliation (καταλλαγῆς) given to Paul and his coworkers (ἡμῖν) in 5:19. The verb καταλλάσσω is not found elsewhere in the letter. The use of ἡμῖν in this element is distinguished from other occurrences by its connection to the ministry/message of reconciliation (καταλλαγῆς).

Overview: Macrochiasm III (4:15—6:2)

A 4:15-18: χάρις (4:15); ἀνακαινοῦται (4:16); ἡμέρᾳ (4:17); πρόσκαιρα (4:18)
  B 5:1-5: θνητόν (5:4); ζωῆς (5:4)
    C 5:6-10: εἴτε, εἴτε (5:9, 10); φανερωθῆναι (5:10)
    C′ 5:11-13: εἴτε, εἴτε (5:13); πεφανερώμεθα/σθαι (5:11a, b)
  B′ 5:14-15: ἀπέθανεν/νον (5:14-15a, 15d); ζῶντες/ζῶσιν (5:15b, c)
A′ 5:16-6:2: χάριν (6:1); καινή/ά (5:17); ἡμέρᾳ (6:2); καιρός (6:2)

A. The Benefit of the Community and the Glory of God (4:15-18) // A′. Now Is the Time: Be Reconciled to God (5:16—6:2)

The first and last units of Macrochiasm III are connected by four sets of parallel terms. Our inner self that is "renewed" (ἀνακαινοῦται) in 4:16 of the A unit parallel the "new creation" (καινὴ κτίσις) and "new things" (καινά) in 5:17 of the A′ unit. The "grace" (χάρις) that abounds in 4:15 of the A unit parallels the "grace of God" (τὴν χάριν) in 6:1

of the A′ unit. The double occurrence of "day" (ἡμέρᾳ) in 4:16 parallels the double occurrence of "day of salvation" (ἡμέρᾳ) in 6:2 of the A′ unit. The things that are "temporary" (πρόσκαιρα) in 4:18 of the A unit parallel the acceptable "time" (καιρῷ) in 6:2 of the A′ unit. All of the particular terms noted above are unique to the A and A′ units of Macrochiasm III.

B. Waiting and Groaning in This Earthly Dwelling (5:1–5) //
B′. Christ Died for All So That All Might Live (5:14–15)

The B and B′ units of Macrochiasm III are connected by the repeated opposition of death/dying (ἀποθνῄσκω) and life/living (ζάω). What is mortal (θνητόν) that is to be swallowed up by life in 5:4 of the B unit parallels the uses of the verb ἀποθνῄσκω in 5:14 and 5:15 of the B′ unit. The life (ζωῆς) that swallows up what is mortal in 5:4 parallels "those who live" (ζῶντες) and who "may no longer live (ζῶσιν) for themselves" in 5:15. Neither term is found elsewhere in Macrochiasm III.

C. Encouraged and Acceptable While Away from the Lord (5:6–10) //
C′. An Opportunity for Boasting (5:11–13)

The C and C′ units of Macrochiasm III are connected by the repetition of the conditional particle εἴτε (5:9, 13) and the verb φανερόω (5:10, 11). "Whether [εἴτε] we are at home or whether [εἴτε] we are away" and "whether [εἴτε] good or whether [εἴτε] evil" parallel a similar structure in 5:13: "if [εἴτε] we are beside ourselves, it is for God, and if [εἴτε] we are of sound mind, it is for you." That we must all appear (πεφανερῶθῆναι) before the judgment seat of Christ (5:10) parallels the fact that Paul and his coworkers are apparent (πεφανερώμεθα) to God and to the consciences of the audience (5:11). The verb φανερόω and the particle εἴτε are not found elsewhere in Macrochiasm III.

Chapter Summary

Overall, the study of chiasms has greatly aided literary analysis of Western literature—ancient and modern—and has been particularly useful in the study of biblical texts. Past chiastic structures proposed for 2 Corinthians are unsatisfactory since most depend on thematic or subjective criteria. In this chapter, however, I propose chiastic structures within 2 Cor 1:1—6:2 that are objectively grounded in lexical and grammatical criteria. In all, there are twenty individual chiastic units and three macrochiasms in the text. The opening and praise sections of the letter (1:1–2 and 1:3–7) are free-standing units. The remaining eighteen chiastic units comprise three macrochiasms. Transitional terms connect the chiastic units to one another and create a cohesive progression through all twenty units.

The first macrochiasm (1:8—2:13) concerns Paul's defense of his administrative and ministerial decisions that occurred between 1 and 2 Corinthians and drew criticism from the community. The section is made up of seven units: (A) 1:8–11; (B) 1:12–14; (C) 1:15–17; (D) 1:18–22; (C′) 1:23—2:3; (B′) 2:4–9; (A′) 2:10–13.

The second macrochiasm (2:14—4:14) compares Paul's ministry to the old covenant, argues for the superiority of Paul's ministry, and affirms his qualification to be a minister to the Corinthian community. The section is made up of five units: (A) 2:14—3:6; (B) 3:7–18; (C) 4:1–6; (B′) 4:7–11; (A′) 4:12–14.

The third macrochiasm (4:15—6:2) concerns the tension in the believers' present state and future glory, as well as Paul's exhortation for the audience to be reconciled to God. The section contains six units: (A) 4:15–18; (B) 5:1–5; (C) 5:6–10; (C′) 5:11–13; (B′) 5:14–15; (A′) 5:16—6:2.

The chiastic structures proposed here will be used in the following chapters for the audience-oriented analysis of 2 Cor 1:1—6:2. The next two chapters will provide a summary of the audience's response to Paul's rhetorical argument as it progresses in the chiastic structures found in 1:1—4:14 (Macrochiasms I and II). Thereafter, I will closely analyze the audience's response to Paul's rhetorical argument as it progresses through 4:15—6:2 (Macrochiasm III), and conclude with the climactic final unit of the argument in 5:16—6:2.

3

Audience Response to 2 Corinthians 1:1—2:13

The audience-oriented study of 2 Cor 4:15—6:2 that will take place in later chapters requires a contextual foundation. For this reason, the present and following chapters will analyze how the authorial audience[1] responds as the letter progresses in 1:1—4:14.

This chapter addresses the introductory material (1:1–7) and the initial rhetorical argument (1:8—2:13). The greeting and blessing establish two things. First, they reaffirm the relationship between Paul and the Corinthian community as between apostle and a church of God's elect. Second, they denote Paul's relationship as theologically symbiotic: the community receives their blessings and grace from God because Paul brought them the message and Paul is affirmed as an apostle because the community receives this message and subsequent gifts of grace and salvation from him.

The body of the letter begins by addressing the most recent events since 1 Corinthians along with the tension in the relationship between Paul and the Corinthians. Throughout this section Paul develops the

---

1. As noted in chapter 1, the "authorial" (or "textual") audience refers to the group of addressees implied in the text. This group may also be called the "implied" or "ideal" audience, and, in order to avoid cumbersome repetition, is also referred to as "the Corinthians," the "Corinthian community," "the community," or "the audience." Thus the audience is in no way simply the modern reader or a heuristic device, but is grounded in textual evidence and presumed to be the group of addressees that the author Paul imagined as he composed the letter 2 Corinthians.

notion of a symbiotic relationship with the community and stresses that their separation is theologically detrimental. Anything he has done—be it change travel plans, writing a harsh letter, or preaching the gospel—has been for their benefit. The section makes clear Paul's emotional concern for the community and their relationship, and shows a more pastoral and contrite tone than is seen in 1 Corinthians.

Introductory Sections: Greeting and Blessing (1:1–7)

Greeting (1:1–2)

A   1:1a Paul, an apostle of *Christ Jesus*,
  B   1b by the will of *God*, and Timothy our brother, to the church of *God*
    C   1c *that is in* Corinth
      D   1d with all the holy ones,
    C′ 1e *those who are in* all Achaia.
  B′ 2a Grace to you and peace from *God* our Father
A′ 2b and the Lord *Jesus Christ*.[2]

In the A and B elements (1:1a, b), the authorial audience hears the author of the letter, Paul, refer to himself as an apostle of Christ Jesus by the will of God (1:1a). That he is an apostle of Christ recalls that Paul was sent to proclaim the gospel (1 Cor 1:17) with the demonstration of the Spirit and power (2:1), that he founded the Corinthians as a community (1 Cor 3:5–11), and that they now serve as the seal of his apostleship (1 Cor 9:2).[3]

    2. The translations presented here attempt to demonstrate what the audience hears. Whenever possible, I try to maintain the word order and verbal connections that are apparent in the Greek. The translations, although wooden at times, serve to demonstrate the aural experience of the authorial audience.

    3. I presume in this study that the authorial (ideal) audience knows of 1 Corinthians and the events that occurred between the composition of 1 and 2 Corinthians (that is, as the events are defined in the text of 2 Corinthians). For example, the authorial audience of 2 Corinthians is aware of the painful visit, the "offender," the "tearful letter," and the issue of the opponents (see the Introduction above). Although these issues are not directly mentioned in the early part of the letter, I may presume that Paul expects the Corinthians to be aware of all pertinent issues at the time of writing. For this reason, I may comment on the possible implications of the opponents and other events even before they are explicitly mentioned in the text itself.

That Paul's apostleship comes by the will of God, according to the B element (1:1b), informs the audience that God affirms Paul's ministry and has given him the gospel as a gracious gift (1 Cor 2:12). Furthermore, they hear that Timothy is with Paul as he writes the letter.[4] Timothy had recently visited the community ahead of the painful visit, suffered some public embarrassment at the hands of the offender, and was henceforth replaced with Titus as Paul's liaison in Corinth.[5] That Timothy is referred to as "the brother" reminds them of the familial relationship that all believers share in Christ, and also that he is a "co-worker" with Paul for their benefit.[6]

The B element (1:1b) reminds the audience that they are a church that belongs to the same God who affirms Paul's apostleship. They are a church of God and thus also the continuation of the "assembly of the Lord," "Israel," God's "true people."[7]

The emphatic wording of Paul in the C element (1:1c) clarifies that he is writing to "the church of God—[the one] that is in Corinth." That they comprise a church of God that resides in Corinth reminds them that they are set apart from their imperial geographic location and exist theologically as God's special people. That they are referred to as being "with all the holy ones" in the D element (1:1d) recalls that they were sanctified in Christ by the gospel that Paul proclaimed (1 Cor 1:2–9) and by their baptism (1 Cor 6:9–11). The preposition "with" informs the audience that their sanctification in Christ joins them with all of God's holy ones throughout the world.

The participial phrase in the C′ element (1:1e) clarifies the identity of the "holy ones" in the D element (1:1d): Paul writes to the church of God—the one that is in Corinth—"with all the holy ones—the ones

---

4. The mention of Timothy in the greeting does not necessarily make him an equal co-author with Paul. The audience still recognizes Paul as the primary author and the holder of apostolic authority (Thrall, *II Corinthians*, 82; Hughes, *Second Epistle*, 3).

5. See, e.g., 1 Cor 4:16; 16:10; 2 Cor 7:12, according to Harris, *Second Epistle*, 132; Barnett, *Second Epistle*, 24. Cf. Thrall (*II Corinthians*, 83), who offers (with hesitation) that Timothy may not have arrived successfully to Corinth as Paul had intended (1 Cor 4:16).

6. Hughes (*Second Epistle*, 3) sees the definite article ὁ as indicating Timothy's relationship to the Corinthians; cf. Furnish (*II Corinthians*, 100), who sees the term as referring to Timothy's relationship as co-worker to Paul (hence, "our brother").

7. LXX Lev 16:17; Num 16:3; 20:4; Deut 23:1–8; 1 Chr 28:8. See Dunn, *Theology*, 128–35; Ridderbos, *Paul*, 328.

who are in all Achaia." Upon hearing the C′ element (1:1e), the audience experiences the D element (1:1d) as the pivotal (or central) point of the greeting section.⁸ The central point of the chiasm draws the audience into communion with all the holy ones in Achaia and thus closer to Paul. They are the church of God "that is in Corinth," that is also "with all the holy ones—those who are in all Achaia," who have been sanctified in Christ by receiving Paul's gospel. The mention of the holy ones throughout Achaia recalls that many others in their region have received salvation through his gospel (e.g., Phoebe from Cenchreae) and thus serves to ratify further the apostleship that Paul received from Christ by God's will (1:1a–b).⁹

That Paul brings grace and peace from God in the B′ element (1:2a) develops the B element (1:1b) in which God ratifies the apostle and in which the audience is described as being a church of God. God, who gave Paul his apostleship (1 Cor 1:9; 2 Cor 1:1b), also sends to the community his "grace," an unmerited gift. This grace and peace that comes through Paul in the B′ element (1:2a) galvanizes the Corinthians as one of God's churches. This identity logically underscores their subordination to Paul, who brings the gospel of salvation to them according to God's will (1:1b).

"Christ Jesus," who sent Paul to proclaim his gospel in the A element (1:1a), is developed in the A′ element (1:2b) as "the Lord Jesus Christ" who sends his greetings to Corinth (along with God the Father) through his emissary. That Jesus is called Lord in the A′ element enhances Paul's authority as his apostle and underscores that the Corinthians' membership with "the holy ones" who are "in Christ" also places them under his sovereign lordship.[10] Since they proclaim Christ as their "Lord," they should afford Paul more respect in receipt of his letter than they would even to a messenger from Caesar. The inversion

---

8. The "experience," in theory, refers to how the authorial audience aurally receives the text as it progresses within the chiastic structure. The purpose of the structure that is presented is to *show* what the authorial audience *hears* in the text. Upon hearing the first prime element of a chiasm, the audience experiences the chiasm begin to fold back towards its initial topic (seen in the A and A′ elements). In the present case, "those who are in all Achaia" in the C′ element (1:1e) points the audience back to "[the Church of God] that is in Corinth" in the C element (1:1c). The unparalleled D element (1:1d), "with all the holy ones," stands out in relief from the parallel elements that flank it.

9. See, e.g., Harris, *Second Epistle*, 135.

10. Martin, *2 Corinthians*, 4. A similar example is found in Heil, *Ephesians*, 52.

of the names from the A element (Christ Jesus, 1:1a) to the A′ element (Jesus Christ, 1:2b) accentuates the chiastic structure of the unit.

In sum, the central point of the greeting is that the Corinthian community is the church of God, the assembly of Israel, who are joined to all the holy ones who are sanctified in Christ, especially "those who are in all Achaia." The complex phrase forces the audience to recognize that they are part of a larger body and that other churches in their region have accepted Paul as an apostle of Christ and his gospel.

The outer elements of the chiasm support this point by first asserting the source of Paul's authority (1:1a–b) and then enhancing its depth (1:2a). As an apostle of Christ, Paul was commissioned to proclaim the gospel to the elect so that they might be sanctified (1 Cor 1:2) in Christ (1 Cor 1:1–9). The problems that transpired between him and the audience after the painful visit and their alliance with the opponents threatened the community's relationship with their founder and their sanctified state. The progression of the chiasm underscores that their salvation and Paul's authority are interrelated: Paul was called to be an apostle of Christ to them so that they may accept the invitation to be God's holy possession in Christ.

Blessing (1:3–7)

A 3 Blessed be the God and Father of our Lord Jesus Christ, the Father of compassion and God of *consolation*,[11] 4 who consoles us[12] in every affliction, so that we can console others in affliction, through the *consolation* by which we ourselves are *consoled* by God.

  B 5a Because just as *overflow*

    C 5b the sufferings of *Christ*

      D 5c to us,

    C′ 5d so too, through *Christ*,

---

11. The verb παρακαλέω may be rendered as "to encourage," "to exhort," "to comfort," or "to console" (BAGD, s.v.). This passage requires that the same term be used in both noun and verbal forms. The last option, "to console, consolation," is preferred in this passage by Matera (*II Corinthians*, 35) and Lambrecht (*Second Corinthians*, 17–19).

12. Many commentators consider Paul to be using the literary plural in this section, meaning that these pronouns refer to Paul alone. Thrall (*II Corinthians*, 105–7) offers a helpful discussion on the matter. Ambiguous plural pronouns remain a problem throughout the letter.

B′ 5e *overflows* our consolation.[13]

A′ 6 If we are afflicted, it is for your *consolation* and salvation. If we are *consoled*, it is for your *consolation*, which is effected through the enduring of the same sufferings that we ourselves suffer. 7 And our hope for you is firm, since we know that just as you are sharers of the sufferings, so too are you sharers of the *consolation*.

The A element (1:3–4) of the blessing develops the previous unit with the transitional words "Lord Jesus Christ." That Paul blesses God "the Father of our Lord Jesus Christ" develops the earlier statement that God was Father to the author and audience, and clarifies that both parties share the same familial relationship with God as does their Lord Jesus Christ. That God is the father of every consolation reveals that he who affirms Paul's ministry and bestows his grace upon his children (1:2) also consoles those who encounter affliction. The consolation that Paul receives from God enables him to console others. The B, C, and D elements (1:5a–c) build on this idea when they state that the sufferings of Christ overflow to Paul with a divine intention.

The elements of the second half of the chiasm elaborate on Paul's affliction and consolation. Upon hearing the C′ element ("so too, through Christ," 1:5d), the audience recognizes that Paul places himself as the pivot of the chiasm in the D element ("to us," 1:5c). He is thus also the center of the affliction-consolation transaction that is presently unfolding. That Christ is the agent of consolation in the C′ element (1:5d) develops the parallel idea in the C element (1:5b) that the sufferings of Christ overflow to Paul. The consolation that overflows in the B′ element (1:5e) reveals the divine intention behind the sufferings of Christ that overflow to Paul in the B element (1:5a).

In the A element (1:3–4), Paul's suffering resulted in the consolation of others. The "others" who benefit from Paul's affliction-consolation transaction in the A element are clarified in the A′ element (1:6–7) with the second-person pronoun. When Paul suffers, it is for the consolation and salvation of "you," the audience. The Corinthian community endures "the same sufferings" (1:6b) that overflow to Paul in the B, C, and D elements (1:5a–c). These sufferings represent the anguish of the cross and

---

13. The term "consolation," as it appears in the B′ element (1:5e), may be distinguished from the occurrences found in the A and A′ elements. In the Greek, v. 5e has the nominative παράκλησις with the pronoun ἡμῶν; however, the occurrences in the A and A′ elements are all in the genitive case, παρακλήσεως.

the "messianic sufferings" that are to take place at the beginning of the new age.[14] Since they share in the same sufferings as Paul, the Corinthians also share in the same consolation (1:6b–7) that comes to Paul in the A element from God the Father and patron of every consolation (1:3).

In sum, in the blessing, Paul emphasizes the bond that he and the Corinthians share in Christ. As mentioned in chapter 1, his afflictions had become an issue with community members and the opponents.[15] Affliction, as a sign of weakness, seemed unacceptable for an emissary of a powerful Lord such as Christ.[16] In the blessing, Paul addresses this issue indirectly by stating that any affliction he may suffer has a divine purpose and bears out consolation and salvation for others, namely "you," the audience.

Macrochiasm I: Paul's Defense of His Recent Administrative Decisions (1:8—2:13)

A. Paul's Suffering in Asia (1:8–11)

A 8 For we do not want you to be unaware, brothers and sisters, *of our* affliction that came about in Asia, in such a way that we were weighed down beyond our power, such that we despaired even of life.

> B 9 Indeed, we have received a *death sentence* in order that we might trust not in ourselves but in God *who* raises the dead,
>
> B′ 10 *who* rescued us from *deadly situations* and will rescue us, in *whom* we hope. And he will rescue us again,

A′ 11 so long as you, for your part,[17] join in solidarity with *us* by your prayer, in order that thanks may be given *on our behalf* from many for the gift given to us by the prayers of many.

---

14. Barrett (*Second Epistle*, 61) considers "the sufferings of Christ" to refer to (1) those sufferings experienced by Christ and that extend to be shared by others, and (2) analogous to the "sufferings of the Messiah," namely, the eschatological sufferings that "usher in the messianic age in a period of woe preceding eternal bliss." Thrall (*II Corinthians*, 107–10) argues that this phrase refers to an internalization of a mystical fellowship with Christ that is grounded in baptism. Through baptism believers are confirmed to Christ's death and thus participate in his sufferings.

15. Matera, *II Corinthians*, 41.

16. Schreiner, *Paul*, 96; Belleville, "Paul's Polemic."

17. So Harris, *Second Epistle*, 160.

The opening element of the A unit (1:8–11) moves from a general discourse on suffering to a specific incident of affliction via transitional words. Paul does not want "you" (the audience) to be unaware of the affliction[18] that came upon him (1:8).[19] In the B element (1:9), he states that his present affliction in Asia has led him to trust that God will rescue him even in the face of death. Paul is weighed down beyond his power. The use of the perfect ἐσκήκαμεν denotes that the impact of the death sentence is still felt as he writes the letter. This degenerate situation inspires him to trust in God who raises the dead (1:9).

In the B´ element (1:10), God, in whom Paul trusts and who raises the dead in the B element (1:9), is further defined as he "who has rescued us" and "will rescue us" and "in whom" he hopes. These pivotal elements contain Paul's central point in the unit: he hopes that God who raises the dead will also rescue him. That Paul has received a "death sentence" in the B element (1:9) is paralleled by the fact that God has previously rescued him from "deadly" situations in the B´ element (1:10). Since ῥύομαι refers to preservation in the midst of turmoil through "God's gracious presence" in scripture (Isa 25:4; Ezek 37:23; 1 Macc 12:15), the element implies that Paul presently feels God's saving presence while he is undergoing this affliction in Asia.[20]

The A´ element (1:11) develops the arguments that were first stated in the A element (1:6–7). Paul does not want "you" (the audience) to be unaware of his situation in Asia (1:8) because "you" are co-workers for his sake through prayer during this affliction (1:11). This prayer from

---

18. The "affliction" was likely a severe relapse of a chronic disease, but there is some debate as to the exact nature of the situation that Paul experienced in Asia. Thrall (*II Corinthians*, 116–17) prefers to see the affliction as an event of severe persecution, perhaps by an act of mob violence that precipitated in a death sentence. However, I follow Harris (see his helpful and detailed excursus in *Second Epistle*, 172–82), who views the affliction as a chronic disease comparable to malaria or an eye disorder. This malady may have relapsed for Paul on three occasions: in Cilicia (2 Cor 12:6–9), in Perga (Acts 13:13–14), and in Troas (2 Cor 1:8; 2:12)—three relapses in a period of thirteen years. The one in Troas was presumably the most severe, such that Paul suspended his ministry. Already distraught over worsening persecution in Ephesus, Paul entered a state of depression; the added calamity of the relapse and the unresolved tension in Corinth exacerbated the situation. See also Harvey, *Renewal*, 16–19.

19. The vague details imply that the audience was already aware of the affliction. See Barrett, *Second Epistle*, 64; Matera, *II Corinthians*, 24.

20. Kaisch, "ῥύομαι"; BAGD, s.v. In particular, the term ῥύομαι connotes for the audience divine intervention in the face of supernatural or eschatological antagonism. See also *Pss. Sol.* 4:23; *T. Reu.* 4:10; *Sib. Or.* 2:344.

many persons occurs so that thanks may be given to God, not just by Paul, but by many on his behalf on account of the gift that was given to him—namely, God's saving presence in affliction that gives him hope in a future rescue (1:8-9).

In sum, in the first unit of the first macrochiasm, Paul is confident that God will rescue him from his affliction. Paul includes the audience within this equation of rescue in the same way that he included them in the consolation equation in 1:3-7. The phrase "join in solidarity" (1:11) affirms the reciprocal relationship of consolation that Paul established among himself, God, Christ, and the community in 1:3-7. Just as God gives consolation to him through Christ in order to console "you," now "you" also take part in God's rescue of Paul from death by "your" prayers (1:11). Within these two equations in 1:3-7 and 1:8-11, Paul describes the relationship between himself and "you," the Corinthians, as symbiotic and beneficial to both parties. Paul's consolation consoles the audience, and their prayers aid in his rescue—both benefit from their relationship and from God, who is the ultimate source of the gifts.

B. Paul's Reason for Writing the Present Letter (1:12-14)

A   12 For our *boast* is this: the testimony of our conscience, that *by* godly holiness[21] and sincerity—not *by* human wisdom, but *by* the grace of God—we have conducted ourselves *in* the world—and even more so towards you.

  B   13a For we do not write to you anything except what *you can read*[22] and *understand*.

  B′ 13b And I hope that *you* will *understand* fully, 14a just as *you* have *understood* us partially,

A′ 14b that we are your *boast*, just as you are ours, *on* the day of the[23] Lord Jesus.

---

21. Witnesses differ on whether the text should read ἁγιότητι or ἁπλότητι. The external evidence favors ἁγιότητι with old and reliable witnesses of wide geographical representation (P^{46} ℵ* A B).

22. "Read" translates ἀναγινώσκω, which in the Greek has an alliterative and lexical connection to γινώσκω ("to understand").

23. For this translation I follow P^{46vid} A C D Ψ M and Ambrosiaster to omit ἡμῶν, which NA^{27} places in brackets as doubtful. The pronoun was likely added by scribes to echo the same phrase in 1:3.

The A element develops the previous unit with the transitional words χάρισμα (1:11) and χάρις (1:12). The grace that Paul received in affliction by means of the community's prayers is further explained as God's own grace that is now made manifest in his ministry. Paul takes pride in the sincerity of his ministry (1:12), in accordance with the testimony of his conscience.[24] He acts with godly holiness and sincerity in the world—not with human wisdom, but with the grace of God. The audience recognizes that Paul has acted with such characteristics even more so to them. As an extension of his pastoral conduct, the audience hears in the B element (1:13a) that Paul writes only what they can read (ἀναγινώσκετε) and understand (ἐπιγινώσκετε).

The B′ (1:13b-14a) and A′ (1:14b) elements present a chiastic progression from the A and B elements (1:12-13a). That Paul writes only letters that "you" can "read and understand" in the B element (1:13a) is developed in the B′ element (1:13b-14a) by the fact that he writes the present letter so that the community may "understand" completely just as "you" have "understood" him partially.

The A′ element (1:14b) presents a chiastic progression from the A and central elements (1:12-14a). That Paul writes so that the audience has a boast in him just as he does in them in the A′ element develops the fact that Paul has a boast in the character of his ministry in the A element (1:12). That Paul now calls on them to have a boast in him underscores the fact that his conscience has testified to the sincerity of his ministry and that he acted with godly holiness exceedingly more toward "you" than to anyone else.

That Paul and "you" are to be mutual sources of pride for one another on the day of the Lord Jesus further develops his reasons for writing in the central elements. Paul hopes for the audience to understand him more fully since it will benefit both parties at the Parousia.

---

24. The expression that underlies "conscience," συνείδησις, means "I know with myself" or "I am conscious." Within the ethical realm, this denotes "self-awareness" before God (Harris, *Second Epistle*, 184). Thrall (*II Corinthians*, 134-35) brings to light that in Greek usage the συνείδησις corresponded to "an element in human nature which passed judgment on a person's past acts" and was able to inflict internal pain upon a person via remorse. Because of the harsh nature of the conscience, this concept was normally viewed in a negative light in the ancient world. For this reason, Thrall sees Paul's usage of it in 1:12 as misplaced. However, I would argue that Paul uses the term precisely to prove his developing point that even his conscience, which has a reputation for being harsh, testifies that he has conducted himself and his ministry in an upright manner.

In sum, in 1:12–14 Paul moves abruptly from his discussion of affliction to an explanation of his reason for writing. The twofold explanation of their symbiotic relationship in 1:3–11 sets up Paul's boasting in 1:12–14. Since he takes pride in the way he ministers to the community, Paul writes so that they may understand him and take pride in him just as he does in them. He hopes that the mutual boast he shares with "you" will lead to a good standing for both parties in the eschatological court of Christ at the Parousia. Paul writes so that "you" may know him fully, which implies that the Corinthians' understanding of his ministry and his gospel is not yet complete.

C. Decision to Change Travel Plans Prior to the Painful Visit (1:15–17)

A   15a With *this* confidence I formerly *decided*
   B   15b to *come to you*, so that you might have a double favor,
     C   16a and by way of you pass through to *Macedonia*,
     C′ 16b and again from *Macedonia*,
   B′ 16c *come to you*, and by you be sent off to Judea.
A′ 17 So when I made *this decision*, was I flip-flopping? Or did I *decide* in a worldly way when I made the *decision*, such that from me it is "yes, yes," and "no, no?"

In the A and B elements (1:15a–b), Paul explains that previously he had intended to visit the community so that they may have a "double favor."[25] A progression from the previous unit (1:12–14) occurs via the transitional second person plural terms in 1:14–16: that Paul made this decision with "this confidence," the audience realizes, follows from the fact that he has a boast in "you" and hopes that "you" will also have a boast in him once "you" understand him completely (1:12–14). The C element (1:16a) further explains that Paul will pass through Corinth to visit Macedonia.

The second half of the chiasm develops the first three elements. That Paul will return from Macedonia in the C′ element (1:16b) parallels that he will go from Corinth to Macedonia in the C element (1:16a).

---

25. The sense of χάρις in 1:15 has been debated. Thrall (*II Corinthians*, 137) combines two meanings: (1) the divine grace that the apostle ministers to the community (as in Rom 1:11), and (2) a mark of goodwill to the Corinthians. Hughes (*Second Epistle*, 30) and Allo (*Seconde Épître*, 26) translate the term as "favor."

That he will "come to you" again in the B′ element (1:16c) parallels Paul's plan to visit Corinth first in the B element (1:15b) and verifies and develops that he intended to give "you," the Corinthians, a "double favor" (1:15a). The audience recognizes that this double favor was the opportunity to have their founding apostle, who was sent to them by Christ to proclaim the gospel for their salvation and sanctification (1:1–2), visit them twice within a brief period of time.

"This decision" in the A′ element (1:17) refers back to the A and B elements (1:15a–b) in which Paul formerly "decided" with "this" confidence to give them a double favor (1:15a–b). The two rhetorical questions (1:17) are overtly sarcastic. Since his decision to come to "you" twice was based on this confidence that comes from his boast in "you" (1:14), the answer to both of Paul's rhetorical questions obviously is "no." The true motive behind Paul's decision was to give a double favor to those in whom he has a boast (1:14), and to whom he acts with exceedingly more holiness, sincerity, and grace than to others (1:12).

In sum, in 1:15–17 Paul addresses his reason for changing his travel plans before the painful visit. The audience thus recognizes that their misunderstanding of Paul's travel change is a priority for him as he attempts again to be worthy of their boast.

D. All Things are "Yes" in Christ (1:18–22)

A   18 But as God is faithful, *our*[26] message to you is not both "yes" and "no." 19a For the Son of God, Jesus Christ, who was proclaimed to *you* by *us*—by myself and Silas and Timothy—

    B   19b he is not "yes" and "no," but *in him* is "yes."

    B′ 20a For as many as are the promises of God, they have their "yes" *in him*.

A′ 20b Therefore, *our* amen is through him to the glory of God. 21 The one who established *us* with *you* in Christ and anointed *us* is God— 22 he who sealed *us* with *you* and gave *us* the down payment of the Spirit in *our* hearts.

In the D unit (1:18–22), the audience experiences the center (pivot) of Paul's apologia for his recent administrative decisions. Paul answers

---

26. The first-person plural pronouns in this verse are likely not literary plurals but rather refer to the team of Paul, Timothy, and Silas.

his own rhetorical questions from 1:17 in the A element (1:18–19a) by explaining that since God is faithful, his "word" to them is not at the same time both "yes" and "no." His apostleship, and thus his gospel and ministry, come through the will of God (1 Cor 1:1; 2 Cor 1:1). Thus Paul's "word" to the Corinthians, whether it is his gospel or a chosen travel plan, can never be less faithful than God himself.[27] This statement regarding his message is expressed further in the B element (1:19b), in which Paul states that his word cannot be both "yes" and "no" because all things are "yes" in the object of his proclamation, Jesus Christ the Son of God (1:19b).

The B´ element (1:20a) presents a chiastic progression from the B element (1:19b) with the repeated phrase "in him." The B´ element (1:20a) clarifies for the community the thesis of its parallel element: "yes" in Christ has arrived to "you" because all the promises of God have become "yes" in Christ.

The A´ element (1:20b–22) presents a chiastic progression from the A element in the repetition of personal pronouns "you," "our," and "us." That through Christ all believers may proclaim "amen"[28] to God on account of the promises of God being "yes" in Christ, and that God has anointed them, sealed them, and given them a down payment of the Spirit in their hearts (1:20b–22),[29] recalls that God is faithful con-

27. Lambrecht, *Second Corinthians*, 28; see also 1 Cor 7:25.

28. For Allo (*Seconde Épître*, 28), "amen" recalls for the audience their own liturgical practices (that were based on synagogue procedures) in which believers affirm their thanks to God (as in 1 Cor 14:16). The exclamation "amen" may also be used by believers to confirm their election (as in 1 Kg 1:36; 1QS 1:18–20; Rev 5:14); see Conzelmann, *1 Corinthians*, 239.

29. The activities of God as described in 1:21—confirming, anointing, setting a seal upon, and giving a down payment of the Spirit to—likely have Paul and the community in view as recipients. Barrett (*Second Epistle*, 79) and Matera (*II Corinthians*, 56) view the referents as Paul and his co-workers alone since Paul is defending his apostolic ministry. However, Harris (*Second Epistle*, 205–6) and Bultmann (*Second Epistle*, 42) argue that grammatically the phrase σὺν ὑμῖν governs the meaning of the verbs and so refers to Paul, his co-workers, and the audience. See also Belleville, "Paul's Polemic." I prefer to follow this line of thinking and add that the phrase σὺν ὑμῖν, when seen elsewhere in Paul (2 Cor 4:5; Col 2:5), includes the audience with the respective contextual action.

The ambiguous plural pronouns are a noted problem at numerous other places in 2 Corinthians. I hold that Paul uses these pronouns at times as a rhetorical strategy to draw in his audience. Three optional referents emerge for the pronouns: exclusive to Paul alone (literary plural); exclusive to Paul and his co-workers; or inclusive of Paul and the audience (or all believers). From an audience-oriented perspective, Paul uses

cerning Paul's gospel that was proclaimed to "you" by Paul and his co-workers (δι' ἡμῶν) in the A element (1:18). In other words, the veracity of "our" word and God's faithfulness in the A element is supported by the Spirit that God placed in "our" hearts in the A′ element (1:20b–22).[30] That God has established Paul with "you" (σὺν ὑμῖν) recalls that he proclaimed to "you" Jesus Christ, the Son of God, in whom all of God's promises are affirmed, and also recalls the unifying and sanctifying activity of their baptism.[31]

By establishing Paul and the Corinthians together (1:21), God is bound in an irrevocable relationship with them and must keep their value intact until the Parousia.[32] The verb "anoint" (χρίω) recalls their baptism and fulfills the divine promises made in Dan 7:22, 27 (also 1 Cor 4:8; 2 Cor 1:19) that the elect will share in the ruling function of the messianic kingdom.[33] In hearing that Paul and the community were sealed by God, the audience understands that they are branded as God's property, validated in proper status in Christ, certified to be agents of God, and secured with his protection to pass examination at the Parousia (as in Exod 31:13, 17; Deut 34:10-12; Ezek 7:4-6; Rev 7:2-8; 4 Ezra 6:5; 8:57).[34] The indwelling Spirit that is received at baptism functions as a down payment. The four key verbs in 1:21-22 develop the force of God's faithfulness in 1:18. The Spirit's activity in the hearts of the Corinthians and the ministry team in the A′ element (1:20b-22) verifies the faithfulness of God and the gospel of Paul and his co-workers in the A element (1:18).

---

the pronouns in a consistent manner. When he is speaking of his apostolic responsibilities or hardships the pronouns are literary or exclusive to himself and his co-workers (1:3b-7, 9-20; 2:14—3:6; 4:1-5, 7-14; 5:11-15, 18b, 19b, 20; 6:1). But when Paul is speaking in terms of the spiritual benefits that all believers might gain from the gospel the pronouns are inclusive of the audience, that is, the authorial audience hears themselves included in pronouns that concern benefits that all believers presume to share (1:1-3a, 8, 21-22; 2:11; 3:12-18; 4:6, 16-18; 5:1-10, 16-18a, 21). This pattern seems consistent throughout 2 Cor 1:1—6:2.

30. The referent for ἡμῶν need not be exactly the same. The oral connection alone points out the development for the audience.

31. Lambrecht (*Second Corinthians*, 29) argues that the aorist participles recall what happened at baptism; see also Thrall, *II Corinthians*, 154.

32. Harris, *Second Epistle*, 205.

33. Thrall, *II Corinthians*, 154.

34. Woodcock, "Seal." See also Barrett, *Second Epistle*, 79; Harris, *Second Epistle*, 207; Thrall, *II Corinthians*, 156-57; Belleville, "Polemic," 545.

In sum, the argument Paul puts forward at the pivotal unit of this macrochiasm is heavily theocentric. God is faithful and makes Paul's gospel and ministry faithful, even if it involves a change in travel plans. All things are "yes" in Christ because all of the promises of God are fulfilled in him (1:20a). Through Christ, the "amen" of Paul and all believers may be given to God (1:20b). In further affirmation of his sincerity in his change of travel plans, Paul states that God has affirmed his apostleship by confirming, anointing, setting a seal upon, and giving a down payment of the Spirit in the hearts of the apostle, his co-workers, and "you," the audience (1:21–22). The evidence of the Spirit in the Corinthians' hearts affirms that God both fulfills his promises and is the genesis of Paul's authority. By having the Spirit, the audience themselves confirm the sincerity and divine origin of his gospel and ministry.

C′. The Change in Travel Plans after the Painful Visit (1:23—2:3)

A 1:23 And I call God as witness against my life that it was to spare you that I did not come again to Corinth. 24 Not that we lord over your faith; rather we work together for *your joy*. For you stand firm in the faith.

  B 2:1 For *this reason* I determined in myself not to come visit you again in *pain*.

    C 2a For if I *cause you pain*,

      D 2b who will be the one who gladdens me,

    C′ 2c if not the one *who is pained* by me?

  B′ 3a And I wrote *this very thing* so that when I do come I might not *be pained* by those from whom I must gain joy;

A′ 3b for I am confident in all of you that my joy will be *your joy* as well.

The C′ unit (1:23—2:3) presents a chiastic progression from the C unit (1:15–17). Just as Paul made "this" decision with "this" confidence to change his travel plans prior to the painful visit in the C unit, so too did he make "this" decision in the C′ unit not to return after the painful visit, and instead wrote "this very thing," i.e., the tearful letter.[35] "This" tearful letter was written so that the two parties would not bring each other mutual pain when in fact they should bring one another joy.

---

35. Batey, "Paul's Interaction," 143–45; Hughes, "Rhetoric," 254; Gilchrist, "Sequence," 54–55, 61.

God serves as a fitting witness in the A element (1:23-24) for the apostle's declaration because he was said to have affirmed Paul's credibility in the previous unit (1:18-22). Paul reveals that he did not follow through with the travel plan and return to Corinth as described in 1:15b because he wanted to spare the community. He immediately adds that he does not lord it over their faith but rather works toward their joy. "Joy" (χαρᾶς) is a play on words that recalls the second "grace" (χάριν) that Paul wished to offer "you" on his second visit in the original travel plan. "For this reason" in the B element (2:1a) refers to the fact that they stand firm in their faith in the A element (1:23-24). The C element (2:1b-2a) develops Paul's reason for not coming that is stated in the A element (1:23) by explaining that he did not return as he originally planned because he did not want to cause "you" pain. For if he causes "you" pain, the D element (2:2b) asks, who will be the one to gladden him?

The second half of the chiasm presents a progression from elements A, B, C, and D (1:23—2:2b). The C′ element (2:2c) parallels the C element (2:2a) and completes the line of thought in 2:2. If Paul pains the Corinthians, no one will be left to gladden him except the group whom he has pained. That he wrote "this very letter" in the B′ element (2:3b) develops the B element (2:1) in which Paul states it was for "this reason" (their faith) that he decided not to return but instead wrote a tearful letter in order to rebuke the community for their poor response to "this one," the offender.[36]

The B′ element (2:3a) also responds to the line of thought in the B, C, D, and C′ elements (2:1-2): Paul wrote in order that when he does come he does not cause pain to those who should give him joy (2:3a). The A′ element (2:3b) completes the chiasm by referring back to the A element (1:23-24). That Paul wishes for his joy to be "your joy" (2:3b) recalls that he works for "your joy" in 1:24 and creates an alliterative echo to the fact that he wished to give the Corinthians a second "favor" (χάριν) in the parallel C unit (1:15).

Between the C and C′ units (1:15-17; 1:23—2:3), the content of the pivotal D unit (1:18-22)—that God's faithfulness serves to justify the sincerity of Paul's ministry—affirms his reasons in 1:23—2:3 for not

---

36. Lambrecht, *Second Corinthians*, 5-6; Barnett, *Second Epistle*, 27-30; Lüdemann, *Opposition*, 81-83.

returning but instead writing a tearful letter. The C′ unit (1:23—2:3) underscores the ideas found in the C unit (1:15-17), namely, that Paul did not act impulsively in his travel changes. Rather, this apostle, who was sent to proclaim Christ by the will of God, acted with selfless concern for the Corinthians' spiritual welfare and development.

B′. The Tearful Letter and the Offender (2:4-9)

A 4 Because in great distress and with a pained heart I wrote to you with many tears, not that you be pained, but *so that you might know* of my love that overflows for you.

  B 5 But if anyone has caused pain, he did not cause pain to me, but, in a way—not to exaggerate—to all of you. 6 The penalty for *this one* by the majority is sufficient 7a so that you should rather forgive and *encourage* him,

  B′ 7b or else *this one* may be swallowed up by excessive pain.
  8 Therefore, I *encourage* you to reaffirm your love for him.

A′ 9 It was for this reason that I previously[37] wrote: *that I might know* your character—whether you are obedient in everything.

The B′ unit of Macrochiasm I develops the B unit (1:12-14) via the chiastic structure. That Paul wrote in order that "you" might know of his "overflowing" love for "you" (2:4) recalls that he acted with godly holiness and the sincerity of God—not by human wisdom—but by the grace of God in an "overflowing" manner towards "you" (1:12). The intensity of Paul's overflowing love reinforces the sincerity of his ministry to "you."

A progression from the C′ unit (1:23—2:3) to the B′ unit (2:4-9) also occurs via the transitional second person plural terms. That Paul wrote to "you" a tearful letter in the present unit (2:4) develops that he does all things for the benefit of "you," the Corinthian community, in the previous unit (2:3).

In the A element (2:4), Paul's sensitivity to causing "you" pain (1:24—2:3) is affirmed when he dismisses the notion that he wrote to pain them. Rather, he informs the audience that he wrote in order that

---

37. The term "previously" is added to show that I do not consider ἔγραψα in this verse to be an epistolary aorist, but rather to refer to the previous tearful letter. See, e.g., Harris (*Second Epistle*, 178-79) and Thrall (*II Corinthians*, 230-31).

"you" might know of his overflowing love.[38] In the B element (2:5–7a), Paul addresses an otherwise unidentified figure, "this one," who caused him pain. The audience recognizes "this one" as the offender who insulted the apostle at the "painful visit."[39] But Paul corrects their understanding of the situation: if anyone was pained by the offender, it was "you." Since the majority had punished "this one" sufficiently in his view, they are now to forgive and console the offender.

The B´ (2:7b–8) and A´ (2:9) elements develop the themes found in the first half of the chiasm. That Paul warns that "this one" may be swallowed up by pain in the B´ element (2:7b–8) underscores that the punishment placed on "this one" in the B element (2:5–7a) was in fact sufficient (2:7a). That he "calls on" the audience to reaffirm "your" love for "this one" in the B´ element (2:8) reinforces that he had asked the Corinthians to forgive and "console" "this one" in the B element (2:6–7a). In the A element (2:4), Paul said that he wrote the tearful letter so that the community might know of his love for them. Now, in the A´ element (2:9), he adds that he wrote the tearful letter in order to know "your" character and obedience. Combined, the A and A´ elements (2:4, 9) explain that Paul wrote the tearful letter for mutual understanding between him and them.

In sum, in the B´ unit (2:4–9), Paul addresses the matters of the painful visit and the offender. He corrects their misunderstanding that he was hurt by the offender ("this one") and emphasizes that within their symbiotic relationship the offense pained the Corinthians as well. Forgiveness of the offender, from both Paul and the rest of the community, reestablishes the symbiotic relationship they all share and allows it to be beneficial to all parties once again (2:8–9).[40] As the B´ unit (2:4–9) closes, the audience realizes that Paul also wrote the tearful letter so that he might know "your" character, namely, whether "you" were obedient and had punished the offender.

---

38. Watson, "Painful Letter"; Barnett, *Second Epistle*, 29–31.

39. Thrall, *II Corinthians*, 61–69; idem, "Offender"; Lüdemann, *Opposition*, 81; Kruse, "Offender"; Barrett, "HO ADIKĒSAS (2 Cor 7.12)."

40. Hughes, "Rhetoric," 355–56.

A′. Paul's Anguish in Troas (2:10–13)

A 10a Anyone you forgive anything, *I* do also. For what *I* forgive—if I have forgiven anything—

    B 10b is for your sake in the presence *of Christ*,

        C 11 so that we might not be outwitted by Satan—for we are not unaware of his schemes.

    B′ 12a When I went to Troas for the gospel *of Christ*,

A′ 12b and a door was opened to *me* by the Lord, 13 I did not have comfort in *my* spirit because *I* could not find Titus, *my* brother. So I left them and went on to Macedonia.

The A′ unit of Macrochiasm I presents a chiastic progression from the A unit (1:8–11). That Paul forgives the audience because he is aware of Satan's schemes (2:11) in the A′ unit adds to the fact that the Corinthians' awareness of his affliction in Asia made possible their participation in his rescue in the A unit (1:8–11). That he does not have rest in his spirit in the A′ unit (2:13) recalls that Paul has in himself a death sentence in Asia as he writes in the A unit (1:10), and thus underscores the affliction that he experienced as he awaited a response from Titus, and reminds the audience that his illness in Troas and anxiety over Titus' report were interrelated.

The A element (2:10a) of the chiastic unit develops the previous unit via the transitional second person plural terms. That Paul forgives anyone whom the community forgives in the present unit reinforces his admonition for them to forgive the offender in 2:7–8. In the B element (2:10b), this point is developed to show that the forgiveness is done for "your" sake before Christ, thus implying an eschatological incentive for the intra-community forgiveness. In the C element (2:11), they recognize that this relationship that is renewed through forgiveness acts contrary to the plans of Satan, whose intention is to slow God's will by disrupting church unity.[41]

Upon hearing the B′ element (2:12a), the audience experiences the pivot of Paul's chiastic argument. That he went to Troas for the gospel of "Christ" develops that everything Paul forgives is for "your" sake before "Christ" in the B element (2:10b). That the gospel of Christ is the goal

---

41. Hughes, *Second Epistle*, 72; Harris, *Second Epistle*, 233–34.

and focus of Paul's activity in the B′ element (2:12a) underscores and develops the fact that the community's good standing before Christ is the goal of his forgiveness in the B element (2:10b).

The A′ element (2:12b) develops the A element (2:10a) of the unit via the chiastic structure. That a door was opened to "me" in the Lord and that "I" did not have relief in "my" spirit because "I" could not find "my" brother Titus in the A′ element (2:12b) underscores the love that Paul has for the audience in the A element when anything "I" forgive "I" do so for "your" sake (2:10a).

The B′ (2:12a) and A′ (2:12b–13) elements state that Paul did not have peace in himself when he went to Troas for the gospel of Christ because there was an un-reconciled matter between him and the community. Instead of following through with a promising ministry in Troas, Paul went on to Macedonia to find Titus and learn how the Corinthians had received his tearful letter. It is clear that the painful visit had taken an emotional and physical toll on Paul, such that he desperately wished to hear good news about the community from Titus.[42] The present chiastic unit, and the macrochiastic unit as a whole, close with the repeated use of the first person singular pronouns in 2:12b–13.

In sum, at the conclusion of Macrochiasm I in the A′ unit (2:10–13), Paul wishes to affirm his love for the audience that he first demonstrated in the opening of the letter (1:1–7) and the A unit (1:8–11). Whether in the midst of certain death (1:8–11) or the abandonment of another community amid illness and depression (2:10–13), Paul's love for the Corinthians moves him to hope for divine rescue or to travel great lengths just to find out the status of their relationship.

Chapter Summary

This chapter presents an overview of how the textual audience responds to Paul's rhetorical argument in 2 Cor 1:1—2:13 and the text's respective chiastic structures. In the greeting and blessing (1:1–2, 3–7), Paul addresses his relationship with them as an apostle to a sanctified people who have received the gospel of Christ. He treats this relationship as

---

42. Murphy-O'Connor, *Theology*, 26–27. Allo (*Seconde Épître*, 43) aptly describes Paul anxiously waiting to be debriefed by his "lieutenant" after returning from a difficult mission.

symbiotic in nature and defends his suffering as one aspect of his ministry that benefits the community's salvation.

In response to doubts and accusations from detractors within the community and the new opponents, Paul puts forward an apology to defend his recent administrative decisions in the first macrochiastic argument (1:8—2:13). In the central D unit of this argument (1:18–22), Paul places God's faithfulness as proof of the sincerity of his own ministry and administrative decisions. In the C and C′ units (1:15–17; 1:23—2:3), Paul addresses his change in travel plans: the first that occurred before the painful visit (1:15–17) and the second that occurred after the painful visit (1:23—2:3). In the B and B′ units (1:12–14; 2:4–9), he treats his reasons for writing to the community. In the present letter, he writes so that they *might know* him as an apostle in a more complete way (1:12–14), and he explains that he wrote his previous letter (the tearful letter) in order that he *might know* of their obedience (2:4–9). The A and A′ units (1:8–11; 2:10–13) affirm the symbiotic relationship that Paul and the audience share: they have solidarity in one another's afflictions through prayer (1:8–11), and their mutual forgiveness edifies both parties (2:10–11). Finally, Paul's love for the community supersedes even the most promising of mission opportunities (2:12–13).

4

Audience Response to 2 Corinthians 2:14—4:14

Macrochiasm II (2:14—4:14): Paul's Defense of His Unveiled Gospel to the Corinthians and a Counterattack on the Opponents

Having addressed in the first macrochiasm (1:8—2:13) the most recent events and sources of tension in their relationship, in the next macrochiastic argument (2:14—4:14) Paul turns his attention more directly to the threat of the opponents. Throughout this section Paul defends his ministry against accusations of fraud and weakness. The outermost units of this argument focus on Paul's relationship to the community and how his qualifications as an apostle are verified in their faith (A. 2:14—3:6; A´. 4:12-14). The next layer of units addresses the glorious status of Paul's ministry due to the nature of the new covenant and the life-giving, transformative treasure of the gospel (B. 3:7-18; B´. 4:7-11). The pivotal and central unit of the macrochiastic argument (C. 4:1-6) presents the illuminative power of the gospel and God's authority as the nexus of Paul's apostolic qualifications.

A. Paul's Qualification to be God's Minister (2:14—3:6)

A 2:14 But thanks be to God, who, in Christ, always leads *us* in a triumphal parade and makes known through us the fragrance of the knowledge of him in every place. 15 Because *we are* the aroma of Christ for God, among those who are being saved and among those who are perishing. 16 For the latter, we are an odor from death to death, and for the former an odor from life to life. And who is *qualified* for this? 17 For *we are* not like the many who sell the *word* of God—but as from sincerity, as *from God*—before God we speak in Christ.

- B 3:1 Are we beginning to commend ourselves again? Or do we need, as some do, *letters* of recommendation to you or from you? 2 You are our *letter, written* on [your]¹ *hearts*, known and read by all people,

- B′ 3 making clear that you are a *letter* from Christ, administered by us, *written* not with ink but by the Spirit of the living God, not on stone tablets but on fleshy *heart* tablets.

- A′ 4 Such confidence we have through Christ toward God. 5 Not that *we are qualified* in ourselves to take credit for anything that comes from us; rather, our *qualification* comes *from God*, 6 who has indeed *qualified us* to be ministers of a new covenant, not of letter but of Spirit. For the letter kills but the Spirit gives life.

The A element (2:14–17) of the first unit of Macrochiasm II develops the previous unit via the transitional term "Christ." That Paul proclaims the gospel of Christ even while undergoing a terrible relapse of a chronic illness in 2:12 is developed further in 2:14 when he gives thanks to God who always leads him in Christ as a prisoner² in a triumphal parade.³ Paul also compares his ministry to incense. Just as the burning

---

1. Although ἡμῶν has external support in the majority of witnesses, I prefer to read ὑμῶν since ἡμῶν was likely assimilated to ἐν ταῖς καρδίαις ἡμῶν from 1:21.

2. The verb θριαμβεύω has been construed to mean that God causes Paul to triumph (as in KJV) or that Paul is being led as a prisoner of war in God's triumphal parade. Some scholars prefer to merge the two options (Martin, *2 Corinthians*, 46; Harris, *Second Epistle*, 245), but the majority prefer the second option alone (Barrett, *Second Epistle*, 98; Thrall, *II Corinthians*, 195; Murphy-O'Connor, *Theology*, 29; Lambrecht, *Second Corinthians*, 39; Matera, *II Corinthians*, 72). See also Delling, "θριαμβεύω." Hafemann (*Suffering*, 12–83) demonstrates that the verb θριαμβεύω is only used (in Greco-Roman literature) to refer to the prisoner who is being led toward execution as a spectacle.

3. The majority of scholars prefer to see the depiction here as a triumphal procession. There are, however, a few dissenters to this view. Furnish (*II Corinthians*, 175) refuses to see an allusion to a Roman triumph and thinks the verb means only "to put on display." Duff ("Metaphor, Motif") believes Paul is referring to an epiphany proces-

powder diffuses an aroma, so too does his suffering ministry diffuse the gospel. He proclaims to those who are being saved and those who are perishing—the former finds life with the gospel and the latter finds death through rejecting it (2:15–16). Paul asks the audience who could be qualified for such a ministry. He is not like the many who sell the word of God; but rather, as with sincerity, he speaks in Christ before God (2:17). The two parties, those "being saved" and those "perishing," recall that the former see the gospel as wisdom, but the latter reject it as foolishness (1 Cor 1:18).

In the B element (3:1–2), Paul asks two more questions—whether he is commending himself and whether he needs letters of recommendation. He then states emphatically that "you," the Corinthian community, are his letter, written on "your" hearts, known and read by all people.[4] To defend his apostleship Paul turns again to an example of what the audience has gained from their relationship with him. He is the apostle from Christ whose proclamation caused the Spirit to indwell the community members and display further that God's promises to his elect are fulfilled in Christ and that his down payment of these promises is already being experienced now with the Spirit (1:21–22).

The B´ and A´ elements (3:3, 4–6) present a chiastic progression from the A and B elements (2:14–17; 3:1–2). That "you" are a "letter" from Christ administered by "us" in the B´ element (3:3) elaborates how "you" are Paul's "letter" of recommendation in the B element (3:1–2) and underscores that the true source of Paul's apostleship is Christ (1:1). That this letter is "written" with the Spirit on fleshy hearts in the B´ element (3:3) explains by what means a letter is "written" on "your" hearts for all to read in the B element (3:1–2) and underscores the importance of the Spirit within the community's sanctification and their relationship to Paul (1:21–22).

The imagery that develops in the B´ element (3:3) regarding Spirit, writing, heart, and stone,[5] recalls the new covenant prophesied by

---

sion that was performed in Roman times to honor the god/goddess for the patronage or gifts they had given the city.

4. I prefer to read the variant ὑμῶν in this verse, thus making the Spirit a present experience within the audience (as in 1:21–22).

5. Stockhausen (*Moses' Veil*, 72) notes instructively that "γράφω and its compounds" in 3:1–6 are an important link between the key covenant texts in Jeremiah and Ezekiel on the one hand and the texts from Exodus on the other hand that Paul's vocabulary

Jeremiah and Ezekiel.[6] Through the progression of the chiastic structure, the audience recognizes that the presence of the Spirit in their hearts is proof that this new spiritual covenant, which was to be written on the hearts of the elect, has finally arrived.

In the A′ element (3:4–6), Paul responds to his own question in the A element (2:14–17) of who can be qualified for this ministry. He states openly that it is by God, not in himself, that he is qualified. That Paul says he does not credit himself as qualified in the A′ element (3:4–6) recalls that Paul is not one who sells the word of God but rather speaks with sincerity in the A element (2:14–17). That the letter kills but the Spirit of the new covenant brings life in the A′ element (3:6) develops the reaction to Paul's gospel from those being saved and those who are perishing in the A element (2:14–17). To the latter who reject it, Paul's gospel brings death; but for the former who receive his gospel, it brings life.

In sum, in the opening unit (2:14—3:6) of Macrochiasm II (2:14—4:14), Paul sets forward a forceful apologia for his qualification to be a minister of the new covenant. The chiastic structure of the unit demonstrates the development of Paul's argument. In the A element (2:14–17), Paul presents himself as a prisoner of Christ and as incense that diffuses the gospel everywhere, and he asks who is qualified for this task. In the central B and B′ elements (3:1–2, 3), Paul responds directly that "you," the Corinthian community, act as his letter of recommendation from Christ, written by the Spirit on "your" hearts. This manifestation of the Spirit in their hearts represents the new covenant that was prophesied

---

reflects. The terms ἐπιστολή, γράφω, γράμμα, μέλας, and πλάξ are all associated with writing and serve to connect Paul's present qualifications as a minister with the stories of Moses and the prophecies of the new covenant. Thus all of 2 Cor 2:14–3:6 serves to draw a "verbal and conceptual link" to Exod 34:27–28; Jer 34:31–34; 39:40; Ezek 11:19; 36:26. Paul is "in dialogue with the whole of the established background at all times," but "he works freely within it, having once entered into it at the point at which the Exodus covenant can be compared unfavorably with the new covenant of Jeremiah [and Ezekiel]." See also Hickling, "Sequence."

6. According to LXX Jer 38:31–34, the new covenant will be written in the hearts of God's people, and all will know God. In Ezek 11:19; 36:26 God assures the prophet that he will replace the disobedient "stony heart" with a new, fleshy heart and a new spirit so that the Israelites will live according to God's will and thus regain their status as God's own people. The audience, who have Paul's commendation letter written by the Spirit of the living God in their hearts, come to understand themselves as an external sign that the new covenant has taken effect.

by Jeremiah (38:31–34 [LXX]) and Ezekiel (11:19; 36:26). In the A′ element (3:4–6), Paul returns to the question of his qualification and directly answers his question in 2:17 that God has made him sufficient to be a minister of the new covenant.

B. Paul's Ministry Makes Known the Glorious New Covenant of Life (3:7–18)

A 7 Now if the ministry of death that was engraved in letters of stone was so *glorious* that the Israelites were not able to look intently on the face of Moses because of the *glory* of his face that was passing away, 8 much more will the ministry of the Spirit be *glorious*. 9 For if the ministry of condemnation was *glorious*, much more will the ministry of righteousness overflow with *glory*. 10 For that which was *glorified* is no longer *glorious* when compared to the surpassing *glory*. 11 For if that which is now passing away was *glorious*, much more will that which remains be *glorious*.

  B 12 Since we have this hope, we act with great boldness, 13 and not like Moses, who placed a *veil* over his face so that the Israelites could not see the end of what was passing away. 14a But their senses were dulled. For to *this day* the *veil* remains whenever the old covenant is read,

    C 14b since it is not revealed that in Christ it is passing away.

  B′ 15 But to *this very day*, whenever Moses is read, a *veil* is placed over their hearts. 16 But for whoever turns to the Lord, the *veil* is taken away.

A′ 17 But the Lord is the Spirit, and where the Spirit of the Lord is, there is freedom. 18 All of us who look on the *glory* of the Lord—as though through a mirror—with unveiled face, are being transformed into the same image from *glory* to *glory*, as from the Lord who is the Spirit.

The A element (3:7–11) develops the previous unit via the transitional terms "minister/ministry," "letter," and "Spirit" and serves as an exposition on the antithetical statement in 3:6.[7] Although Paul has indicted the old covenant for bringing condemnation and death (3:6), he is careful not to say that it was without glory. Instead, in the present element, he

---

7. Kertelge, "Letter and Spirit," 124–25.

argues that the old covenant did in fact come in glory, but this glory was limited.[8] Moses' veil hid from the Israelites the fact that the covenant of condemnation was already passing away. The Israelites were unable to look on Moses' face, and condemnation (and thus death) came as the result of the covenant's limitations (3:7–11). The new covenant is eternal, of the Spirit, and brings righteousness, whereas the old is temporary, written in stone, and brings condemnation. The new covenant is then considered far more glorious than the old.[9] The terminology of varying levels of glory in this element recalls the mention of the "former glory" of the first Temple and the "new glory" that will come from God with the new Temple (Hag 2:1–9). For Paul and the audience, the future that is looked to in Haggai has arrived in part already in their spiritual experience in Christ (2 Cor 1:21–22; 3:1–3).[10]

In the B element (3:12–14a), Paul acts with great confidence because the new covenant that he administers is far superior to the covenant of Moses. In 3:13–14, Paul alludes to Exod 34:29–35,[11] in which Moses

---

8. It would be incorrect to infer from this passage that Paul had conveyed an entirely negative view of the Mosaic Law to his community in Corinth. As Kruse ("Law and the Spirit") points out, Paul describes both positive and negative aspects of the Law to the Corinthians. The Law was given to humanity for a temporary purpose (2 Cor 3:11). It unfortunately became an "unwilling ally of sin," such that it enslaved humanity further (1 Cor 15:56). The Law, however, testifies to the gospel of Christ (2 Cor 3:14–15), and believers in Christ are free from the Law's regulations (1 Cor 9:20–21; 2 Cor 11:24).

9. Räisänen (*Paul and the Law*, 254–56) points out that Paul is not so much a systematic theologian as he is a traveling missionary who responds to different pastoral situations in several different letters. His feelings on the Law demonstrate well his inconsistency. Paul struggles with the reality that God's divinely instituted law has been "abolished through what God has done in Christ." Instead of saying this, though, Paul argues that his gospel apart from the Law in fact fulfills it—an illogical, yet personally necessary assertion for Paul to make. What is most evident is that Paul's views on the Law are determined by his preliminary conversion experience (Gal 2:1–14) and the ongoing interaction with his predominantly Gentile communities who have been incorporated into Christ and the new Israel. Thus a divine institution finds tension within a divinely instituted reality. Paul's arguments regarding the Law, although at times contradictory, are attempts at maintaining both the divine tradition and the present spiritual reality, without demeaning either one.

10. Renwick, *Temple*, 113–21.

11. Hafemann (*Moses*, 429) believes the scope of Paul's allusion may include all of Exod 32–34, and thus refer to the golden calf incident. If this theory is correct, then one may deduce the following pattern in Paul's thought: Israel's inability to keep the Law was made clear by the golden calf incident, yet "this inhibitor is being overcome in the new covenant people of God who are the elect eschatological community."

places a veil over his face[12] when he speaks to the Israelites because he has been transformed during his counsel with God.[13] Because of this veil, Israelites from Moses' time to Paul's were unable to see that the glory of the old covenant was fading (3:13–14).[14] The Law, like Moses, does not disclose its own temporary nature of limited glory but retains a veil. In other words, "Moses' veil rests, no longer on his face, but on the reading of (v. 14) or the understanding of" (v. 15) the Law.[15] Based on the argument put forward by Paul in 2:14—3:6, the audience realizes in the pivotal C element (3:14b) that it is Paul's gospel, as the superior ministry, that reveals that in Christ the old covenant is fading away.

That the "veil" on Moses' face[16] "to this day" remains when the Law is read in the B element (3:12–14a) is underscored in the B´ element (3:15–16) by the fact that "to this day," whenever Moses (i.e., the Law) is read, a veil remains over the hearts of those who do not belong to the eschatological community who are in Christ. [17] Since they heard in the

12. Belleville (*Reflections of Glory*, 77–80, 297) traces the tradition of Moses' veiling and finds similar examples in Philo, Samaritan documents, Qumran, and other materials. This evidence closely associates the glory of Moses' face with the glory of the Law. Paul does not really interpret Exod 34:28–35 in a new way but rather develops his own haggadic expansion of the text with the use of preexisting Moses-δόξα traditions.

13. Thrall (*II Corinthians*, 259–61) gives a concise list of motives proposed by scholars for Moses' veiling: (1) biblical teleology, meaning that the results show the original intent of God. (2) The concealment was educational and preparatory (Matera, *II Corinthians*, 92; idem, "Renewal," 55), (3) occasioned by the Israelites' flaws (Martin, *2 Corinthians*, 68; Lambrecht, *Second Corinthians*, 52), or (4) developed as a response to opponents. Two other options are that Moses (5) acts with reverent motives or (6) points forward to Christ. I prefer option (1) since Paul often connects a result with God's original intention (e.g., Rom 1:18–32; 9:14–29; 1 Cor 1:18–31). See also, McDermott, "Sequence," 59.

14. Stockhausen (*Veil*, 23) notes that the *Assumption of Moses* attributes Moses with receiving "a grand vision of the heavenly realms and with a privileged prophetic revelation of the future of Israel and the world" during the forty days and forty nights that he was on Sinai in conversation with God (Exod 24:18).

15. Stockhausen, *Veil*, 171.

16. According to Räisänen (*Paul and the Law*, 45–46), the images of Moses' face and ministry are not intended to point to particular events, but rather serve as symbols of the old system of the Law, and hence "denote more a slavery to written precepts and ordinances, as implied by the abrupt mention of 'freedom' in 3:17."

17. The term καρδία ("heart") refers to the inner part of the person that governs religious and moral decisions; this faculty may be differentiated from the ψυχή that served as the animating force of the σῶμα ("body") (Baumgärtel, "καρδία"). The term καρδία becomes the imperative source of morality in Jewish apocalyptic literature, particularly in the *Testaments of the Patriarchs* (e.g., *T. Dan* 5:6–13; *T. Sim.* 4:5; 5:2; *T. Gad* 5:3).

C element (3:14b) that it is in Christ that the old covenant is passing away, the audience comes to understand in the B′ element (3:15–16) that the only way to remove the veil is to turn to Christ, of whom Paul is an apostle (1 Cor 1:1; 2 Cor 1:1). The C element (3:14b) thus establishes the centrality of Christ in the transition from the glorious old covenant to the more glorious new covenant.[18]

In the A′ element (3:17–18) the audience hears the powerful conclusion to this unit. Those who look to the Lord have an unveiled understanding of the Law (i.e., Moses, 3:14–16) and therefore gain freedom (3:17). This is freedom from the Law (i.e., the old system of the written precepts and ordinances) so that they might live for God (1 Cor 6:19–20).[19] That those who look on the glory of Christ with unveiled face as through a mirror[20] are transformed[21] from glory to glory to the same image in the A′ element (3:18) underscores the centrality of Christ in proper perception in the B, C, and B′ elements (3:12–16). The glory of Christ also recalls the multiple references to the respective levels of glory of the old and new covenants in the A element (3:7–11). That recipients of Paul's gospel look on Christ and are presently transformed into a likeness of his glory in the A′ element clarifies in what way the new covenant comes with a glory surpassing the old in the A element (3:7–11).[22] What the believers see in the A′ element is thus Christ "who is himself God's glory." This glory and subsequent transformation come from the covenant that Paul administers (as stated in the A element, 3:7).[23]

Previously, in 1 Cor 15:45, as mediator of God's power to renew humanity, Christ is "a life-giving Spirit." In 3:18, the believers' glorious

---

18. See Davis (*Antithesis*, 213), who argues "in 2 Cor 3 Paul figuratively represents Torah as written, veiled, and mediated—always in contrast to direct experience with God through the Spirit for those in Christ."

19. Sanders, *Palestinian Judaism*, 468; Räisänen, *Paul and the Law*, 45–46.

20. "Seeing as though through a mirror" is the proper rendering for κατοπτριζόμενοι in this passage, according to Belleville (*Reflections*, 49) and Lambrecht ("Transformation").

21. The verb μεταμορφόω means "to remodel" or "to change into another form." In Hellenistic culture there was widespread belief that gods would transform themselves into humans to walk on earth. In mystery religions transfiguration was tantamount to deification. Transformation was intended to lead one out of the earthly reality and into a spiritual existence. See Behm, "μεταμορφόω"; von Rad, "εἰκών."

22. Through his resurrection Christ became the Lord of glory (1 Cor 2:8), and hence is endowed with God's glory and power. See Grabner-Haider, "Meaning," 30.

23. Lambrecht, "Transformation," 245; Renwick, *Temple*, 158.

transformation is again accomplished by Christ, "the Lord who is the Spirit (3:17)."²⁴ By being transformed into his likeness, believers regain in Christ the glory that Adam had lost and that the Law was unable to give.²⁵

In sum, in the B unit (3:7–18) of Macrochiasm II (2:14—4:14), Paul presents his ministry as superior to that of Moses. Moses' ministry brought death and condemnation (3:7, 9), but Paul preaches with confidence because his ministry brings life. Moses' veil hid the fading glory of the old covenant from the Israelites, but those who receive Paul's gospel have the veil removed in Christ. Since it is in Christ that the veil is taken away to reveal the limited glory of the old covenant in relation to the new (3:14b), those who look on Christ do so with an unveiled face. And, since they also have the Spirit written in their hearts (3:3), the audience members realize that they who look on Christ [the Lord], who is the Spirit,²⁶ do so as though looking in a mirror. Having received this mystical "insight,"²⁷ they understand that looking on Christ transforms

---

24. Scroggs, *Last Adam*, 106.

25. According to Scroggs (*Last Adam*, 96), Christ manifests God's glory because he is the image of God (4:4). Paul's ministry is far superior to Moses' because the new covenant makes known in Christ God's glory. Christ holds the glory that humanity was intended to have at creation; now, at the new creation, Christ will transform believers to his own glorious divine image.

26. Debate surrounds whether God the Father, Christ, or the Spirit is the proper referent for κύριος. The works of Fee (*Presence*, 198–202), Dunn ("2 Corinthians III. 17"), and Wong ("Lord") have been influential in the study of this exegetical problem. However, following the work of Hughes (*Second Epistle*, 98) and Barrett (*Second Epistle*, 123), I prefer to see Christ as the referent to Lord in 3:17a for the following reasons: (1) κύριος without a modifier almost always refers to Christ in the Corinthian correspondence (sixty-three times total; in twenty occurrences the title is modified by Jesus Christ; in forty occurrences Jesus is deduced as the referent by the contextual activity, such as judging, returning, etc.); (2) in particular, κύριος, when seen with πνεῦμα (1 Cor 6:17; 12:4–6), refers to Christ; (3) κύριος as Christ corresponds to early Christian understanding of the Spirit when considered with 3:17b (e.g., Acts 8:39); (4) the activity of "the Lord" in 3:16 corresponds to the activity that occurs "in Christ" in 3:14c. Thus all available data for the textual audience to this section of the text points to Christ as the logical referent for κύριος in 3:17a. See also Grundmann, "Teacher," 109.

27. Hays (*Echoes*, 123–24) argues that in 2 Cor 3 (particularly in 3:12–17) Paul puts forward an ecclesiocentric hermeneutic in which Scripture is "rightly read as a word addressed to the eschatological community," and thus "the Church is meant to read and understand scripture as a text that concerns their present time, which is the end of days." In a sense, then, Paul felt he and other believers in Christ had been given "new eyes" by which they are able to interpret Scripture for the church's present escha-

them from one glory to another: namely, from the limited glory of the old covenant to the surpassing glory of the new.[28]

C. Paul's Ministry Is Unveiled (4:1–6)

A 1 For this reason, since we have this ministry just as we have been shown mercy, we are not discouraged. 2 But we renounce the shameful hidden things, since we do not act with trickery, nor do we falsify the word of God; rather, with honest transparency we commend *ourselves* before God to everyone's conscience.
  B 3a And even if our *gospel is* veiled, it *is* veiled
    C 3b *to* those who are perishing—
    C′ 4a *to* those, the unbelieving, whose minds the god of this age has blinded,
  B′ 4b so that they might not see the light of the *gospel* of the glory of Christ, who *is* the image of God.
A′ 5 For we do not proclaim *ourselves* but Jesus Christ as Lord, and *ourselves* as your servants for the sake of Jesus. 6 For God who said, "From darkness let there be light," has set in our hearts the light of the knowledge of the glory of God on the face of Christ.

In the C unit (4:1–6) of Macrochiasm II, the audience experiences the pivot of the macrochiastic argument. In the A element (4:1–2), Paul makes known that he renounces the shameful hidden things, acts with transparency, and does not teach in a deceitful manner.[29] That he has been shown mercy to attain his ministry recalls that he was made trustworthy by God's mercy (1 Cor 7:25). The term ἐλεέω also marks Paul as one among the eschatological people (Isa 14:1; Wis 3:9; 4:15; 2 Macc 2:7; 7:29) and as one of the righteous who can boast of God's favor (Pss 40:10; 63:3; 88:11; Isa 63:7).[30]

---

tological context. This "proper reading" of Scripture is prevalent throughout Jewish apocalyptic literature, including Dan 9, the peshers of Qumran, and Acts 2.

28. So Furnish (*II Corinthians*, 215), who offers that "glory to glory" refers to 2 *Apoc. Bar.* 51:1–10, in which "believers find an increase of glory over against the diminishing glory of Moses." See also Stanley, "Last Adam," 21.

29. The verb δολόω has the sense to ensnare or use bait for trickery; see Harris, *Second Epistle*, 325.

30. Bultmann, "ἔλεος, ἐλεέω."

That he speaks to everyone's conscience in God's presence recalls that Paul called God to witness the sincerity of his ministry (1:23), and that he speaks before him with sincerity in Christ (2:17). Since Paul is found to be faithful and stand the test before God and even his own conscience (1:12), he is ipso facto able to commend himself to every human conscience to have each affirm the validity of his gospel and his ministry.

That Paul defends his gospel as being allegedly "veiled" in the B element (4:3a) recalls that the opponents or some detractors within the community had accused Paul of deception. The inability of first-century Jews, Gentiles, and the opponents to see the quality of Paul's gospel parallels the inability of ancient Israelites in the desert to see God's glory (3:12–18). This spiritual nearsightedness implies that the former three groups will share an eschatological fate that parallels the physical fate of the ancient Israelites.

Those to whom his gospel is veiled are in fact perishing (according to the C element, 4:3b), as are those who perceived Paul to be an odor from death to death (2:16) and those who rejected his gospel as folly (1 Cor 1:18). The audience is not presently among those perishing since they have accepted his gospel (1 Cor 15:52; 2 Cor 2:17), but they could join this group's fate if they dismiss Paul and side with the opponents.[31]

The C′ element (4:4a) clarifies that those who are perishing, those to whom Paul's gospel is veiled, according to the B and C elements (4:3a, b), are the ἄπιστοι ("unbelievers").[32] The B′ element (4:4b) builds on the discussion of the unbelievers found in the pivotal C and C′ elements (4:3b, 4a) by revealing further that if some allege Paul's gospel to be veiled (4:3a), it is because Satan[33] has blinded these ἄπιστοι from seeing the light of his gospel. That Satan dulls the unbelievers' senses parallels the dulled senses of the Israelites who were thus unable to see the temporary status of Moses' covenant (3:14a).[34] Because of this spiritual blindness that Satan inflicts, those who are perishing are not able to see Christ, the image of God. That Christ is the "image" of God develops that the audience is transformed into the same "image" of the glory of

---

31. Paul has related to the Corinthians previously that it is possible to lose the sanctified state before the time of judgment (1 Cor 6:7–20; see also 2 Cor 11:1–3).

32. Beale, *Worship*, 220–40.

33. Literally, "the God of this age." See Arnold, *Powers*, 93.

34. Behm, "νοῦς, νοέω," 960.

Christ when they look upon his face (3:18) to mean that they are in fact transformed into glory of the image of God (4:4b).³⁵ The phrase also leads the audience to link Christ with Adam who was created in the image of God (Gen 1:26).³⁶

That Paul proclaims not himself but Christ as Lord in the A′ element (4:5–6) develops the fact that he can commend himself before every conscience in the A element (4:1–2). Paul may commend himself because the content of his message, Christ, is the light that conveys the glory of God to all who receive the gospel (4:4). That God has set a light "in our hearts" (τῆς καρδίαις ἡμῶν) recalls that God set his Spirit in the hearts of all believers (τῆς καρδίαις ἡμῶν, 1:21–22) and that "you," the Corinthian community, bear the promise of the new covenant with the Spirit written in "your" hearts to commend Paul as a qualified minister (3:1–3).³⁷

The light that illuminates the face of Christ recalls the veil on Moses' face that covered the glory of God from the Israelites (3:11–15) and the transformation³⁸ that overtakes believers as they look with unveiled face on the glory of the Lord Christ (3:18).³⁹ The fact that the content

---

35. Scroggs, *Last Adam*, 99. In both 3:18 and 4:4–6, the terms εἰκών and δόξα are nearly synonymous.

36. The phrase "image of God" may allude to a tradition found in Philo that distinguished between the heavenly man who was made in God's image (Gen 1:26) and the earthly man who was made out of dust (Gen 2:6). See Kittel, "εἰκών." Von Rad ("εἰκών," 390–92) argues that the "image of God" remains with humanity after the fall, although the glory of Adam is lost (Gen 5:1, 3; 9:6).

37. Some scholars (e.g., Belleville, *2 Corinthians*, 118) who believe Paul is referring to his conversion on the Damascus road in 4:6 argue that ἡμῶν should be exclusive for Paul alone. But the wording of 4:6 has no lexical similarities to 1 Cor 15:10–11. It is more likely that since Paul says all are looking with unveiled face on Christ, so too do the hearts of all believers who look on Christ (3:18; 4:4) receive the light of the knowledge of the glory of God. See, e.g., Plummer, *II Corinthians*, 121.

38. Pate (*Adam Christology*, 110, 112) argues that the transformation noted in 3:18; 4:4, 6 refers to the believer regaining the glory that Adam lost at the fall. This "inaugurated eschatology" presents the age of the last Adam, which is "characterized by the renewal of the image of God in the heart of the believer."

39. The references to "light" in conjunction with proper interpretation of Scripture recall the Palestinian Jewish concept of illuminated interpretation of which Paul and the audience are aware. Qumran texts (e.g., 1QH 4.5–6, 27–29; 1QSb 4.24; 1QS 2.2–4) speak of Torah as the illuminating source. In the same way, the audience of 2 Corinthians understands Christ's face as a pool that reflected light (illumination, knowledge) to inform their interpretation of Scripture. This illumination aids the audience's under-

of Paul's gospel, the Lord Jesus Christ, transforms its hearers who are given new "sight" according to the A′ element (4:6) further underscores why Paul is able to commend himself before every conscience in the A element (4:1–2). The light of the knowledge of the glory of God refers back to the insight that all believers receive when their interpretation of the Law is unveiled in Christ by the gospel.

In sum, in the central unit (4:1–6) of Macrochiasm II, Paul again turns to defend his gospel. If his gospel seems veiled at all, it is because those who reject it are in fact among the perishing ἄπιστοι. This group of unbelievers is determined by God to be blinded by Satan so that they do not see the light of Christ, who is the image of God (4:4). Paul's gospel cannot be "veiled" because those who receive it gain in Christ an unveiled interpretation of the Law.

God, who shone light onto the world at creation (Gen 1:9), also shone onto Moses to reveal his glory to humanity; but he shone on Moses' face, not his heart (Exod 34:29–35; 2 Cor 3:12–17). Paul, who has been qualified to succeed Moses as a minister of a new and more glorious covenant (2:14—3:6; 3:7–11), has been given a gospel to proclaim so that the elect might be illuminated by God's light in their hearts, so that they might understand God's glory clearly in Christ and the new covenant and not only in the veiled and temporary ordinances of Moses.[40]

This internalization of his qualification within the audience and himself has no external evidence (such as in letters of recommendation or a glowing countenance) on Paul. Rather, the light of the new covenant is manifested as "the divine glory as fully revealed on the face, not the back, of Christ, who is the glorious Image of God himself."[41] Believers who are now able to look on Christ (3:18) are able to look on God's own image (4:4) and gain the knowledge of God's glory (4:6). All of this comes to the audience because of Paul's gospel. Paul's point is that no minister could have a finer credential on his résumé than the result found in the recipients of his gospel: they are able to see God in Christ, become illuminated with the knowledge of God's glory, and thus gain further access to his presence. This credential, in the end, is the most qualifying.

---

standing of the new covenant. See Martin, *2 Corinthians*, 80–81; Stockhausen, *Veil*, 31; and Fitzmyer, "Glory," 76–78.

40. Stockhausen, *Veil*, 174.

41. Ibid.

B′. Paul's Mortality Makes Known the Life of Christ (4:7–11)

A 7 But we hold this treasure *in* jars of clay, so that the surpassing power may be of God and not of *us*.

   B —8 In every way we are afflicted *but not* constricted, confused *but not* at a loss,

   B′ 9 persecuted *but not* abandoned, beaten down *but not* destroyed—

A′ 10 always bearing the death of Jesus *in* our body, in order that the life of Jesus may also be manifest *in our* body. 11 For we who live are always being handed over to death for the sake of Jesus, so that the life of Jesus may be manifest *in our* mortal flesh.

The B′ unit of Macrochiasm II presents a chiastic progression from the B unit (3:7–18). The glory of the new covenant that "surpasses" even that of the old (3:10) parallels the "surpassing" power of God that is manifested in Paul's participation with Christ's suffering (4:7, 10–11). The glory of the new covenant in which believers are transformed according to the B unit (3:7–18) is developed as the glory of the knowledge of God on the face of Christ that is set in the hearts of believers because of Paul's ministry, according to the pivotal C unit (4:1-6). The B′ unit (4:7–11) develops this glory as a "treasure" that Paul carries within his fragile body. In line with God's will, Paul's weak disposition and ministry of suffering manifest the life of Jesus in the face of death and shows the true source of this surpassing glory to be God. In both the B and B′ units (3:7–18; 4:7–11), then, Paul's gospel is indirectly portrayed as "surpassing" the audience's present opinion of him and his ministry.

The A element (4:7) develops the previous unit via the transitional term "God." Although God has shone in the hearts of believers the knowledge of his glory in 4:6, Paul carries about this treasure in his mortal body, like "jars of clay," so that the power may be shown to be from God and not its human carriers (4:7).[42] That is, Paul's ministry, which brings the knowledge of God to those who receive the gospel, is only successful if its hearers recognize the true message of the gospel that weakness bears out glorification. The glory that the audience has gained from the gospel is not visible but internal (1:21–22; 3:1–3, 18; 4:6).

---

42. Scholarship is in fair agreement that the referents for "we" in 4:7b–11 are Paul or Paul and his co-workers, and do not include the audience. The phrases "affliction" and being handed over to "death" recall 2 Cor 1:3–11 in which Paul speaks of his illness.

Paul's reference to his own vulnerability recalls the defense of his ministry in the face of affliction (1:3–11). The point in 4:7, that this power comes from God, recalls the arguments of Paul's sufficiency in 2:14–17; 3:4–6. In addition, the audience hears that his vulnerability exists within a divine teleology (as in 2:16–17; 3:14–15; 4:1–4).[43] It occurs so that people recognize that the power comes from God and not from its human messenger. The list in the B element (4:8) suggests that although the afflictions show his limitations, the afflictions themselves have a limited impact on him. That he is afflicted but not constrained (4:8) recalls that even while Paul is under severe affliction (1:8) he still has hope that God will rescue him (1:11).

The language used in the B´ element ("persecuted but not abandoned, beaten but not destroyed," 4:9) develops and reframes the hardships of the B element ("afflicted but not constricted, confused but not at a loss," 4:8) with echoes of the faithful suffering psalmist. That Paul is not abandoned (ἐγκαταλειπόμενοι) recalls the righteous sufferer who has faith that God will not abandon (ἐγκαταλείπω) him (LXX Ps 26:25, 28, 33).[44] That he is "not destroyed," according to the B´ element (4:9), recalls those who are "on their way to destruction (2:15; 4:3) because they have not heeded the gospel."[45] It is Paul's wholehearted acceptance of the gospel, even to the edge of death (as in 1:8–11), which keeps him among those who are being saved and apart from those who are spiritually perishing.

In total, the list of afflictions and their limitations that serves as the pivot of the present chiastic unit further defines Paul's ministry. The list describes his survival through several categories of affliction: personal (4:8a), psychological (4:8b), eschatological (4:9a), and physical (4:9b). In this list of sufferings, Paul amalgamates Stoic affliction lists with the faith of the righteous suffering psalmist to show that, although his life situation often appears desperate, he has the same faithful conviction that he will escape annihilation as does the suffering psalmist.[46]

43. According to Ahern ("Fellowship," 42, 45), this emphasis on divine teleology echoes both Isaiah (2:11; 30:15) and Paul's earlier letter to the Corinthians (1 Cor 1:31) that emphasize God's plan to humble the mighty by displaying his own might through weak instruments.

44. Thrall, *II Corinthians*, 328. Other examples include LXX Pss 15:10; 26:9; 37:22; 70:9, 18; 115:8; 139:9.

45. Matera, *II Corinthians*, 109.

46. See Savage, *Power*, 162; the excursus in Thrall, *II Corinthians*, 329–31.

The A′ element (4:10–11) presents a chiastic progression from the A element (4:7). That Paul carries the "death of Jesus" in his body in order that Jesus' life may be seen in his body, and that he is always in danger for Jesus' sake so that Jesus' life may be seen in his mortal body in the A′ element, develops the fact that Paul carries the illuminating treasure of the gospel as if in a jar of clay in the A element (4:7).[47] Because of the afflictions described in the pivotal elements, Paul is able to manifest the death of Jesus all the more in his body.[48]

In sum, in the B′ unit (4:7–11) of Macrochiasm II (2:14—4:14), Paul again wrestles with the audience's perception of his suffering. "Jars of clay" are symbols of weakness and cheapness. They are easily broken—yet Paul is not. His afflictions should not cause others to doubt his credibility as an apostle, but rather allow them to recognize the glory of God that is apparent despite his mortal limitations. By questioning Paul on the issue of his suffering, the Corinthians show that they understand him and God's plan only in part (1:13). Now, as he explains how his afflictions reveal the glory of God all the more, they come closer to understanding him in a more complete way (1:14). Paul also rallies against the opponents in this section. The opponents had insisted that signs and wonders were indicators of God's Spirit, but Paul counters that suffering in solidarity with Christ is what truly manifests the Spirit, and thus also the power of God.[49]

---

47. For Héring (*Second Epistle*, 32), this section reopens for the audience the eschatological matter in which the apostle shares in the sufferings of Christ "in order to kill the old Adam so that the new Adam may emerge."

48. The death of Jesus may refer either to a process of suffering or to the event of the cross. Thrall (*II Corinthians*, 234) denotes three possibilities: (1) Paul suffers as Jesus suffered; (2) Paul's suffering and the death of Jesus are linked by baptism; (3) the death of Jesus is revelatory, in that "the apostolate is the early manifestation of the gospel, and apostolic suffering plays a part in this." Most commentators prefer the third option, which fits the context best. Lambrecht (*Second Corinthians*, 73) believes νέκρωσις is a process of mortification that refers to the death of Jesus as it is present in all human suffering, particularly in the apostle. Harris (*Second Epistle*, 345–46) adds that Greek physicians used the term to describe a "withering or mortification of the body or of a sick member." See also Bultmann, "νέκρωσις," 895.

49. Schreiner, *Paul*, 96. Koester, "Suffering Servant," 105: "Paul is here fighting miracle-working super-apostles, who claimed to be imitators of the powerful . . . Christ."

A'. Paul Proclaims His Faith for the Life of the Community (4:12-14)

A 12 So death is at work in us, but life *in you.*

   B 13a Since, then, we have the same Spirit of faith, according to what is written, "I *believed,* therefore I *spoke,*"

   B' 13b we too *believe* and therefore *speak.*

A' 14 Because we know that the one who raised Jesus will also raise us with Jesus and set us *with you.*

The A' unit presents a chiastic progression from the A unit. That Paul believes and therefore speaks (4:13) recalls that he speaks in Christ with sincerity before God (2:17). That it is written in Scripture, "I believe, therefore I speak" (LXX Ps 115:1), develops that his letter of commendation is written with the Spirit on "your" hearts for all to read (3:1-3). The term ἐγγεγραμμένη in both units denotes the divine passive. What is written in Scripture by God's will (3:1-6) encourages Paul to proclaim further the gospel in the A' unit (4:12-14). The Spirit, written in the hearts of believers in the A unit (2:14—3:6), commends him as a minister of this new covenant that is far superior to Moses' (3:7-11), transforms believers (3:17-18), and manifests the life of Christ in Paul's mortal body (4:7-11).

That Paul "speaks" with the same Spirit as the suffering psalmist according to what is written in the A' unit (4:12-14) explains how he can "speak" with sincerity in Christ before God in the A unit (2:14—3:6). Since he speaks from what is written by God's will in Scripture to proclaim Christ, Paul speaks sincerely about Christ as though in the presence of God. This point underscores the sincerity that he claims to bring in his ministry to the community (2 Cor 1:14; 2:14).

The A element (4:12) develops the previous unit via transitional terms. The "death" to which Paul is being offered for the sake of Jesus in 4:11 is explained further as one antithetical result of his ministry, namely, that "death" is being worked in him, but life is being worked in "you" (4:12). The more he suffers, the more his life flows out for the audience.[50] That his affliction works for the benefit of "you" recalls that God consoles Paul in his affliction so that he might console others (1:3-7). They themselves are proof that Paul's afflictions are not in vain.

50. Héring, *Second Epistle,* 32-33.

The Corinthians are able to pass from life to death because his ministry brought to them the gospel of the new covenant, the Spirit, sanctification, and life in the new age.[51]

In the B element (4:13a), Paul echoes the suffering psalmist from LXX Psalms 114–16, whom God had rescued previously from death (LXX Ps 114:8). While undergoing new anxiety, the psalmist speaks confidently that God will rescue him again (LXX Ps 115:1). In the B′ element (4:13b), Paul speaks with the same Spirit that informed the psalmist to believe and thus speak regarding his future rescue by God. Paul is able to speak with faith (4:1) about God saving him because the same Spirit by which the psalmist spoke also inspires his own understanding of his afflicted ministry. The verb λαλέω refers to all that the apostle has spoken of to this point in regard to his faith in the resurrection, especially in 4:7–12.[52] He interprets for the audience what he has just said, namely, that God's power is at work in him. For this reason, he manifests the life of Jesus in his sufferings.

The A′ element (4:14) expounds further that Paul speaks as he believes because he knows that God, who raised Jesus, will at one time also raise and set him with "you." The content of 4:14 shows a connection to the A element (4:12): just as Paul suffered with Christ (4:12), he will also be raised with Christ (4:14). The Corinthians will join Paul, partly because of the suffering ministry that he endures for them. His hope that Jesus' resurrection prefigures his own recalls that during his severe affliction Paul put his hope in God who raises the dead (1:8–11).[53] The resurrection of the believer is a central point in his proclamation, along with the fact that Jesus is Lord and God raised him from the dead.[54] The

---

51. Hughes, *Second Epistle*, 145.

52. Murphy-O'Connor, "Faith and Resurrection."

53. Murphy-O'Connor (ibid., 547) argues that the "life of Jesus" in 4:11 has an existential sense (as in 2 Cor 2:16) rather than an eschatological sense. Paul's resurrection in 4:12, 14 then logically takes on an existential meaning, in his understanding. *Pace* Murphy-O'Connor, the categories of existential and eschatological are not mutually exclusive in 2 Cor 2:16 or 4:11–14. Rather, even if the "life" in 2:16 were taken to be existential/figurative in the turn of the ages period, there is little question that Paul and the audience understand the categories to have a very real eschatological result in the imminent future. The problem with Murphy-O'Connor's theory is that Paul's suffering, as he has presented it through the letter to this point, has been displayed with eschatological vocabulary and contexts (1:3–11, 14; 2:8–13; 4:1–6, 8–9). See also Lambrecht, "Eschatological."

54. Ridderbos, *Paul*, 55.

content of 4:12–14 thus encompasses the very heart of Paul's first message to the Corinthians. These "fundamentals" are the greatest assets to their salvation. That God will set Paul with "you" recalls that his afflictions work toward "your" resurrection life (4:12). With this affirmation of Paul's actions for the community's benefit, the audience experiences the closure of the A′ unit (4:12–14) and of Macrochiasm II (2:14—4:14) as a whole.

In sum, in 4:12–14 Paul addresses the Corinthian's concerns about his weakness by emphasizing his hope in the resurrection and how this perseverance results in life for them. They have already criticized Paul regarding his physical weakness and illness, but the text demands that they reconsider their own Greco-Roman standards for divine power.[55] Paul's view of apostolic suffering contradicts their delusion of superficially oriented status. They should instead view Christian life through the lens of the cross. When they can do this, they will "come to understand" Paul more fully (2 Cor 1:14). His afflictions are not a disqualification from the ministry but rather serve as the fulfillment of God's will. In his suffering, Paul manifests the weakness of the cross and thus also the power of the resurrection.

Chapter Summary

Having dealt with his administrative decisions in 1:8—2:13, in the second macrochiastic unit (2:14—4:14) Paul answers accusations about his apostleship and his qualifications to be a minister of the gospel. At the center of this argument (the C unit, 4:1–6) is the case that God has shown a light in the hearts of the gospel's recipients (see also 1:21–22; 3:1–3) so that the greatest demonstration of Paul's apostolic qualifications is not external. Rather, only those who are able to "see" Christ gain the knowledge of God's glory and understand the true nature of Paul's ministry. The opening units (2:14—3:6; 3:7–18) first address the source of Paul's qualifications to be a minister of the gospel and compare Paul to Moses, the minister *par excellence*. The apostle and his new covenant are more glorious than Moses and the old covenant because it is from Paul's gospel that the audience gains the insight in Christ necessary to interpret the Law properly and to see and regain God's glory (3:7–11, 14–15, 18).

55. Cousar, *Cross*, 152.

The C unit (4:1–6) serves to cap and support the arguments in units A (2:14—3:6) and B (3:7–18) and also preemptively supports the B´ (4:7–11) and A´ (4:12–14) units that follow. Since Paul is qualified to be superior to Moses by God's illumination of believers in their hearts (4:6), the afflictions that he suffers superficially do not disqualify him as an appointed minister of the gospel. Rather, these afflictions serve to glorify God further and manifest the life of Christ to those who receive his gospel (4:7–11). Because of his qualification and commission from God, Paul speaks with the same Spirit as did the suffering psalmist to proclaim Jesus as Lord (4:13). Furthermore, this faith is centered by the focus of his gospel: since Christ suffered and was raised, Paul will also suffer in solidarity in his missionary activities for the benefit of the audience and will subsequently be raised, as was Christ, to be joined with those who received his gospel (4:12–14).

Having dealt with his administrative issues in Macrochiasm I and defended his apostleship against the opponents' accusations in Macrochiasm II, in the third macrochiasm Paul will call for the audience to be fully reconciled to his ministry and to God. It is to this section, 4:15—6:2, that I will now turn in the following chapters.

5

Audience Response to 2 Corinthians 4:15—5:15

The recent chapters have provided preliminary relevant aural context in which the authorial audience receives Paul's call to reconciliation in 2 Cor 5:16—6:2. The present chapter examines 4:15—5:15 as the most immediate context to that climactic exhortation. In this section Paul continues his counterattack on the opponents that he began in the second macrochiasm (2:14—4:14), but also aims to pull the Corinthian audience closer to himself and away from the opponents. He does this by centering his argument and rhetoric around the seen/unseen aspects that separate his gospel from the ministry of his opponents.

Paul argues that these opponents boast in and judge others by appearances, but his gospel and the salvation of the community are determined by the unseen blessings that they have received from his ministry: sanctification, illumination, renewal, and preparation for the resurrection. Everything Paul does—whether attractive or not—is for the community's benefit (4:15; 5:11–13). The Spirit renews the inner person of the audience members daily, even though their outer selves are in decay. Can the opponents say the same thing? Paul's counterattack builds to a crescendo as he inverts the opponents' strength and his weakness.

Macrochiasm III: Paul's Continued Defense and Call to Reconciliation

A. For the Benefit of the Audience and the Glory of God (4:15–18)[1]

A   15a For *all things*[2] are for your benefit

> B   15b in order that the grace, which overflows among the growing number of believers, may increase the thanksgiving for the *glory* of God.
>> C   16a So we are not discouraged: *even though our* outer self is continually decaying,
>>
>> C′   16b *yet our* inner self is being renewed day by day.
>
> B′   17 For the temporary, light burden of our affliction is working out for us an eternal weight of *glory* out of all proportion,[3]

A′   18 since we are not concerned with the *things* that are seen, but with the *things* that are not seen. Because the *things* that are seen are temporary, but the *things* that are not seen are eternal.

A. All Things Are for "Your" Benefit (4:15a)

Having just described his hope in the resurrection despite affliction, Paul proceeds to discuss how his ministry benefits the audience, all believers, and God. The clause that introduces 4:15 connects the statement that "all things" are for "your benefit" with the discussion of hope in the resurrection that precedes in 2 Cor 4:12–14. The second-person plural pronouns act as transitional terms to link the chiastic units 4:12–14 and 4:15–18. That God will raise Paul and set him "with you" in 4:14 defines

---

1. Most commentators and translations prefer to group v. 15 with what precedes (e.g., 4:7–15) rather than what follows. As noted above, I delimit the section 4:15–18 for the following reasons: both 4:15 and 5:1 begin with γάρ clauses; the ὅτι clause in 4:14 concludes the section 4:11–14; and 4:15 presents a shift in subject from Jesus Christ (4:11–14) to the glory of God (4:15–18).

2. Although neuter plurals in Greek are collective (e.g., "everything"), this rendering in English would lose the aural connection between 4:15a and 4:18 since the former would be rendered "everything" and the latter "what is seen/not seen." The translation offered here is preferred for this particular study since retaining the plural *shows* the present reader what the authorial audience *hears*, namely, an aural connection between the phrases τὰ πάντα in 4:15a and τὰ (μὴ) βλεπόμενα in 4:18.

3. So Barrett, *Second Epistle*, 147.

"your benefit" in 4:15. Paul's ministry that preaches life in the face of affliction testifies to hope in the resurrection for the benefit of "you" and for all believers.

The phrase "all things" (τὰ πάντα) refers to both the content of Paul's preaching and the affliction that he endures.[4] That everything is for "your benefit" recalls several instances in the letter that stress his concern for the audience. Previously, Paul argued that his affliction worked out consolation and salvation for the Corinthians (1:5–6). His travel plans (1:23; 2:3) and forgiveness of the offender (2:10) were for their own good. His suffering also brings them transformation to glory (3:18) and hope in new life (4:12). Recalling these points as they hear the A element, the audience recognizes that Paul has made a significant investment in their spiritual success. At the very least, he has faced physical harm (1:3–7), embarrassment (1:23—2:4), and even death (1:8–11; 4:7-11) to bring them a message of life. It is not hyperbolic when Paul describes his preaching and suffering as "all things."

B. Grace and Thanksgiving for the Glory of God (4:15b)

The ἵνα clause presents to the audience the assertion that Paul's activity for them has a higher purpose, namely, that God's grace among the growing number of believers may further exalt God.[5] Through aural similarities, the B element (4:15b) points back to Paul's statements in 2 Cor 1:11. In the earlier passage, the "gift" (χάρισμα) refers to the rescue that Paul hopes to receive from God through the prayers of the many on his behalf. He claims that God will rescue him from his affliction as long as the audience works in solidarity to give thanks (εὐχαριστηθῇ) on his behalf.

Now, in 4:15, Paul's ministry serves the Corinthians and all believers by adding more converts with God's grace. "Grace" (χάρις) here refers to the divine gift that is embodied in the gospel and benefits the audience.[6] "All things" are for "your" benefit so that the "gift" that is being given by the growing number of believers may cause "thanksgiving" (εὐχαριστίαν) to overflow to God's glory.

---

4. See, e.g., Furnish, *II Corinthians*, 259; Harris, *Second Epistle*, 356. See also 2 Cor 4:2–3, 5, 7, 8–12.

5. Matera, *II Corinthians*, 113.

6. Polhill, "Reconciliation," 348.

Both passages demonstrate a cyclical relationship. The aural similarities recall as well as reinforce Paul's point that the audience is a part of a larger body of growing believers (1 Cor 1:2; 2 Cor 1:1) who act in solidarity through prayer for the benefit of all within their symbiotic relationship.

"Glory" (δόξα) here has a subjective sense (i.e., the exaltation of God), but the term itself recalls the previous demonstrations of glory in the letter. The new covenant comes with a greater "glory" than the old (3:7–11). Believers who accept the gospel and look on the "glory" of Christ are transformed "from glory to glory" (3:18). The gospel brings to light for the elect "the glory of Christ," who is "the image of God" (4:4). This "knowledge of God's glory" comes to the believers by the light that is reflected on the face of Christ (4:6).

The "glory" that believers receive in Christ expresses further the impact of "all things" that Paul does for "your benefit," and why these activities should lead the audience to give thanks to "God's glory." Since Paul's gospel makes "God's glory" present in their lives, the proper response is for the audience to give thanks to "God's glory" (i.e., God's exaltation).

C. Confident While in Decay (4:16a)

The earlier elements of the unit explain how Paul's ministry contributes to God's glory and his people. The pivot and conclusion of the unit will address what is so glorious about this ministry. That believers are not discouraged[7] in the C element recalls that they have received in Christ

---

7. The identity of first person plural pronouns in 2 Corinthians is at times unclear. As mentioned above, I hold that Paul often uses these ambiguous pronouns as a rhetorical strategy to draw in his audience. As the ensuing analysis has shown, Paul's method is effective: at many points these inclusive pronouns emphasize important theological themes that not only support the defense of his ministry, but also heal the bond with the community to whom he feels obligated (1:21–22; 2:11; 3:12–18; 4:4–6). These points are supported by the fact that within 1:1—6:2 (the focus of this study) the pronouns are exclusive when Paul is discussing the duties, authority, or obligations of his ministry (1:3–7, 9–20; 2:14—3:6; 4:1–5, 7–14; 5:11–15, 18b, 19b, 20; 6:1), but they are inclusive when he addresses the spiritual benefits of the gospel that have come in Christ to all believers (1:1–3, 8, 21–22; 2:11; 3:12–18; 4:6, 16–18; 5:1–10, 16–18a, 21).

In the present context, the literary plural ("we are not discouraged") adds to the argument's rhetorical effect. Paul here continues to discuss his ministry (from 4:7–14), but the literary plural draws in the audience. Paul and his ministry are the particular focus, but the hope expressed can be held by all believers (as seen in 4:15). (See also

the fulfillment of God's promises to his eschatological people (1:18–22), which is made evident in their hearts (3:1–6). In the same way, the content and character of Paul's ministry and the new covenant (3:7–16), the ensuing transformation to a new glory (3:18), the knowledge of God's glory (4:6), and hope in the resurrection (4:11–14) offer encouragement while awaiting the Parousia.

"Our outer self" (ὁ ἔξω ἡμῶν ἄνθρωπος) is the aspect of the person that is material and subject to decay and points back to the "jars of clay" of 4:7. The audience recognizes the decay of "our outer self" as a real condition that is presently occurring.[8] The verb διαφθέρω implies that the body is rotting like a corpse in a grave (Job 33:28; LXX Pss 15:10; 29:10; 54:24) prior to the resurrection of the body and the attainment of the spiritual body (σῶμα πνευματικόν; 1 Cor 15:48).

C′. Daily Renewal of the Inner Self (4:16b)

With the second of the central elements in the unit, the audience experiences the pivot of the chiasm's argument, which centers around the daily renewal of the believer. In particular, the pivotal elements express how "our inner self" is renewed while "our outer self" is in decay.

The repetition of ἀλλ' . . . ἡμῶν, differentiated by the respective antithetical properties ἔξω and ἔσω, establish the contrasting yet equally present situations of the believer's self. "Even though" (ἀλλ') "our outer

---

Harris, *Second Epistle*, 363 n. 28 [citing Rom 8:18].) The benefits that all believers share from the gospel include the endowment of the Spirit (1:21–22), transformation (3:18), and the light of the knowledge of the glory of God (4:4–6), all of which intone inclusive first person plural pronouns.

Furthermore, within audience theory, both authorial intent and audience response are governed by the progression of the text. Thus, even if one argued that Paul intended for his ministry to be the exclusive referent of ἡμῶν in 4:16 (or elsewhere) based on the apologetic context, the text has conditioned the audience to recognize pronouns within shared points of faith to be inclusive of them, such as 1:21–22; 3:18; 4:6. The apologetic context does not necessarily support exclusive force since throughout the letter Paul has used the Corinthians as proof of his ministry. Since the aspects of the faith mentioned in 4:16—5:10 are fundamental to all believers, the audience members recognize themselves as being among the "we/our/us" who are not discouraged and whose outer self is in decay but whose inner self is being renewed because of the gospel.

8. See Jewett, *Anthropological Terms*, 397; Collins, *First Corinthians*, 136. The pronoun ἡμῶν is likely inclusive. Aune ("Anthropological Duality," 235) argues that when Paul uses ἡμῶν here he is "speaking *a pluralis sociativus*, i.e., Paul is speaking on behalf of those he is addressing," and so is speaking for the individual "I" of each member of the ideal audience.

self" (ἔξω ἡμῶν ἄνθρωπος) is in decay, "yet" (ἀλλ') "our inner self" (ἔσω ἡμῶν) receives daily renewal. The C′ element (4:16b) thus progresses and completes the line of thought regarding the "self" from the C element (4:16a). That the inner self is being renewed daily informs the audience further of why Paul is confident in the face of a decaying external body. "Our inner self" is renewed daily so as to counteract the decay that "our outer self" undergoes.[9]

---

9. The terms "outer" and "inner person" present some exegetical problems. From a diachronic perspective, the ἔξω ἄνθρωπος appears only here and ἔσω ἄνθρωπος occurs only here and in Rom 7:22; Eph 3:16; 4:24. Betz ("Inner Human Being," 315–41) points to 1 Cor 15:21–54 and notes that here Paul sees two types of humanity: those who share the image and characteristics of Adam and those who share such aspects of Christ. But in 2 Cor 4:16, rather than saying there are two types of humanity, Paul now says that there are two aspects to the human person, which is now described as a composite entity. Paul's use of these terms contradicts the Platonic dualism that was possibly shared among some Corinthians. Instead, he speaks of two aspects that analogize "the contradictions of human life in this world."

According to Schnelle (*Apostle Paul*, 537–38), Paul is using with a new name the Hellenistic image of the "person within" (ὁ ἐντὸς ἄνθρωπος), which was the conscience by which the rational person separated himself from external stimuli (see also Aune, "Duality," 215–40). The external person, however, was dominated by stimuli and thus also passions and anxiety (see Philo, *Worse*, 23). Jeremias ("ἄνθρωπος," 364–66) considers the terms to be widely used in Hellenistic Jewish cultures, and thus widely understood by Paul and his audience.

Among scholars today, definitions of these terms have some points of agreement. According to most commentators, "our outer self" concerns the whole body—muscles, mind, and perception—that is in a constant process of decay (Hughes, *Second Epistle*, 153; Matera *II Corinthians*, 113; Hoehner, *Ephesians*, 479). It is comparable to the jars of clay (4:7), body and mortal flesh (4:10–11), the earthly dwelling (5:1), and that which is mortal (5:4), and thus is a metaphor for the physical body (see Aune, "Duality," 220–21). According to Behm ("ἔσω," 699), Ladd (*Theology*, 477), and Hoehner (*Ephesians*, 479), "our inner self" and heart both effectively receive God's grace in a similar way. Another comparable internal aspect is the "I" (Rom 7:22) that is receptive to the Law of God (Dunn, *Romans 1–8*, 393–94) and, in being receptive to Paul's gospel, enables the believer to be eschatologically transformed into God's holy people (Jewett, *Anthropological Terms*, 597; Matera, *II Corinthians*, 115).

These explanations, while helpful in the diachronic sphere, are not as useful for this study since the authorial audience of 2 Corinthians would not be aware of the texts in Romans or Ephesians. More helpful is Thrall (*II Corinthians*, 353–54) who sees the terms as pointing both backward to the transformation in 3:18 and forward to the eternal glory in 4:17. Thus, the renewal of "our inner self" is identical to the glorious transformation in 3:18 (I add also 4:4–6), but awaits the glorious consummation of the resurrection body in eternal glory (4:17; 5:1–10). Within the polemical context of the letter, the "outer/inner" contrast also underscores the opponents' lack of vision. They see Paul's devolving appearance but fail to see the internal glory that renews him

B´. Temporary Affliction Produces Eternal Glory (4:17)

In the B´ element, the audience hears a progression from the B element (4:15b) regarding the "glory" (δόξα) motif. The subjective "glory of God" (i.e., "God's exaltation") that is the purposeful result of Paul's ministry to the ever-growing numbers of believers in the B element (4:15b) is paralleled with the weight of divine objective glory, that is, an eternal weight of "glory" (δόξης) from a divine source, in the B´ element (4:17). The B´ element (4:17) elaborates on the believers' reason for giving thanks in the B element. Believers who receive the gospel are able to give thanks to God's "glory" (4:15b) with the hope that their daily decay will yield an "eternal weight of glory" (4:17) at the resurrection.

The temporary "affliction" develops the idea that God consoles believers in every affliction (1:4) and that the audience participates through prayer in Paul's rescue from affliction (1:8, 11) in Asia. That glory follows affliction develops the theme in 1:4–5, 7, 8–11 that the community will receive consolation through Christ even as it endures the affliction of his sufferings (1:6).

This glory is not only future. It is also experienced in the present consolation and the ongoing transformation into a divine likeness (3:18; 4:4–6).[10] Glory in the present refers to the transformation (3:18) and the renewal of the inner self (4:16b). The resurrection body (i.e., the "spiritual body"; 1 Cor 15:44, 53) is the glory (δόξα) that has yet to come.[11]

A´. Things Seen and Things Unseen (4:18)

The audience experiences an aural connection to the beginning element of the unit with the repetition of the neuter plural with definite article in 4:18. "All things" that Paul endures in his ministry enable the audience to prioritize between two different sides of reality—that which is visible and that which is not. To say it a different way, "all things" (τὰ πάντα) that Paul suffers for the community's benefit in the A element (4:15a) bring believers the gospel of the light of Christ (4:4–6) so that they may look

---

daily in the divine likeness. In a similar manner, the Corinthians fail to see the internal evidence of Paul's credibility (1:21–22; 3:1–6, 14–18; 4:6) within their inner self.

10. Collange (*Enigmé*, 178) argues for only a future sense to the glory. Thrall (*II Corinthians*, 353) and Barrett (*Second Epistle*, 148), however, point to the present tense of κατεργάζεται and the experiences of 2 Cor 3:18 as evidence for both a present and future sense to the glory that is produced by affliction.

11. So Thrall, *II Corinthians*, 354; Barrett, *Second Epistle*, 148.

with proper sight to be concerned not with "things seen" (τὰ βλεπόμενα) but with "things unseen" (τὰ μὴ βλεπόμενα) in the A′ element (4:18).

The paradox of Paul's ministry in 4:17–18 mirrors that found in 4:10–11. In the latter, he bore the death of Jesus in order to manifest the resurrection life. In the present unit, affliction produces eternal glory and the invisible things endure beyond what is seen.[12]

The clause "since we are not concerned" (genitive absolute) informs the audience that what follows in the A′ element is a presumed cause of the reality described in the B′ element (4:17).[13] This temporary affliction is working for "us" an eternal glory *because* the eschatological people of God who are in Christ have a preexisting focus that is paradoxical in nature. The pronoun "we" refers to those whose outer self is in decay,[14] yet whose inner self is being renewed daily by the indwelling of the Spirit (3:3), the transformation in Christ (3:18), and the light of the knowledge of God's glory that is "seen" by faith on the face of Christ (3:18; 4:4, 6). The content of Paul's gospel, Christ, is not physically visible to those who hear it. The central points of the gospel—the death and resurrection of Christ—remain outside of the believers' viewpoint. They can only be part of a confession of faith in the resurrection when affliction is all that is visible (4:7, 13, 15–16).[15]

The audience recognizes both the genitive absolute and the γάρ clause as presenting real preexisting situations. The content within the chiasm, then, in a sense, is given in reverse order. It is the knowledge that things seen are temporary and things unseen are eternal (4:18b) that enables believers to remain confident and to realize that the present affliction will lead to future eternal glory (4:17), even though their outer self is presently in decay (4:16a).[16] By being concerned with "things unseen" and realizing the knowledge of God that is brought to them through "all things" that Paul does in his ministry for them (4:15a),

---

12. So Matera, *II Corinthians*, 116.

13. Harris, *Second Epistle*, 363.

14. As in 4:16 and 17, the literary plural ("we," ἡμῶν) in this verse is ambiguous. Paul and his ministry are the particular focus of the unit; yet the topics at hand, in that they encompass basic principles of faith in the resurrection, include all believers, and thus also the Corinthian audience. See Barrett, *Second Epistle*, 148; Harris, *Second Epistle*, 362; Hughes, *Second Epistle*, 157.

15. Matera, *II Corinthians*, 116.

16. Barrett, *Second Epistle*, 147.

the audience may take comfort in the fact that their inner self is being renewed daily (4:16b) and further give thanks to God's glory (4:15b).

B. Waiting and Groaning in This Earthly Dwelling (5:1–5)

A 1 For we know that even if our earthly dwelling, a tent, is *destroyed*, we have a building from *God*—an eternal building not made by hands—in heaven.
  B 2 For even *in* this *we groan*, desiring to put on in addition our heavenly residence,
    C 3 so that when we put it on[17] we will not be found naked.
  B′ 4a For while we are *in* this tent, *we groan* anxiously, because[18] we do not wish to be unclothed but to be further clothed,
A′ 4b so that what is mortal may be *swallowed up* by life. 5 The one who has *conditioned us* for this matter is *God*, who has given us the down payment of the Spirit.

A. The Spiritual Body That Awaits Believers (5:1)

Having stated in the last unit that the present affliction is working out for believers eternal glory because of their focus on unseen eternal things (4:15–18), the present unit affirms and develops this theme of eternal future glory in the resurrected body.[19] The A element (5:1) provides for the audience an accompanying image for their future reward via the transitional terms in 4:17–18 and 5:1. Whereas the reward was previously expressed as an "eternal" weight of glory (4:17) that believers receive because they look to the "eternal" things that cannot be seen (4:18), now the audience hears that they have an "eternal" building from God awaiting them in heaven (5:1). "We [believers][20] know" of this fu-

---

17. External evidence favors the reading ἐνδυσάμενοι (read by RSV, GNV, ASV, NASB, NIV, NJB; Matera, *II Corinthians*, 116). The variant ἐκδυσάμενοι (read by NAB [1980] and NRSV) is preferred with some reservation in the NA27 (Metzger, *TCGNT*, 580). I follow the majority of scholars and translations in favoring ἐνδυσάμενοι.

18. The force of ἐπί here is debated, but the sense is most likely causal, as it is in Rom 5:12; Eph 2:10 (Wallace, *Grammar*, 389).

19. See Polhill, "Reconciliation," 348.

20. It is debated whether the first person plural form of οἴδαμεν includes the Corinthians or just Paul and his ministry. Thrall (*II Corinthians*, 357) sees only Paul in view here (but see, 362–63, where she concedes that all believers are included later

ture eternal building because "we" have the proper sight to focus on the unseen things that are eternal (4:18) and to remain confident that "our inner self" is being renewed while "our outer self" is decaying (4:16).

The earthly tent that can be destroyed (5:1) serves as a metaphor for the believers' mortal bodies. The image is cogent with the Greek perspective that the material body is the dwelling place for the immaterial soul and recalls the breakable "jars of clay" that hold the immeasurable treasure of the knowledge of God's glory (4:7). Such a fragile existence defines the life of apostles in particular and Christians in general.[21] However, at the same time, the wording recalls the image of the believers' bodies housing God's Spirit like a temple (1 Cor 6:19).[22] Their earthly bodies are fragile, but the destruction of the visible body is not the endpoint for believers. The Spirit indwells "our hearts" (1:21; 3:1–3), renews "our inner self" daily (4:16b), and enables "us" to look with faith towards an unseen (4:18) body that is "our" true destination (5:1).

That "we" have a house "from God" in heaven (5:1) develops the point in 4:18 that "we" are concerned not with things that are seen but with things that are not seen. This house from God refers to the individual resurrection body of 1 Cor 15:44–48.[23] The resurrection body is not made of human hands, but is eternal, in heaven, and from God. This future gift is prefigured by God's active role in the lives of the elect, such as when he consoles them in the face of affliction (1:3–11), and confirms, sets his seal upon, and gives them the down payment of the Spirit in their hearts (1:18–22; 3:1–3; 4:4–6).

B. Desiring Our Heavenly Residence (5:2)

The B element (5:2) develops the content of the A element (5:1). "For even" informs the audience that their groaning "in this" (ἐν τούτῳ) is a real, ongoing situation (5:2). "In this" points back to the "tent of our

---

in the section). Martin (2 *Corinthians*, 124), Collange (*Enigmé*, 154), and Gillman ("Thematic Comparison," 445), among others, see the audience included in 5:1–10, as it was in 4:15–18. For Gillman, the audience is included in the οἴδαμεν of 5:1 just as they are in the εἰδότες of 4:14. Here, as in 4:16, I favor the view that the audience experience themselves among the "we" who hope and are courageous because of the benefits of the gospel.

21. Barrett, *Second Epistle*, 153.
22. See Thrall, *II Corinthians*, 358; Barrett, *Second Epistle*, 153.
23. Harris, *Second Epistle*, 372–74; Thrall, *II Corinthians*, 359.

earthly dwelling" from the A element (5:1). Groaning (στενάζομεν) is defined by, and comes about because of, "our" desire to don the heavenly dwelling from God (5:2).[24] That "we desire to don" this promised dwelling develops further what believers might attain in the future. The weight of eternal glory that is a heavenly dwelling from God (5:1) and born from affliction (4:17) in the A element is now a heavenly residence that believers "put on" like a robe (5:2).

The double compound verb ἐπενδύσασθαι (5:2) can be rendered "to put on over/in addition to,"[25] meaning that the dead believer puts on the immortal body in addition to the mortal body. This view is similar to, but also a slight development of, the image presented in 1 Cor 15:53: "For it is necessary that this corruptible body put on [ἐνδύσασθαι] incorruptibility and for this mortal body to put on [ἐνδύσασθαι] immortality." In Paul's view, the mortal body is not found naked, even when dead.[26] However, in this latest correspondence with his audience, Paul emphasizes that the new body is not only "put on," but is in fact "put on in addition to," the corruptible mortal body that the believer presently holds. This clothing event dramatically transitions believers from the earthly body to a body that is completely guided by the Spirit.[27] The "heavenly residence," then, is not heaven *per se*, but the glorious body (i.e., the σῶμα πνευματικόν).[28] The new body is the future fulfillment for what "we" presently experience in the daily renewal of "our inner self" (4:16).

C. Regaining and Wearing God's Glory (5:3)

The C element states a logical progression from this fact, albeit tautological. It is hoped that when "we" put on God's glory, "we" will not be found "naked" (γυμνοί). To be "naked" recalls the loss of glory by Adam (Gen 3:7).[29] Believers regain glory by being transformed into the same image as Christ (3:18), who is the image of God (4:4), and thus put on

---

24. Barrett, *Second Epistle*, 153; Hughes, *Second Epistle*, 172.

25. Thrall, *II Corinthians*, 371.

26. According to Polhill ("Reconciliation," 349–50), this view contradicts the Greco-Roman perspective that the soul is left naked when it is separated from the body at death.

27. Gillman, "Comparison," 447.

28. Thrall, *II Corinthians*, 363–68.

29. See Pate, *Adam Christology*, 145.

the glory of God (as in Bar 5:1; see also 2 Cor 4:6, 17). For Paul, if God's divine son can become human, then humanity in him can attain God's glory. It is possible that the opponents or the anti-Pauline Corinthians preferred the Greek view that the self was essentially left "naked" when separated from the material body at death.[30] Paul's statement is a clear refutation of that point.

What is gained within this transformation is the glory that Adam held prior to the fall (Gen 1:26).[31] The audience realizes that when "we" put on the glory of Christ, "we" will no longer be found "naked" as the rest of humanity is in their glory-less, Adam-like state. Rather, now being in Christ, the New Adam (1 Cor 15:11–15), "we" will be found clothed in God's eternal glory with the resurrection body, and regain humanity's original and intended glorious status.[32]

B′. Wishing to Be Clothed (5:4a)

The motif of groaning while in this earthly situation of decay progresses from the B (5:2) to the B′ (5:4a) element within the chiastic unit. That "we groan" (στενάζομεν) "in this" (ἐν τούτῳ) earthly situation as "we desire" to don "our" heavenly residence in the B element (5:2) is developed further in that "we groan" (στενάζομεν) anxiously while "in this tent" (ἐν τῷ σκήνει) because "we" wish to be clothed (5:4a). The B′ element (5:4a) affirms that ἐν τούτῳ in 5:2 refers to the earthly dwelling/tent of 5:1. The added anxiety of the B′ element (5:4a) comes from the possibility of being naked, as stated in the C element (5:3). The progression underscores to the audience the anxiety that believers encounter as they await the fulfillment of glory in the attainment of their resurrection body. Believers are at present being transformed to the same glory as Christ (3:18), but that transformation will not be complete until they have put on the resurrection body and attained the eternal glory of God that was intended for them (1 Cor 15:48–53; 2 Cor 4:17).

That "we groan" because "we" desire to don "our" heavenly goal in the B element is developed further in the B′ element (5:4a) in that "we groan" anxiously. The anxiety comes because "we" do not wish to be

---

30. So Harris, *Second Epistle*, 388–89; Polhill, "Reconciliation," 350–51; see also Thrall, *II Corinthians*, 361.

31. Hooker, "Interchange," 26–41.

32. Scroggs, *Last Adam*, 94.

unclothed but to be clothed. That is, "we" desire to receive the glory that is both present and yet will not be complete until death or the Parousia arrives. This desire and wish flow from the knowledge of the future eternal house in heaven (5:1) and the proper focus that allows "us" to look not on things seen that are temporary but on things unseen that are eternal (4:18).

The desire to don the heavenly body is a response to the fear of being naked (5:3) or unclothed (5:4), that is, a state without the future completed glory (i.e., the σῶμα πνευματικόν) that believers are intended to receive (1 Cor 15:52; 2 Cor 5:1–4).[33] The desire is to be away from the present situation of affliction that requires daily renewal, and instead to be in the promised future state of constant incorruptibility and immortality (1 Cor 15:53–54; 2 Cor 5:2).

A´. That Mortality May Be Swallowed Up by Life (5:4b–5)

A repetition of terms and aural patterns connect the A (5:1) and A´ (5:4b–5) elements for the audience. Within these elements, the destructive experience of the believers while in this earthly dwelling in the A element (5:1) is contrasted with the creative activity of God who gives the Spirit to prepare believers for the victory of life over death in the A´ element (5:4b–5).

God's prominent role in the preparation for, and the believers' attainment of, the resurrection body is underscored by his placement in the primary and ultimate elements of this unit (5:1, 4b–5). That we have a heavenly house from "God" if "our" earthly dwelling is destroyed, according to the A element (5:1), is developed by the fact that "God" has conditioned "us" for the victory of life over death by giving the Spirit as a down payment, according to the A´ element (5:4b–5).

---

33. Some scholars (e.g., Harris [*Second Epistle*, 388–89] and Barrett [*Second Epistle*, 155]) do not consider "unclothed" and "naked" to be equivalent terms. Accordingly, "unclothed" refers to the state of being without the resurrection body, but "naked" refers to the body that has passed away, been buried, and awaits the consummation of the Parousia. This view, however, neglects the emphasis on Adam's loss of glory and the hope of regaining it in Christ. *Pace* Murphy-O'Connor (*Theology*, 53), the context of the sentence directly places "naked" as antithetical to that of "being clothed." They are mutually exclusive properties. Naturally, "unclothed" is also antithetical to the state of being "clothed." The statement, then, contains three terms that describe two separate statuses: one status is "clothed," the other is "unclothed," which is equivalent to "naked."

The three verbs (καταλύω, καταπίνω, κατεργάζω) that share the preverb κατα- also serve to aurally link God's conditioning of believers and the defeat of death in the A´ element (5:4b–5) with the destruction of the earthly body in the A element (5:1). "If," as the A element (5:1) states, the believers' earthly dwelling "is destroyed" (καταλυθῇ), the A´ element (5:4b–5) gives two reasons to retain hope: (1) death will be "swallowed up" (καταποθῇ, i.e., utterly defeated) at the resurrection, and (2) God "has conditioned" (κατεργασάμενος) believers to attain the future heavenly dwelling by giving them his Spirit as a down payment.

The terms "mortal" (θνητόν) and "swallowed up" (καταπίνω) echo and confirm for the audience the unit's aural link to 1 Cor 15:54.

> 1 Cor 15:54 And when this corruptible body *puts on* incorruptibility and this *mortal* body *puts on* immortality, then the word that is written will come to pass, "Death is *swallowed up* in victory!"

> 2 Cor 5:4 But we do not wish to be unclothed but to *be clothed*, so that what is *mortal* may be *swallowed up* by life.

The transformation that takes place at the Parousia in 1 Cor 15:52–54 is now spread, to some extent, into the present experience of the believer (3:18; 4:4–6, 16–17; 5:1–4), and yet still retains its place at the consummation of the new age (5:5). With this connection to the parallel in 1 Cor 15 complete, the audience recognizes that the nakedness that is referred to in the C (5:3) and B´ (5:4a) elements refers to the situation of corruptibility and mortality that they are in. That is, believers are presently naked like Adam after the fall (Gen 3:7), but ultimately they will be clothed with God's glory when they put on the σῶμα πνευματικόν in addition to their mortal bodies.[34]

That what is mortal "might be swallowed up" (5:4b) entails a complete defeat of death. In 1 Cor 15:54–55, it is death itself that is to be swallowed up, after which Paul "places himself at the end of time, mocking death as already defeated and no longer able to exercise its sting."[35] Recalling Paul's previous statements on the resurrection and the victory over death, the audience of 2 Corinthians at this point gains further hope in the attainment of a spiritual body. Death is the final opponent (1 Cor

---

34. As in 4:16 and 5:1 above, the first person pronouns and verbs continue to include the audience.

35. Barrett, *First Epistle*, 383.

15:26), but its future defeat is certain. Since death is swallowed up (1 Cor 15:53–55), so too is that which is mortal (2 Cor 5:4). The swallowing up of what is mortal by life acts as the capstone to the transformation that has been taking place in believers who look with faith on Christ (3:18) and receive daily renewal to sustain their focus on things unseen in order to attain the future glory (4:16, 18; 5:1–4).

This future hope is meant to be attained by believers. According to 1 Cor 15:53, it must (δεῖ) be attained by believers.[36] The presence of the Spirit is what guarantees this conclusion (5:5). To condition them for this, God has placed the Spirit in their hearts as a down payment (ἀρ ραβῶνα, see also 1:22).[37] Although the Spirit is the agent, the statement has the same theocentric force as 2 Cor 1:18–22.[38] God's central role in defeating what is mortal recalls for the audience that God who consoles the afflicted also raises the dead (2 Cor 1:9).[39] "This very thing" refers to the resurrection, the "ultimate investiture with the glorified body"[40] that God has prepared for us. As a pledge for this future glory, God gives believers possession of his divine Spirit.

The Spirit, who prepares believers for life, was placed in their hearts by the living God (1:20). "Life" here in 5:5 refers to the resurrection life (as in 4:12–14), not life personified.[41] The believers' preparation begins at baptism, in which God seals them and secures them as his own to receive the promises that are made "yes" in Christ (1:19–22). But the preparation extends far beyond one event. The Spirit remains within their hearts to confirm the arrival of the new, spiritual covenant

---

36. According to Collins (*First Corinthians*, 581), δεῖ "bespeaks the eschatological certainty and divine imperative of what Paul describes."

37. Most scholars prefer to interpret ἀρραβών as a down payment that is a present experience of salvation (see in particular the NRSV, among others). Kwon ("Ἀρραβών," 525–41) argues that the term has a narrower meaning of "pledge" that precludes a present experience implied in a down payment. *Pace* Kwon, in light of the present experience that is found in the present transformation (3:18), knowledge of God's glory (4:6), daily renewal (4:16–17), and proper vision/knowledge (3:14–16; 4:18; 5:16–17), the present experience of salvation, and thus the meaning of "down payment" in ἀρραβών, is logically realized by the authorial audience.

38. Hughes (*Second Epistle*, 173) confirms that the name "God" is emphasized in the Greek by its placement at the end of the clause.

39. Matera, *II Corinthians*, 123.

40. Hughes, *Second Epistle*, 174.

41. *Pace* Polhill, "Reconciliation," 352.

that was prophesied (3:4–6) and to enable the believers to look clearly upon the face of Christ and be transformed into the same glory (3:18). The Spirit also validates Paul's ministry. After all, the Corinthians first received the Spirit from his proclamation of the gospel (1 Cor 1:30; 2 Cor 1:18–22; 3:1–6). Paul's ministry, then, may be seen as another part of how God prepares believers, particularly the audience, for the future glory of the resurrection.[42]

C. Courageous and Acceptable While Away from the Lord (5:6–10)

A 6 So we are *always* courageous—although we know that while we are at home in the body we are away from the Lord— 7 for we walk by faith, not by sight.

  B 8a But we are courageous, although we prefer *to be away* from the body

    C 8b and *at home* with the Lord.

    C′ 9a So we aspire, whether we are *at home*

  B′ 9b or whether we *are away*, to be acceptable to him.

A′ 10 For we must *all* appear before the judgment seat of Christ, so that each one may receive recompense for what one did in the body, whether good or whether evil.[43]

A. Courageous Because We Walk by Faith (5:6–7)

Having heard that God has conditioned "us" with the Spirit to attain in Christ the glory that Adam had lost, the audience is now further informed about their future dwelling. In the A element (5:6–7), "we"[44] are courageous even while "we" are away from the Lord. "So great is the

---

42. Matera, *II Corinthians*, 123.

43. A number of good witnesses (P^{46} B D F G Cl) read κακόν, but since φαῦλον (ℵ C) is the less common word, it is also more likely original.

44. According to Furnish (*II Corinthians*, 301), among others, the participle that presumes a first person plural referent (θαρροῦντες, "we are encouraged") has an expanded sense that includes the audience. Much like the section in 4:12–14, 16–18 and 5:1–5, even if the Pauline apostolate is the primary referent, the attitude and belief of the statements are shared by all believers.

glory within, and so strong the guarantee of the promise made with the Spirit," that there is no room for doubt.⁴⁵

The contrasting pairs that contain ἐκ- and ἐν-preverbs in 5:3–4 and 5:6 act as transition terms that link the B (5:1–5) and C (5:6–10) units. In the previous unit, being clothed (ἐπενδύομαι) signified a glorified state for the believer in Christ, whereas being unclothed (ἐκδύω) represented the glory-less state of Adam-like humanity. Now the audience hears that the believer prefers to be away (ἐκδημέω) from the body and at home (ἐνδημέω) with the Lord. Using antithetical parallelism, Paul continues to compare this earthly realm and the future glorious one. The "old" and "new" are mutually exclusive categories. For believers to cross from one to the other they must be utterly transformed. The radical inner transformation (4:16) foreshadows the external transformation that is promised to take place (4:17; 5:1–5).

That the body is described as distant from the Lord (5:6) recalls that "our outer self" is in decay (4:16) and can be destroyed (5:1), but "we" who are in Christ are transformed and await to put on the eternal glory of God that Adam had lost (5:3–5).⁴⁶ Although believers are always "in Christ" so long as they are members of his sanctified community (e.g., 1 Cor 1:2, 4, 30; 3:1; 4:10; 16:24; 2 Cor 2:17; 3:14), Paul's present point is that they are not so near to him now as they will be when they finally join him at the resurrection of the dead.⁴⁷

The audience is informed that "we" are courageous while "we" are away from the Lord because "we" walk by faith and not by sight (5:7).⁴⁸ That "we" do not walk by sight recalls and develops the idea that believers are not concerned with things seen but rather with things unseen (4:18). Productive faith does not come from objective evidence; rather, "it trusts in the indemonstrable" figure of Christ, who is no longer visible to the living, but whose coming "lies in the unknown future."⁴⁹

---

45. Barrett, *Second Epistle*, 157.

46. Pate, *Adam Christology*, 147.

47. See, e.g., Martin (*2 Corinthians*, 110), Thrall (*II Corinthians*, 386), and Matera (*II Corinthians*, 124–25).

48. The force of εἴδους, whether active or passive in force, is debated. The latter is preferred by Thrall (*II Corinthians*, 387): "we live by faith, not in the presence of his visible form." This translation, however, seems overdrawn. The active force, "sight," is preferred by most commentators (e.g., Hughes, *Second Epistle*, 175) and most translations (RSV, REB, JB, NAB, NJB, NRSV, KJV, NASB, GNV).

49. Barrett, *Second Epistle*, 158.

B. Preference to Be Away from the Body (5:8a)

The B element (5:8a) restates that "we" are encouraged even though "we" prefer to be away from the body. This new image refers to death.[50] The believer prefers to be away from the body because it is in a state of decay (4:16). The inward feeling "to prefer" develops the previously stated notions of desiring (5:2) and wishing (5:4) to be clothed in God's eternal glory. Given the future realities that "we" hope for in 4:16–18, it is understandable for the audience to prefer to be away from the present glory-less body that is undergoing decay and affliction.[51]

C. Preference to Be at Home with the Lord (5:8b)

The C element (5:8b) completes the line of thought in the B element (5:8a) and asserts positively the preferred location for the believer as being not only away (ἐκδημῆσαι) from the body but, more importantly, at home (ἐνδημῆσαι) with the Lord. The prepositional phrase "with the Lord" informs the audience that they will share not just close proximity with Christ but will have "dynamic, interpersonal communion with him" at the point of death.[52] The verb ἐνδημέω acts as the grammatical antithesis to ἐκδημέω, but its similar sound serves to stress aurally the contrasting situations in life: Paul and the Corinthians are presently ἐκ-, but they prefer/desire/wish to be ἐν-. The description of being away from, and at home with, the Lord recalls the imagery of earthly and heavenly houses in 5:1–5. In both cases, the latter condition is preferred over the former.[53]

C´. Aspiration Whether We Are at Home with the Lord (5:9a)

With the repetition of the verb ἐνδημέω in the C´ element (5:9a), the audience experiences the completion of the unit's pivot, which centers

---

50. Thrall, *II Corinthians*, 390–91.

51. Hughes (*Second Epistle*, 177) and Murphy-O'Connor (*Theology*, 55) point out that Paul is in no way wishing that he die prior to the Parousia. The passion with which he defends his apostleship and attempts to reconcile himself with the Corinthians gives every impression that he intends for this letter to succeed and to visit the community yet again.

52. Belleville, *2 Corinthians*, 140.

53. According to Harris ("Watershed," 56), the faithful become "close in proximity to Christ at the moment of death." It is at this moment that they receive the new, spiritual body, which is comparable to Christ's.

around the theme of being at home with the Lord. In the first half of the chiasm, the B (5:8a) and C (5:8b) elements explain that believers are courageous even though they prefer to be away from the body and "at home" with the Lord. The C´ element (5:9a) develops the believers' internal feelings. The result of their preference to be "at home" (ἐνδημῆσαι) with the Lord in the C element (5:8b) is aspiration in the C´ element (5:9a), whether at home (ἐνδημημοῦντες) with the Lord or not. That they "aspire" adds to the inventory of internal gestures that believers have as they await the future glory: desire (5:2), anxiety (5:4), wish (5:4), courage (5:6), and preference (5:8).

B´. Acceptable Whether We Are Away (5:9b)

In the B´ element (5:9b), the audience hears a completion to the line of thought in 5:8–9 and a development and progression from the B element (5:8a). That "we" aspire to be acceptable to the Lord whether at home or away (ἐκδημοῦντες) in the B´ element (5:9b) develops the idea that "we" prefer to be away (ἐκδημῆσαι) from the body and at home with the Lord in the B (5:8a) and C (5:8b) elements.

To be "acceptable" has liturgical and sacrificial connotations. In particular, it refers to a "sacrifice which is pleasing to God" (Lev 19:5; 22:19; Isa 56:7; LXX Ps 19:14).[54] It also points back to the assertion that "we" walk by faith and not by sight (2 Cor 5:7). That "we" aspire to be acceptable to the Lord not only when at home but also when away affirms and underscores the intense emotion with which "we prefer" to be at home with him and, in light of what was said earlier, to attain eternal glory (4:15—5:5).

The inward desire to be with the Lord is so strong that it directs "our" conduct while "we" are in this earthly tent just as much as it would if "we" were already with the Lord in heaven.[55] This preference for the Lord's home, then, cooperates with the believers' focus on the unseen things (4:18) so that they can desire the unseen glory and aspire to be acceptable to the Lord; and this is all accomplished through walking by

---

54. Schrenk, "εὐδοκία," 742–43.

55. Some see the need to please the Lord, "whether home or away," as suggesting that there is a moral choice that continues in the new state with Christ (see, e.g., Matera, *II Corinthians*, 125). This question, however, misses Paul's point that pleasing the Lord should be a central aspiration for the believer since they will soon be "near" the Lord in judgment (5:10).

faith (5:7). The end product of this faith-directed emotional conduct is that they remain able to "put on" the glory and not be found naked in the Parousia or at death (5:3).

A´. Before the Judgment Seat of Christ (5:10)

The repetition of the adjective πᾶς aurally connects for the audience the stated cause in the A´ element (5:10) with its effect in the A element (5:6–7). Why are "we" "always" (πάντοτε) courageous according to the A element (5:6–7)? Because, the A´ element (5:10) explains, "we" must "all" (πάντας) appear before Christ's judgment. The middle elements of the unit explain further why this courage aids "us" (the elect): the preference to be at home with the Lord and to be acceptable to him makes believers even more courageous in their earthly existence to walk by faith, not by sight. The judgment of Christ, as seen in 5:10, serves as the ultimate motivation to be courageous in this life.

By remaining encouraged and not becoming weakened or dismayed, believers maintain their focus on the things unseen and thus desire the future glory, prefer to be with the Lord, and aspire to be acceptable to him. The sufferings of believers gradually transform them "from glory to glory until they attain the resurrection from the dead";[56] this is all prepared by God and orchestrated through his Spirit. The Corinthians' commitment to the faith must be renewed constantly up to the moment of judgment,[57] and their bodies must be raised in order to be judged before Christ.[58]

C´. An Opportunity for Boasting (5:11–13)

A 11 Therefore, since we know the fear of the Lord, we try to persuade others. We are apparent *to God*, and I hope we are also apparent to your consciences.

> B 12a We are not commending ourselves to you again but are giving you an opportunity *of boasting* on behalf of us,
>
> B´ 12b so that you may have something to say to *those who boast* of external appearance rather than of the heart.

---

56. Matera, *II Corinthians*, 125
57. Ibid.
58. Betz, "Concept," 315–41.

A′ 13 For if we are beside ourselves, it is *for God*; if we are of sound mind, it is for you.

Chiastic Progression from the C Unit (5:6–10)

With the C′ unit (5:11–13), the audience experiences the second half of the macrochiastic structure's pivot, which centers around the theme of things seen/unseen, through lexical and aural connectors. The occurrences of the verb φανερόω in 5:10 and 5:11 serve as linking terms that connect and indicate parallel qualities within the pivotal C (5:6-10) and C′ (5:11–13) units. In both the C and C′ units, the contrast of things seen/unseen takes a central role. In the C unit (5:6–10), the deeds of the body and the aspiration to be acceptable to the Lord, whether at home with him or not, emphasizes the importance of the things unseen (4:18). These eternal aspects allow the believers to walk by faith (5:7), give them courage while they are away from the Lord (5:8), and cause them to aspire to be acceptable to the Lord (5:8-9) in anticipation for when their deeds, whether good or bad, are judged (5:10). In the C′ unit (5:11–13), Paul wishes to stress that the power of the gospel comes from God and not from the external skill of a charismatic speaker (see 1 Cor 2:1-4).[59] If Paul speaks poorly (as some in the community and the opponents allege), then it is for God's glory. If he must speak well in order to "persuade" others (2 Cor 5:11), then it is for the benefit of God's elect in Christ. The εἴτε clauses in the C unit (5:6-10) that stress the internal and external spheres as mutually exclusive groups that have

---

59. The clause in 5:13 and the meanings of ἐξίστημι and σωφρονέω have experienced a variety of interpretations. Some claim that Paul is boasting in his ability to have ecstatic experiences (e.g., Matera, *II Corinthians*, 135), while others argue that Paul is defending himself from criticism that he is overly emotional (e.g., Hughes, *Second Epistle*, 90-91). A third, conciliatory position states that Paul did in fact have ecstatic experiences but that he is warning the Corinthians not to focus on such external expressions of the Spirit (e.g., Martin, *2 Corinthians*, 126–27; Barnett, *Second Epistle*, 224). However, I prefer to follow Hubbard ("Out of His Mind," 39–64) who, after a rhetorical analysis of 1 Cor 2:1–5; 2 Cor 2:14–17; 4:1–5, argues that the terms σωφρονέω and ἐξίστημι, in this context, refer to rhetorical skill. The former term infers rhetorical talent while the latter denotes its absence. Paul, who is defending his method of speaking in 5:11–13, is saying here that if he ever speaks well it is for the benefit of the Corinthians whose infantile spirituality prefers such external qualities. However, if he speaks poorly (as they accuse him of doing) it is so that the gospel does not lose its cruciform focus and that all might recognize the true "power" of the message to come from God (as in 1 Cor 2:4).

opposite results for believers serve to foreshadow and shed light on the elliptical εἴτε clauses in 5:13 in the C′ unit (5:11–13).

This emphasis on eternal, unseen things in the C (5:6–10) and C′ (5:11–13) units underscores for the audience the importance of focusing on things unseen even while here on earth where external, temporary things can distract one from the true reality of salvation. Paul has made the things unseen the focus of his ministry, and thus is apparent to God when he speaks. By this logic, he should also be "apparent" to the Corinthians who had first accepted his gospel. That is, they should recognize the validity of his gospel so that they can focus on unseen things in order to aspire to be acceptable to the Lord (5:9); this will prepare them to "appear" before Christ's judgment (5:10).

A. We Are Apparent to God, and Should Be to You (5:11)

In light of 4:15—5:10, which speaks of the hope that his gospel brings for the audience's future glory, Paul in the C′ unit (5:11–13) returns to directly defend his ministry. That the A element (5:11) begins with "therefore" informs the audience that what follows is a logical progression from the argument heretofore, that is, in the first half of the macrochiasm (4:15—5:10).

That "we know the fear of the Lord" recalls the audience's hope that they will be in good standing when all humanity must appear before the judgment seat of Christ (5:10).[60] The "fear" then is a healthy recognition of, and respect for, Christ's judging authority. The content of 4:15—5:10 leads Paul and his co-workers to persuade others, that is, to win them over with the gospel of Christ.

That "we[61] try to persuade" (5:11) others points to the accusation from some in the community that Paul uses insincere rhetoric in his preaching as if he were peddling his own philosophy (e.g., 1 Cor 2:1–5; 2 Cor 4:1–4). Using the terminology of his opponents' accusation, Paul argues that even if he is "persuading" people, this activity makes him even more apparent to God.[62] That Paul hopes to be apparent to the

---

60. "Lord" here, within the context of 5:10, refers to Christ. See, e.g., Lambrecht, *Second Corinthians*, 91.

61. As opposed to the first person plural pronouns found in 4:16—5:11a, the "we" who persuade others in 5:11b refers to Paul and his co-workers. The rest of the content in 5:11–15 concerns Paul's ministry directly (as did 4:1–5).

62. Bultmann, *Second Letter*, 147; Lambrecht, *Second Corinthians*, 91.

audience is underscored by the assertion that he is already apparent to God and is able to commend himself before every human conscience (4:1–2).

B. A Return to Commendation and Boasting (5:12a)

Paul again denies that he is commending himself, much like when he began his apologia (2:14—3:6). The apostle has no need to commend himself because the presence of the Spirit in the hearts of the Corinthians speaks for him (3:2–3). In 4:1, however, Paul states that with the open declaration of the truth he will commend himself to others, even in the sight of God. In both 3:2–3 and 4:1, it is his confidence in the content of his gospel that avails Paul to speak boldly regarding the validity of his ministry. He has no need to commend himself, because Christ (1:18–19), the Spirit (1:21–22; 3:1–3, 17–18; 5:5), and the glory of the future resurrection (5:1–10)—all of which are received from his gospel—verify Paul's ministry.

Paul wishes to give the Corinthians some response by which they can defend his apostleship against the opponents' accusations.[63] If they had boasted in him when the opponents first came, the situation would not have deteriorated to its present status. That Paul is giving the audience an opportunity to boast in him recalls that he hoped that they would boast in him (just as he boasts in them, 1:14). This, according to the text, was the reason for writing the present letter. If the audience cannot boast in Paul, that is, if they cannot recognize that his suffering ministry has brought them the light of the knowledge of the glory of God and life in Christ, then their "faith" and his ministry are in vain.[64]

B´. Those Who Boast in External Appearance (5:12b)

In the B´ element (5:12b), the audience experiences the pivot of the unit and a progression from the parallel B element (5:12a). That Paul wishes for "you" to have a response to "those who boast" (καυχωμένους, 5:12b) in external appearance explains why he wishes to give "you" an opportunity to have a "boast" (καυχήματος, 5:12a) in him. The audience recognizes "those who boast in external things" as the opponents who boast in spiritual gifts and rhetorical aptitude. The opponents' boast in

---

63. Harris, "2 Corinthians," 351.
64. Bultmann, *Second Letter*, 148.

external things sets them in opposition to everything that was stated in 4:15—5:10 regarding the eternal unseen things. This group does not walk by faith but by sight (cf. 5:7).

The opponents' priorities, in other words, are misdirected. External things are temporary and subject to decay, as was the glory attending to the old covenant and the glory of Moses' face (3:11–15), the outer self (4:16a), and the things seen (4:18). Paul, in contrast, grounds his boast in things unseen.[65] In particular, what the "heart" receives from the gospel serves as a prominent example of God's unseen glory. God places in the hearts of believers his Spirit (1:21–22; 3:3; 5:5) and the light of the knowledge of his glory (4:4–6), both of which give credence to Paul's apostolic ministry (3:2; 4:7). Since the presence of the Spirit confirms his apostleship (3:2), Paul is right to boast in unseen things and matters of the heart.

Even more important is the idea that these unseen gifts that God places within believers are the very things that seal them as God's property (1:21–22), transform them into Christ-like glory (3:18), renew them daily (4:16b), and prepare them for (and guarantee for them) the future glory of the resurrection body (5:5). Since these unseen things truly bring salvation, believers should not be distracted by external things; nor should they follow "apostles" who are. Rather, they should boast in Paul's ministry that has brought them the gospel and begun their transformation to glory.

A´. If We Are beside Ourselves,[66] It Is for God (5:13)

The A´ element (5:13) presents a chiastic progression from the A element (5:11). The γάρ clause indicates that the unit explains the cause of the previous statements. That Paul is beside himself "for God" (θεῷ) in the A´ element (5:13) develops the idea that he is apparent "to God" (θεῷ) in the A element (5:11). He is apparent to God because of his selfless and sincere proclamation of the gospel (2:14–15; 4:4). Whereas his opponents boast in letters of commendation and other external signs of authority, Paul discounts his own rhetorical skills and boasts of internal

---

65. Bultmann, *Second Letter*, 149.

66. Here I follow Hubbard ("Out of His Mind," 45–55) to view ἐξίστημι and σωφρονέω as referring to respective levels of rhetorical skill.

gifts. The wisdom of his message is found in the power (δυνάμει) of God (1 Cor 2:1–5).[67]

Since 2 Cor 2:14, Paul has argued that his ministry succeeds in intangible categories while the Corinthians judge only by tangible standards. As in 4:7–11, the audience is again challenged to reconsider their manner of judging the quality of Christ's apostle. Whether or not Paul has any external examples of his ministry, such as letters of recommendation or rhetorical skill, should not persuade the community in any way. For Paul, the power of his message comes not from his own speaking abilities but from God. The community should recognize the innate wisdom of the gospel, made clear in plain and wise speech (1 Cor 1:14), that benefits them and affirms Paul's credibility. External expressions of skill, such as excellent rhetorical ability, are distractions; and appreciation of such things alone could endanger the Corinthians' focus on the unseen things, and in turn jeopardize their future glory.

B´. Compelled to Live for the One Who Loved All and Died for All (5:14–15)

A   14 For the love of Christ compels us: we are certain that since one
     died for[68] all, therefore all have *died.* 15a He *died for* all,
  B   15b so that *those who live*
  B´ 15c may no longer *live* for themselves,
A´ 15d but for him who *for their sakes died* and was raised.

Chiastic Progression from the B Unit (5:1–5)

With the B´ unit (5:14–15), the audience again hears the contrast of life and death that was seen in the B unit. That Christ died for all so that all might live, according to the B´ unit (5:14–15), parallels and develops for the audience that we desire to be clothed so that mortality may be swallowed up by life in the B unit (5:4). The death/life transference, described in the B´ unit (5:14–15), explains further how the glory

---

67. See Hubbard, "Out of His Mind," 51–55.

68. Some have proposed that the preposition ὑπέρ here has a substitutionary meaning (BAGD, s.v.; Wallace, *Grammar*, 383, 387), as in Gal 3:13. However, a combined meaning of substitutionary and representative traits is also persuasive (e.g., Hooker, "Interchange," 121; Matera, *II Corinthians*, 149).

believers will attain in Christ may result in life swallowing what is mortal, as described in the B unit (5:1–5). Since one died (ἀπέθανεν) for all and was raised, what is mortal (θνητόν) will be swallowed up for all those who are raised with him into the resurrection life.

Christ's death for all those who now live prefigures the victory over what is mortal (5:4–5; see also 1 Cor 15:54) at the resurrection. For Paul, Christ's exchange on the cross and his subsequent resurrection guarantee the future glory for believers. If one died for others and was raised so that they might live, those who received life through his death will be raised like him (2 Cor 5:14–15).

A. Compelled by the Love of Christ (5:14–15a)

The first-person plural pronouns in 5:12b and 5:14 act as linking terms that connect the C′ (5:11–13) and B′ (5:14–15) units. That the love of Christ[69] compels "us"[70] (ἡμᾶς, i.e., Paul and his co-workers) in 5:14 serves as further basis for why the Corinthians should boast in "us" (ἡμῶν, i.e., Paul and his co-workers) in 5:12. Having commenced the apologia for his ministry in the C′ unit (5:11–13), Paul builds on how he is apparent to God and "you," the audience. He hopes that they will boast in him because his ministry is driven by no ambition other than to serve the one who died for him. It is the love of Christ that compels him and his co-workers to proclaim the gospel and bring life to the elect (4:12–14, 15).[71]

Paul makes his next argument based on the certainty of the cross: "Since one died for all, therefore all have died" (5:14). Christ is the one who died for all by redeeming them with his own blood (1 Cor 6:19–20). For this reason, "all have died," that is, as the audience recalls that their bodies are no longer their own, they have, in a sense, died to themselves.[72] In regards to Paul's ministry, the example of Christ precludes any self-centeredness in the life of an apostle. All have died, but this is

---

69. The phrase "the love of Christ" is most likely subjective, that is, "Christ's love for [Paul]" (so Gloer, "2 Corinthians 5:14–21," 355; Barnett, *Second Epistle*, 287).

70. As in 5:11b–13, in which Paul is evidently defending his own ministry, here in 5:14–15 the first person pronouns appear to be exclusive to the apostle and his ministry team. Paul is compelled (5:14) by the love of Christ to speak before God and persuade people by the gospel (5:11–13).

71. Harris, "2 Corinthians," 351.

72. Furnish, *II Corinthians*, 328; Hughes, *Second Epistle*, 195.

not a physical death. Those for whom Christ died receive the death to sin and self that is involved in Christian living.[73]

B. Those Who Live (5:15b)

Christ died for all so that they might live. The verb ζάω that is found in the B element (5:15b) directly contrasts the verb ἀποθνῄσκω that is found in the A element (5:15a). Christ's death brings about the opposite result for those for whom he died. The audience recognizes themselves as those who live with hope for future glory.

B´. Might No Longer Live for Themselves (5:15c)

The B´ element (5:15c) creates a chiastic progression from the B element (5:15b). Those who might no longer "live" (ζῶσιν) for themselves, according to the B´ element (5:15c), clarifies the cruciform obligations of "those who live" (οἱ ζῶντες), according to the B element (5:15b). Following Christ's death, the focus of living has been reoriented away from the self, such that those who die in him are obligated to follow his example and live for others.[74] The audience recognizes that Paul hopes they understand his motives in preaching the gospel as well as their own obligations to follow Christ's selfless example. Their lives, in a sense, were no longer their own (1 Cor 6:19–20).

A´. Living for the One Who Died and Was Raised (5:15d)

With the A´ element, the audience hears the conclusion to the chiastic unit (5:14–15). That those who live may live no longer for themselves but for him who died (ἀπέθανεν) for them, according to the A´ element, develops the point that since one died (ἀπέθανεν) for all, all have died (ἀπέθανον), according to the A element (5:14–15a). This ultimate element completes the causal line of thought in the chiastic structure that one died for all so that those who live might live for the one who died for them and was raised. Christ is the new focus for those who live after the crucifixion.

The audience recognizes that this unit advances Paul's apologia. Here he is presenting the content of his self-sacrificing ministry as the

---

73. Furnish, *II Corinthians*, 328.
74. Harris, *Second Epistle*, 423.

logical product of the Christ event.[75] He is certain that Christ's death for all reorients the lives of the living to such a degree that his love compels Paul to perform his ministry not for himself but for the one who died for him.[76] Thus Paul carries out his ministry in a way that presents his life as belonging no longer to himself but to Christ. This point again recalls the imagery of redemption seen in 1 Cor 6:19–20, in which Paul explains that believers have been redeemed at a price. In this case, Paul repays life with life. Christ gave his life as a ransom for Paul out of love, and now Paul returns his life in service to the one who died for him.

The A' element (5:15d) also explains how Christ's death brought life for "all" in the B' element (5:15c), and also how mortality might be swallowed by life in the B unit (5:1–5). Those who have died in Christ have also been raised with him (4:12–14). Christ died for all so that in him they might die to sin and in him also be raised. This element then merges the substitutionary and representative aspects of Christ's death.[77] Christ died in place of all; but God completes his plan for humanity in Christ, their representative, who is raised to prefigure their own future life in the resurrected body (5:1–10).[78] Christ died and was raised for their benefit. The only appropriate response is for believers to live for him but to die to self and sin. This is the model and motive for Paul's ministry and, he hopes, for the Corinthians' lives as well.

The life/death contrast underscores the prevailing dichotomy of things seen/unseen (4:15—5:13). The "life" that one sees now is not true life, and the "death" that one sees now is not true death. Everything has been redefined in Christ's sacrifice. It is the death and resurrection of Christ, unseen to the audience, that allows them to die truly to sin in Christ and with Christ to live truly in the resurrection.

---

75. Harris, "2 Corinthians," 351.

76. Hughes, *Second Epistle*, 196.

77. According to Hooker ("Interchange," 121), the Christ event may be seen as both substitutionary and representative. Christ ransomed believers with his death on the cross (1 Cor 6:19–20), but his resurrection raised them up from slavery to sin and death (1 Cor 15:50–55; 2 Cor 4:12–14, 15–18; 5:1–10; Rom 6:5–9). Christ must both pay the ransom and bring them out of their former master's house to complete their freedom. Being free now from sin and mortality, believers are obligated to live for their new master who, by his example, calls them to live for others.

78. So Matera, *II Corinthians*, 354.

Chapter Summary

The preceding analysis of the macrochiastic structure in 2 Cor 4:15—5:15 demonstrates how the ideal audience hears and responds to Paul's defense of his ministry as he calls on them to recognize their identity as a new creation in Christ and be reconciled to God. The A unit (4:15–18) centers around the theme of the renewal of *"our" inner self* (4:16) despite the decay of *"our" outer self* (4:17). Receiving this daily renewal, believers increase their thanksgiving to God's *glory* (4:15b) because they are confident that this present affliction is working out for them an eternal weight of *glory* (4:16). The outer elements explain that Paul undergoes all *things* for the Corinthians' benefit (4:15a) so that they might focus not on *things* seen but on *things* unseen (4:18).

The B (5:1–5) and C (5:6–10) units both contrast life on earth with life in God's heavenly presence. The pivot of the B unit emphasizes that the resurrection of the believer will not separate the soul from the body (5:3). That *"we" groan while in* this earthly situation because "we" desire to put on the promised heavenly residence (5:2) is clarified by the point that *"we" groan in* this tent because "we" wish to be further clothed in the glorious resurrection body (5:4a). God's actions bracket this unit: believers take confidence in the hope that *God* has made for them a heavenly dwelling (i.e., the resurrection body) for the time after their earthly body is *destroyed* (5:1), with the effect that what is mortal is *swallowed up* by life. Furthermore, *God* has given believers the Spirit to *condition* them for this glorious body (5:4b–5).

The C unit (5:6–10) concerns the antithetical characteristics of being at home with, or being away from, the Lord. The former is preferred to the latter; yet the hope to be with the Lord is what encourages believers to be acceptable to him even while they are away (5:8–9). These antithetical properties are flanked by two foundational ideas: "we" are *always* courageous while "we" are away from the Lord because "we" walk by faith and not by sight (5:6–7); and "we" must *all* appear before the Lord's judgment seat to receive recompense for "our" earthly deeds (5:10). These bracketing elements emphasize the immensity of Christian hope and the inevitability of future judgment that fully penetrate the believers' activities as they aspire to be at home with the Lord while they are still away.

The second half of the macrochiasm moves from general matters of Christian hope to a more pronounced apologia of Paul's ministry. In particular, the motif of contrasting things seen/unseen, which was broached in 4:18, will become prominent throughout the rest of his argument. The C′ unit (5:11–13) emphasizes this distinction as it centers around the true location of an apostle's boast. Paul contends that while his opponents have their *boast* in appearance, he boasts in the heart, that is, in the internal gifts with which God has blessed believers (5:12a). For this reason alone, the Corinthians should have a *boast* in Paul when confronted by the opponents regarding his credentials (5:12b). As in the B unit (5:1–5), God flanks and supports Paul's core argument within the unit. Since Paul is apparent to *God*, he should also be to the Corinthians (5:11); and regardless of his preaching acumen, they should still have a boast in him since his occasional eloquence benefits them but his poor preaching glorifies *God* (5:13).

The B′ unit (5:14–15) is structured around the antithetical properties of life and death. At the center of the unit is the present life of believers (5:15b, c). Paul is certain that this life comes about because one *died* for all (5:14b, 15a). For this reason all have *died* (5:14c), and may no longer *live* for themselves (5:15b) but instead *live* (5:15c) for the one who *died* for them and was raised (5:15d). Christ's love compels Paul in his ministry and, he argues, should be a model to the audience in their new lives. The next chapter will analyze how the authorial audience responds to the culmination of these units in Paul's exhortation for them to be reconciled to God and his ministry in 5:16—6:2.

6

Audience Response to 2 Corinthians 5:16—6:2

Paul's Climactic Call to Reconciliation (the A´ unit of Macrochiasm III)

A 16 As a result, from *now* on we regard no one in a worldly manner; even if *we once knew* Christ in a worldly way, we do not *know* him so *now*. 17 As a result, whoever is in Christ is a new creation. The old things have passed away; *behold*: new things *have come*!

  B 18 And everything is from God, who has *reconciled* us to himself through Christ and given *us* the ministry of *reconciliation*,

  B´ 19 to the effect that God was *reconciling* the world to himself through Christ, not counting their transgressions against them and placing on *us* (ἡμῖν) the message of *reconciliation*. 20 So we are ambassadors on Christ's behalf, as though God were pleading through us. We implore on Christ's behalf: *be reconciled* to God.

A´ 21 He made the one who did not *know* sin to be sin for us so that we *might become* the righteousness of God in him. 6:1 Working in unison then, we plead with you not to receive the grace of God in vain. 2 For it says: "At an acceptable time I heard you, and on a day of salvation I helped you." *Behold*: *now* is the[1] acceptable time! *Behold*: *now* is the day of salvation!

Chiastic Progression from the A Unit (4:15–18)

Four sets of terms or aural similarities, involving three central themes, connect for the audience the A (4:15–18) and A′ (5:16—6:2) units of the macrochiastic structure in 4:15—6:2. The theme of renewal is experienced in 4:17 and again in 5:17. That "our inner self" is "renewed" (ἀνακαινοῦται) daily in the A unit (5:16—6:2) is recalled and developed in the A′ unit by the declaration that all who are in Christ are a "new" (καινή) creation and that now in Christ "new things" (καινά) have arrived.

The theme of grace is experienced in 4:15 and 6:1. That God's "grace" (χάρις) through Paul's ministry abounds to believers who then reciprocate by giving thanks to God's glory in the A unit (4:15–18), is recalled in Paul's warning to the Corinthians to not reject God's "grace" (χάριν) that had arrived to them in his gospel in the A′ unit (5:16—6:2).

The third theme involves temporal terms. The things seen which are "temporary" (πρόσκαιρα) in the A unit (4:15–18) are echoed in the A′ unit (5:16—6:2) with the double occurrence of καιρός in Paul's Scripture citation and exhortation to recognize "now" as the very acceptable "time" (καιρός) to be reconciled to his ministry and to God. In the same way, the exhortation in the A′ unit (5:16—6:2) to recognize "now" as the day (ἡμέρα) of salvation foretold by Isaiah ("on a day of salvation, I helped you," 49:8) recalls that the believer's inner self is being renewed "daily" (ἡμέρᾳ καὶ ἡμέρᾳ) in the A unit (2 Cor 4:15–18).

Since both echoes from Isaiah concern renewal, Paul's placement of them in the primary and ultimate units of this macrochiastic argument underscores for the audience the rhetorical call to renewal and reconciliation with his ministry and, because of their conflict with a divinely appointed apostle, with God as well.[2] Paul's argument is that

---

1. Definite articles do not appear in the Greek, but the contextual marker of "now" determines that the definite article should be included in an English rendering. Hence, by saying "now," Paul is specifying a time that is ipso facto definite, and I include the article to show this emphasis.

2. Witherington, *Conflict*, 397; Hubbard, "Out of His Mind," 51–55; Matera, *II Corinthians*, 149.

renewal and reconciliation are needed in the audience's lives and their relationship with him and God. Renewal comes through accepting his gospel of reconciliation with God in Christ. But more importantly, the "time" to effect this renewal is "now."

A. Now Those Who Are in Christ Are a New Creation (5:16–17)

The result clause in 5:16 that begins the new unit alerts the audience that what follows in this concluding unit of the macrochiastic argument builds on what they have heard to this point. In particular, the audience realizes that Paul's line of thought is founded on the new life that believers have in Christ since they have died to themselves and live for Christ (5:15).

The linking term ἀλλά lexically connects the B´ unit (5:14–15) with the present unit (5:16—6:2). The arguments of both units center around strong contradictions. Believers no longer live to themselves "but," rather, live for the one who died for them (5:15) in the B´ unit (5:14–15). In the A´ unit (5:16—6:2), even if believers[3] knew Christ in a worldly way[4] before, "but" now they do so no longer (5:16). In both units, the strong conjunction serves to contrast the old life of the believers before the reception of the gospel with their new life in Christ, "now," after having received the proclamation from Paul. Seen within the context of his preceding discussion on "things seen/unseen" in 4:15—5:15, Paul is also stating that his ministry, which he defends in 5:11-15, cannot be judged by worldly standards.[5]

---

3. Here (in 5:16-18a), as in 4:16-18; 5:1-11a, the audience experiences themselves within the "we" who know in a new way.

4. The majority of scholars read κατὰ σάρκα adverbially (e.g., Allo, *Seconde Épître*, 167), thus "seeing in a worldly manner." Bultmann (*Second Letter*, 155) dissents from the majority and reads the phrase with the substantive: "Christ as he can be encountered in the world, before his death and resurrection." If εἰ in v. 16b is taken as a real condition (i.e., "though we did know Christ"), then one may infer that Paul is admitting knowledge of the historical person of Jesus prior to his death and resurrection (so Hughes, *Second Epistle*, 197; Lambrecht, *Second Corinthians*, 96). Other scholars read the clause as an unreal condition. But Thrall (*II Corinthians*, 165) argues that Paul may have presented this unreal clause as a rhetorical response to the opponents' boasting of their relationship with Jesus during his ministry.

5. Beale, "Reconciliation," 552.

"Now" Is a New Era

The audience understands "now" (5:16) to mean the new eschatological age that they presently experience in the Spirit but that will be consummated only at the return of Christ. Having received the gospel from Paul and the down payment of the Spirit in their hearts (1:21–22) that will transform them to attain Christ's glory and prepare them for the resurrection body (3:18; 5:5), "now" the audience must put aside the old and embrace the new. Since vision is transformed with the gospel of Christ's saving death (4:18; 5:7, 14–15), so too is knowledge. The old way of knowing "according to the flesh" (5:16) is no longer acceptable. Even those who knew Christ "according to the flesh" have an outdated knowledge of him. Believers who look on the face of Christ are being transformed to the same glorious image (3:18) and gain the illumination of the knowledge of the glory of God in their hearts (4:6) which renews them daily (4:16). The knowledge that the audience has "now" is no longer of the flesh but is the glorious, transforming knowledge of God's glory.

"Now" is further defined for the audience as something that is "new." Believers "now" no longer know Christ according to the flesh because those who are in Christ are a "new creation" (5:17). As opposed to the old things that have passed away, Paul alludes to Isa 43:18–19 as he writes, "Behold: new things have come!"[6] The "new things" involve the new eschatological reality, the messianic age in which believers presently reside as they await the consummation of God's kingdom with the return of Christ.

New Creation in Christ

The "new things" (5:17), as harbingers of the new age, guarantee its completion.[7] The audience, having received the Spirit in their hearts and been incorporated into Christ, is part of the "new things" that have arrived. They themselves are proof of the new covenant's effect (3:4–6) and thus also stand as proof of the new age. That those who are in Christ are a new creation recalls that "our inner self" is "renewed daily" (4:16b), and this process is paralleled by the believers' transformation

---

6. There is significant agreement among scholars that Paul makes several lexical connections to Isa 43:18–19 (ἀρχαῖα, ἰδού, καινά, νῦν, γνώσεσθε).

7. Gloer, "2 Corinthians 5:14–21," 399.

into Christ's same glory (3:18). Since they are a "new creation," or "new creatures," the audience's epistemology should be reoriented toward the spiritual realm and no longer based on worldly standards.[8]

The phrases "new creation" and "new things" (5:17) recall what God promised through his prophets to do for his people Israel. The new exodus from exile and renewal of Jerusalem (Isa 40:1–5; 42:9; 43:18–19) manifest God's love for Israel and completely transform heaven and earth (Isa 65:17; 66:22). This same display of God's creative and transformational power, for Paul, is "precisely what has happened in Christ. To participate in the death of Christ is to be brought into this new world."[9]

B. Reconciled into a New Relationship (5:18)

As in 1:21–22 and 5:1–5, Paul emphasizes God's central role in saving the elect. God has reconciled "us," all believers, to himself in Christ.[10] The new things that have come, including the newness of the audience members' own selves, are entirely by God's doing ("from God," ἐκ θεοῦ). How does God effect such newness in his elect? God entirely renews his elect, i.e., makes them new creatures, by reconciling them to himself in Christ. Their newness is thus both personal (3:18) and relational (5:18). God recreates in Christ both the elect individual and his/her relationship with himself. The result is a total transformation of the creature, not only in itself but also in his/her standing with God.

Reconciliation entails that the relationship between two parties once at war with each other is now free of enmity.[11] Humanity was at

---

8. It appears reasonable to accept both the cosmological view (as in Barrett, *Second Epistle*, 173–74) and the anthropological view (as in, e.g., Hubbard, *New Creation*, 183) since creation would include both the cosmos and people (most importantly in 1 Cor 15:50–55; but see also Gal 5:16). This amalgamation is represented in Cousar, "II Corinthians 5:17–21."

9. Cousar, "II Corinthians 5:17–21," 181.

10. The inclusive status of the first person plural pronouns here in 5:18a is retained from 5:16–17.

11. The activity of reconciliation at Paul's time generally concerned the entreaty between two military rivals during a confrontation on the battlefield (Fitzmyer, "Reconciliation," 164–66). The theme is considered central to Paul's overall thought, such that justification and reconciliation are nearly synonymous (Barrett, *Second Epistle*, 177; Thrall, "Salvation"). Reconciliation was not figurative but entailed a dramatic shift in status from being in conflict to being at peace. So too, in Paul's understanding, did

one time at odds with God and deserving of his wrath. "Now" they are no longer enemies of God; rather, the relationship is renewed to neutral status.¹² The process of reconciliation was also common in the domestic sphere, and was of particular interest in everyday Hellenistic life.¹³ The authorial audience, familiar with the preexisting and common ideas behind the term καταλλάσσω and its cognates, recognizes Paul's utilization of this secular term within a theological context. Christ mediates this reconciliation to the elect through his death on the cross that he suffered for all (5:14–15).

Reconciliation and the Ministry of the New Covenant

In addition to reconciling "us" to himself through Christ (5:18a), God has also given "us" (ἡμῖν, Paul and his co-workers) a ministry of reconciliation (5:18b).¹⁴ Paul has already stated that his ministry is in line with the new covenant prophesied by Jeremiah and Ezekiel and that is now manifest by the Spirit in the hearts of the audience (3:1–6). His ministry, for which God qualified him, is superior to that of Moses because the new covenant is far more glorious than the old (3:7–11). This ministry had, in line with the new covenant, brought about righteousness and life because the gospel enabled believers to be gloriously transformed in Christ by faith (3:6, 7, 18). Now the audience hears that Paul's ministry also brings reconciliation with God (5:18b). The

---

the world gain a renewed status with God through Christ (Martin, *Reconciliation*, 108). See also Turner, "Ministry"; Denney, *Death*, 85–88; Bultmann, *Theology*, 285–87; Ladd, *Theology*, 450–56; Ridderbos, *Paul*, 182–93; Martin, *Reconciliation*, 90–110; Dunn, *Theology*, 228–30, 387–88; Schreiner, *Paul*, 222–25; Matera, *Theology*, 140–42.

12. In particular, see Porter, "Concept"; idem, "Reconciliation."

13. Fitzgerald ("Paradigm Shifts") argues that Paul here is using καταλλάσσω in its Hellenistic sense of diplomatic and domestic relations (as denoted by the catch words "joy/grace," "ambassador," and "implore/plead"). These are secular terms, not religious; but Paul shifts them into the religious sphere so that they are consonant with the theological idea of atonement.

14. Lambrecht ("Diakonia," 425) argues Paul has all Christians in view when he says "God has reconciled 'us' to himself," but excludes them when he says that "God gave 'us' a ministry of reconciliation." Others, however, see the ministry as being given to all Christians (e.g., Harris, *Second Epistle*, 359; Gloer, "2 Corinthians 5:14–21," 403). This latter view seems awkward within the present context in which Paul defends his own ministry to the audience and exhorts them to be reconciled to God. Thus the "us" in 5:18a, which speaks of salvation that is shared by all believers, is inclusive, but the "us" in 5:18b that concerns Paul's ministry in particular is exclusive to Paul and his co-workers.

genitive clause, following the declaration of God's activity in Christ, is one of content,[15] thus expressing that reconciliation is part of the message (λόγος, 1:18) that God qualified Paul to bring to the audience (3:1–2). God gave this ministry to Paul so that he might make known to the elect the transformative power of Christ (3:18; 4:16b; 5:17) and the light of the knowledge of God's glory (4:6). Paul's message is indeed good news: in Christ the elect and their status with God are completely made anew. Transformation, renewal, and reconciliation are synonymous in the saving mediation of Christ.

B´. God Was Reconciling the World in Christ (5:19–20)

Not Counting Transgressions

The effect in the B´ element (5:19–20) refers to both actions of God stated in the B element (5:18)—his mediation of reconciliation in Christ and his mediation of the message in Paul's apostolic ministry. God's reconciliation through Christ is effected only as hearers of the gospel believe and accept the content of its teaching, as well as the Spirit in their hearts, to begin the process of transformation (3:18) and renewal (4:16b; 5:17). Since the content of Paul's message is reconciliation through Christ (5:18b), Paul's ministry is by necessity part of the reconciliation process.

This element (5:19–20) makes explicit what was implied in the B element (5:18) regarding the agency of Christ. In the B element (5:18), God was "reconciling" (καταλλάξαντος) "us" (all Christians) to himself in Christ and giving to "us" (ἡμῖν, i.e., Paul and his co-workers) "the ministry of reconciliation" (διακονίαν τῆς καταλλαγῆς). Now, in the B´ element (5:19–20), the audience hears that God is "reconciling" (καταλλάσσων) the world to himself in Christ by not counting their transgressions against them and by setting on "us" (ἡμῖν, i.e., Paul et al.)[16] "the message of reconciliation" (λόγον τῆς καταλλαγῆς). The

---

15. Lambrecht ("Diakonia," 422–28) denotes four options for the genitive phrase διακονίαν τῆς καταλλαγῆς: (1) genitive of quality—a ministry characterized by reconciliation; (2) objective genitive—the ministry that proclaims reconciliation; (3) genitive of content—reconciliation is the content of the ministry's message; (4) genitive of respect—reconciliation as far as the ministry is concerned. Within the context of Paul's apologia for his ministry, options (2) and (3) seem most appropriate.

16. The term "world" clarifies that the pronoun "us" in 5:18a is inclusive of all believers (and creation). The exclusive sense of the ministerial pronouns in 5:18b and

process is again described in two parts that involve both Christ's activity on the cross and Paul's activity on the road. Christ's death on the cross for all has the effect of wiping away the transgressions of the world. This verdict of acquittal redefines the transformation to Christ's glory—the cross effects an interchange that brings death to God's Son but life to God's elect.[17] By accepting Paul's gospel of reconciliation, the audience also accepts the effects of the cross and begins the transformation process to a new glory and subsequent daily renewal.

Ambassadors for Christ

Having already heard twice that God has given him a ministry of reconciliation (5:18, 19), the audience now hears Paul deduce, "Therefore we [Paul and his co-workers] are ambassadors on Christ's behalf" (5:20). Paul is an apostle of Christ who was sent within God's will (1 Cor 1:1–2; 2 Cor 1:1–2). With this ambassadorial status, Paul speaks on Christ's behalf as though God were speaking directly to the community.[18] That Paul includes both God and Christ in his apostolic activity in 5:20 affirms the effect of both in the reconciliation of "us" and "the world" to God himself in 5:18–19. To regain what God prepares for them in Christ (5:14–15, 17–19), the audience must first be reconciled to their apostle "since he is the legal ambassador" of God and Christ (5:20).[19]

The exhortation to "be reconciled" (καταλλάγητε) to God (5:20) implies that the reconciliation mediated by Christ has not yet been effected for the audience.[20] How is this possible? The previous tension between the community and Paul regarding the activity of his apostleship and his message is a likely reason. Many within the community at Corinth had rejected Paul's apostolic authority over them for superficial reasons. Paul

---

5:19b is affirmed in 5:20 by the self-designation by Paul of his team and himself as "ambassadors for Christ," through whom God is making an appeal.

17. Hooker, "Interchange," 114–16.

18. According to Witherington (*Conflict*, 396–97), Paul's status as ambassador not only affirmed his credibility as an apostle to the community but also emphasized his status as an accomplished orator.

19. Beale, "Reconciliation," 552; Witherington, *Conflict*, 397.

20. Some scholars (e.g., Harris, *Second Epistle*, 448–49) have difficulty accepting that reconciliation is not yet complete among "the holy ones." But the majority (e.g., Matera, *II Corinthians*, 154; Boer, "2 Corinthians 5:14—6:2," 543; Thrall, "Reconciliation," 145–46; Hubbard, *New Creation*, 223) understand Paul to mean that reconciliation is not yet complete for the Corinthian audience.

now informs them that by rejecting him they have also rejected his ministry of reconciliation. As a consequence, they cannot fully receive the reconciliation that is mediated by Christ and proclaimed by Paul. God has indeed reconciled the world to himself in Christ, even to the extent of annulling transgressions; however, by offending his ambassador the audience remains in need of full reconciliation with God. Reconciliation can only come through Christ, and the audience can only fully know Christ through Paul's ministry.[21]

The primary reason that Paul gave for writing this letter (that the Corinthians might boast of him, 1:14) is developed further. Beyond a mere renewal of their relationship, the underlying issue throughout the letter is now laid bare: Paul is writing to call back the audience after their rejection of him as God's true apostle of the message of reconciliation.[22] Even though they only intended to diminish ties to an assumedly embarrassing apostle (with no intentions of losing the glorious benefits of the Spirit), Paul's argument is that tossing him aside also puts their salvation in danger because of the symbiotic relationship that their faith and his apostleship share.

A′. Behold: Now Is the Day of Salvation (5:21—6:2)

Inversion and the Righteousness of God

The A′ element begins by reaffirming God's primary role in the salvation process. "He" (God) made "the one who did not know sin" (Christ) to be "sin" for our benefit (5:21).[23] This action again points to Christ's

---

21. Paul does not rule out the important role that other ministers play, such as with Apollos (1 Cor 3:1–4) and his own co-workers (2 Cor 1:1–2, 18–20; 2:10–13), but holds himself as having a special relationship with the community at Corinth (1 Cor 1:9; 4:1–10; 9:1–4). Whether or not they could receive the gospel from other apostles (such as from the super-apostles), Paul's point is that they evidently began their transformation to glory from his gospel, and should receive him again to complete God's reconciliation in Christ with them, lest they receive the grace in vain. To borrow from a common bumper sticker: Know Paul, know Christ; no Paul, no Christ.

22. Beale ("Reconciliation," 552) cites 3:1–5; 5:12; 10:10; 11:6–8, 16–18; 13:3, 7.

23. The term may be taken to mean either "sin" or "sin offering." The first sees Christ's death in a forensic milieu, and the second in a cultic. Supporters of the second option ("sin offering") include Talbert (*Reading*, 168), Harris (*Second Epistle*, 453) and Dunn (*Theology*, 217). Allo (*Seconde Épître*, 172) concedes that the second option makes good sense; however, he argues that ἁμαρτία is never used to mean a sin offering in the NT. In addition, since ἁμαρτία in the participial phrase means sin *qua*

mediation of reconciliation on the cross (5:14–15, 19). God, who reconciled the world to himself in Christ on the cross for all (5:14–15, 18–19), made Christ to be sin for "us," that is, the elect who are able to receive reconciliation.[24] That Christ did not "know" (γνόντα) sin parallels and develops how the audience no longer "knows" (ἐγνώκαμεν) Christ in a worldly way. To know Christ "now" is to know him experientially[25] by living faithfully, aspiring to be acceptable before his judgment (5:8–10), to be transformed and renewed (3:18; 4:16) in him, and to gain from his face the light of the knowledge of the glory of God (4:6).

This sacrifice on the cross happens in order that "we" believers might become something entirely new and free from sin, namely, that "we might become the righteousness of God in him." To put it another way, "the one totally innocent individual is made to be the godless, weak, alienated sinner" so that "we" the "godless, weak, alienated sinners" may in turn "become the righteousness of God."[26]

That "we might become" (γενώμεθα) the righteousness of God (5:21) in the A′ element recalls and develops the idea from the A element (5:16–17) that new things "have come" (γέγονεν), namely, "we" who are a new creation in Christ (5:17).[27] The transformation to glory (3:18) and daily renewal (4:16) is also a transformation to righteousness, which is a quality that the new covenant was intended to bring

---

sinful wrongdoing, the majority of modern scholars prefer the first option ("sin"). This view is in line with Gal 3:13: God allowed Christ to become a curse in order to save those under the curse of the law. This activity of Christ that parallels Isaiah's servant (53:3–5) carries both representative and substitutionary meanings, just as do 5:14–15 (Matera, *II Corinthians*, 144). Other scholars who favor the first option include Ladd (*Theology*, 450), Bultmann (*Theology*, 277), Murphy-O'Connor (*Theology*, 62), Furnish (*II Corinthians*, 344), and Hughes (*Second Epistle*, 215).

24. The "us" in 5:21 must be inclusive of all Christians (as opposed to the pronouns in 5:18b, 19b, 20) because the activity of this verse concerns the salvation that all believers may receive (5:18a, 19a). See Hooker, "Righteousness," 369, 373–74.

25. The verb γινώσκω, as opposed to οἶδα, concerns experiential knowledge (BAGD, s.v.; Barnett, *Second Epistle*, 243).

26. Cousar, "II Corinthians 5:17–21," 303.

27. The "we" here in 5:21 and in 5:16–17 include all Christians, as denoted by the "all" for whom Christ died in 5:14–15 (see Hooker, "Righteousness," 369, 373–74). As noted above, when Paul refers to his ministry, the "we" often includes only himself or himself and his co-workers; but when the text concerns spiritual benefits that all Christians receive from the gospel, the "we" includes the Corinthian audience and all believers.

(3:7–11). This image recalls that Christ "became" (ἐγενήθη) for us the wisdom, "righteousness, sanctification, and redemption" from God (1 Cor 1:30). Believers who become a new creation in Christ (such that they are transformed to his same glory and gain life from his death) also gain in him righteousness from God.[28] All things are "from God" (ἐκ θεοῦ, 5:18), particularly righteousness, which the audience may attain because God made his Son to be sin for them.

Given that a glorious transformation and righteousness are so near to them, it makes the audience's ongoing dispute with Paul seem incredibly minor in comparison. Are doubts about Paul's credentials or rhetorical talents worth losing these wonderful blessings that he brings with his ministry? The immediate answer is "no." Whatever his flaws may be, it is the power of the gospel that proclaims renewal and reconciliation in Christ that is more important. In rejecting Paul the audience has also rejected his message. Now is the time to turn back to God and his ambassador.

---

28. The meaning of "the righteousness of God" in 5:21 may be put in two grammatical categories: (A) the righteousness is a quality of God; or (B) the righteousness is a status predicated of humanity. Each of these has two subcategories: (A1) possessive genitive—righteousness is a quality or attribute of God; (A2) subjective genitive—righteousness is an activity which God enacts; (B1) objective genitive—faith is righteousness which humans commit before God; (B2) genitive of origin—righteousness is a human status which results from God's gracious action, equivalent to "righteousness from God" (see Wright, "Righteousness," 200–208). The first option (A1) is rarely held today.

Within the subjective genitive position (A2), held by Käsemann ("Righteousness"), Wright ("Becoming"; idem, *Saint Paul*, 161–64), and Hooker ("Righteousness," 373–75), Paul sees himself and his compatriots transformed into the righteousness of God since they are acting as ambassadors for God and thereby embody his righteous persona. Paul's invitation to the Corinthians at 5:21—6:2 is for them to be reconciled to God, be open to his ministry, and thus become the righteousness of God as well.

Other scholars emphasize the aspect of transformation that believers manifest (e.g., Lambrecht, *Second Corinthians*, 100–101), meaning that "righteousness" refers to the quality that believers become (B1), that is, "God's righteous people" (so Harris, *Second Epistle*, 455) or "those justified by God's action" (so Ladd, *Theology*, 487).

Of the options listed above, the genitive of origin (B2) seems the most correct (so Bultmann, *Second Letter*, 158), given the accompanying phrase "all things are from God" (5:21), and the explicit use of ἐκ θεοῦ in the similar passage 1 Cor 1:30. Matera (*II Corinthians*, 144) follows this perspective, stating that this is "righteousness that God grants in Christ resulting in acquittal and justification for humanity," i.e., "humanity stands in the condition of a God-given righteousness because Christ has stood in the sinful condition before God."

The Ambassador's Emphatic Plea

At this point, Paul restates his plea for the audience to accept his message (6:1). Since God makes his appeal for reconciliation through Paul (5:20), the apostle sees himself as a co-worker of God and Christ. The audience is already aware of this self-designation of apostles (1 Cor 3:9) and of his ministry of reconciliation that was stressed at the community's founding.[29] Because of the tension that the audience has had with him to this point, they have received the grace of God in vain, that is, the "word" of reconciliation that he preached to them (1:18; 5:19). This is not what Paul wants for them. Since his calling, Paul has felt compelled by the love of Christ to carry out his apostolic activity to all so that they might receive righteousness, renewal, and life in the new age.[30] God's grace is evident in his reconciling "us" and the world to himself in Christ's death on the cross so as to annul their transgressions. This grace can only be effected through receiving God's ambassador who brings this good news.[31]

Following Paul's harsh charge of their status with God, the audience hears Paul turn to Scripture to support his pleas. This citation of Isa 49:8 contains direct parallels to the A element. "Now" in 6:2 points, as in 5:16, to the eschatological "now."[32] Since they know Christ "now" ($νῦν$) in a new way because of Paul's ministry in the A element (5:16–17), they should recognize Paul as Christ's ambassador and be reconciled to God by reestablishing their relationship to him "now" ($νῦν$) in the A′ element (5:16—6:2). The Isaian allusion and its new reference to God's promise of salvation being fulfilled in Christ also points back to 2 Cor 1:19, in which Paul claims that all of God's promises are made "yes" in Christ.[33]

---

29. See, e.g., Matera, *II Corinthians*, 149; Beale, "Reconciliation," 560.

30. Some debate surrounds Paul's understanding of the "servant" reference within the Isaiah allusions in 2 Cor 5:16—6:2. A few scholars (e.g., Beale, "Reconciliation," 560–62; Harris, *Second Epistle*, 243; Barnett, *Second Epistle*, 317) consider Paul to be using the allusions to present himself as the "servant" of Isa 40–55 who is suffering to bring a message of salvation to the Gentiles. I prefer to follow Lambrecht ("Favorable Time") and Gignilliat ("2 Corinthians 6:2"), who argue that, for Paul, Christ is the "servant," in whom all of God's promises of salvation are fulfilled.

31. Witherington, *Conflict*, 397.

32. See, e.g., Beale, "Reconciliation," 565.

33. Gignilliat, "2 Corinthians 6:2."

Behold: Now Is the Day of Salvation!

Given the eschatological emphasis that Paul has presented throughout this letter (1:12–14, 18–22; 2:4–9; 3:4–5; 3:14–18; 4:1–6, 15–18; 5:1–10, 16–17), the audience recognizes that his present exhortation implies that their salvation could be in jeopardy. They must be reconciled "now"; otherwise, God's grace, given to them by Paul's ministry, will be in vain.[34] There is no better time than "now" to recognize the acceptable time and the day of salvation and accept Paul, God's ambassador of reconciliation and new creation in Christ, in order to effect the reconciliation that was made possible on the cross.

The exclamatory "behold!" (ἰδού), used twice here by the ambassador to accentuate the Scripture citation, commands the audience's attention for his climactic point. Everything stated until now serves as prologue to his present exhortation. In the A element (5:16–17), Paul deduced for the audience that if those who are in Christ are a new creation then they should "behold!" (ἰδού) and recognize that they are proof that new things have come. As a bookend to his climactic exhortation, in the A´ element (5:21—6:2) Paul calls on the audience, "behold!" (ἰδού) "now" is an acceptable time, and, for emphasis, "behold!" (ἰδού) "now" is the day of salvation—that is, *if* they are reconciled to God. Otherwise, God's grace will be in vain. "Now," the moment that this letter is being performed and heard, is the time to choose.[35]

The logic of Paul's argument to this point is clear: the audience has gained much from Paul's ministry, and these present spiritual benefits aid both Paul's defense and his exhortation to the Corinthians. Because of Paul, "now" they are indwelt by the Spirit and sealed as God's elect (1:21–22; 5:5); "now" they hold the proof of the new covenant in their hearts (1:21–22; 3:1–3); "now" they are being transformed to a new glory (3:18); "now" they hold the knowledge of the glory of God in their hearts (4:6); "now" they see by faith and not by sight (5:7); and "now" they are a new creation in Christ and understand in a new way (5:16–17), so as to hope in the future glory of the resurrection (5:1–10). The text's

---

34. Matera (*II Corinthians*, 149) considers "the grace of God" to refer to Christ's activity on the cross and not Paul's ministry. I am persuaded, however, by Harris (*Second Epistle*, 385) and Beale ("Reconciliation," 560), who see "the grace of God" as referring to the content of Paul's message within his ministry of reconciliation (as in 1:18–22; 1:23—2:5; 4:15b).

35. Matera, *II Corinthians*, 150.

arguments have rendered a full understanding of Paul's ministry (see 1:12–14), in so far as the audience understands him to be sincere and qualified to be an apostle of Christ to them. They themselves are proof of his apostleship, and they bear this proof in their present spiritual experience and hope in a future glory. Having gained all these things through Paul, they are also implored "now" to renew their relationship with Paul and be reconciled with God through Christ (5:20—6:2).

Chapter Summary

5:16—6:2

The application of life and death to his own paradoxical ministry in 4:15—5:15 is continued and finds its climax in the final unit of 5:16—6:2. The new life for believers is characterized as *now*, that is, as the messianic age that has *come* following Christ's death and the reception of the gospel. The old ways of *knowing* and living are obsolete. This is because Christ, who did not *know* sin, was made to be sin, so that those in him might *become* the righteousness of God (5:21). At the center of the unit is the theme of reconciliation. In Christ God was *reconciling* "*us*" to himself, and this activity was the content of Paul's ministry of *reconciliation* (5:18). That is, the activity of *reconciling* the world that occurred in Christ was the "word" or message of *reconciliation* that Paul and his co-workers ("*us*") first preached to the Corinthians. As an ambassador of Christ who speaks for God, Paul exhorts the Corinthians to be *reconciled* to God (5:20) so that the saving activity of the cross may be made effective. In the meantime, their reconciliation with God remains incomplete. The "time" for the audience to embrace Paul's ministry is *now*. Just as they were told, "*behold!*" that new things have come as proof that the new era has arrived *now* in Christ (5:16-17), at the conclusion of the unit they are given the directive, "*behold!*" that *now* is a very acceptable time and *now* is the day of salvation (6:2).

5:16—6:2 as the Close of Macrochiasm III (4:15—6:2)

As a whole, the macrochiastic unit in 4:15—6:2 defends Paul's ministry within the categories of things seen and things unseen. In particular, believers are called to recognize through faith the unseen blessings that they have received from the gospel. "Now" is the time for them to recognize that they are a new creation in Christ and be reconciled to God. They can accomplish this only by understanding fully the selfless nature of Paul's ministry and the internal, unseen glory that comes from God's grace.

The pivot C and C′ units (5:6–10; 5:11–13) indicate that "we" walk by faith and not by sight because "we" are confident that aspiring to be acceptable to the Lord—*whether* at home with him or *whether* away—will prepare "us" to *appear* before him for judgment of "our" deeds, *whether* good or *whether* bad (5:7–10). Paul's preaching has made known to the Corinthians this proper focus on things unseen; for this reason he is *apparent* to God, and should be also to the Corinthians (5:11). His external appearance should not be an issue, even though his opponents boast in such things. Paul contends that his preaching is for the Corinthians' benefit and God's glory, *whether* in their estimation he preaches well or *whether* he preaches poorly (5:13).

The theme of life's victory over death in the B and B′ units (5:1–5; 5:14–15) is presented as the core of Paul's gospel and serves further to persuade the audience to recognize him as a true apostle of Christ. Because of the gospel, he is confident that the *mortal* body will be swallowed up by *life* when the resurrection body is put on (5:4b–5). Furthermore, Paul is compelled by the belief that since one *died* for all, therefore all have *died*. Christ's sacrificial example means that even though one *died* so that others might *live*, those who *live* now do so no longer for themselves but for the one who *died* for them and was raised (5:14–15). Christ's resurrection prefigures the future glory that believers may attain and explains further how what is mortal is swallowed up by life in the B unit (5:1–5).

The A (4:15–18) and A′ (5:16—6:2) units of the macrochiastic apologia are connected by three themes: new creation, glory, and time. Believers who are *renewed* daily despite external affliction (4:17) are also a *new* creation in Christ and among the *new* things that mark the arrival of the messianic age (5:17). The *grace* that abounds to believers because of Paul's ministry (4:15a) is also the *grace* from God that the audience may yet have received in vain (6:1). They should instead be reconciled to God and his chosen ambassador. Just as the *temporary* things seen (4:18) and the *daily* renewal of the believer are limited periods of time with a fixed endpoint, so too is the present time limited for the believers to be reconciled to God. Paul thus calls emphatically for the Corinthian audience to behold "now" as an appropriate *time* to be reconciled and to behold "now" as the *day* of salvation (6:2).

The macrochiastic outline presented above demonstrates the structure and line of thought of Paul's main apologia to the Corinthians: the goal of the letter is to call the Corinthians to reconciliation with Paul, his ministry, and with God. At the center of this apologia, Paul engages the tension over his external appearance and speaking skills and turns his liability into an asset. The text's emphasis on the unseen future glory, new creation, and reconciliation in Paul's gospel reorients the Corinthians' focus to what they have already gained from his ministry and what they have yet to gain in Christ. The life/death contrast parallels the seen/unseen contrast and supports Paul's credibility as an apostle: the audience gains the promise of life from his message of new creation and reconciliation.

The audience's cultural standards are insufficient for them to understand that they are a new creation in Christ because of Paul's ministry. This glorious transformation can only be seen through eyes of faith ("for we walk by faith and not by sight," 5:7; see also 3:14–18; 4:4–14, 16–18; 5:16–17). The apologia's structure thus reorients the Corinthians' focus towards the eternal unseen things (4:18) so that they can "behold!" the new creation that they have become in Christ (5:17). Only after the audience—as a new creation—understands Paul and his gospel in a new way and accepts him as an apostle, will they fully be reconciled with God and allow the sacrifice of Christ's death to be effective for their salvation.

7

Summary and Conclusions

Purpose and Method

The purpose of this study has been to evaluate how the Corinthian audience responds to Paul's rhetorical arguments in 2 Cor 1:1—6:2 as the letter is performed orally. In particular, this study has focused on how the audience experiences the climactic call to reconciliation in 5:16—6:2. This audience-oriented method is "text-centered" in that it studies how the authorial audience (i.e., the "textual," "ideal," or "implied" audience) responds to the performance of the letter.[1] This method demonstrates for modern readers what the textual audience experiences within the text's performance, that is, this method *shows* what the audience *hears*. Within this method the exegete "listens" carefully to repeated terms, themes, and structures that are aurally evident to the textual audience. This present work represents the first major audience-oriented study of 2 Corinthians 1:1—6:2.

---

1. The authorial audience is not progressively created by the reader, as some reading theorists suggest. Rather, in audience theory, the "authorial" (or "textual") audience refers to the group of addressees implied in the text. This group may also be called the "implied" or "ideal" audience, and, in order to avoid cumbersome repetition, is also referred to as "the Corinthians," the "Corinthian community," or "the community." Thus the audience is in no way simply the modern reader or a heuristic device, but is grounded in textual evidence and presumed to be the group of addressees that the author Paul imagined as he composed 2 Corinthians.

The textual audience and author are deduced from the text itself and are not historically reconstructed or created within the reader's mind as the text progresses. The author is the apostle Paul who founded the Christian community in Corinth. The audience is the group of intended addressees that Paul envisioned as he composed the letter with his staff and planned its performance. The audience-oriented method understands the previous events and correspondence alluded to within the text to be presumed by both author and audience.

The situation surrounding 2 Corinthians thus encompasses the breadth of Paul's relationship with the community: its founding, the issues within 1 Corinthians, the changes in travel plans (2 Cor 1:15–17; 1:23—2:3), the painful visit (2:5–8), the letter of tears (2:3–4, 9), and the arrival of ministerial opponents (3:1–3; 4:1–4).[2] The audience-oriented method evaluates how the ideal audience experiences Paul's rhetorical arguments that serve to defend his ministry, answer accusations or questions, attack the opponents, and exhort the Corinthians to renew their relationship with him and be reconciled to God.

Chiasms

No successful rhetorical performance lacks structure, and 2 Corinthians is no exception. The structures I put forward here are predicated on an audience-oriented "hearing" of the text, that is, they are intended to *show* what the audience *hears* in 2 Corinthians. These structures are a consistent chain of chiasms, in that they are inverted patterns of repeated terms or sounds that indicate the progression of the author's argument.

As seen above, chiastic structures are widely present in ancient literature. In particular, they served as a common part of Greco-Roman education, from learning the alphabet to the composition and performance of advanced oratory. Such structures have been found often in Paul's letters, with varying levels of complexity. This study is the first to present 2 Cor 1:1—6:2 as a series of twenty chiastic units, involving three larger macrochiasms.

Each unit has an objective basis determined on lexical grounds. This method is supported not only by the consistent occurrence of

---

2. This study addresses the unity of 2 Corinthians and the identity of the audience in the Introduction.

chiasms but also by the presence of linking terms at the beginning and end of each unit. These linking terms show that the chiasms are not random or disjointed structures but are part of a coordinated argument that is both aesthetically attractive to the intended audience and rhetorically effective in its flow and structure.

At times within academic disciplines the presentation of chiasms has been overly subjective, and many are considered to be *forced* rather than *found*. For this reason, many are hesitant to receive a structure that is presented within the so-called "chiastic method." But such reservations need not be applied to this study. The structures demonstrated here have an objective basis grounded in lexical and grammatical criteria. In this way, they are not unlike those that have been offered at times by historical-critical scholars on the bases of lexical connections.[3]

A helpful analogue to the findings of this study may be seen in form criticism. This long-standing method, based on the premise that the content of oral correspondence has an ordered form, determines the structure of a text by sets of generic criteria.[4] In an analogous way, this study has demonstrated that 2 Cor 1:1—6:2 consists of repeating examples of a particular genre that organize the content of an oral argument. Each unit contains the necessary generic characteristics of a chiasm, in that each has an inverted set of repeating terms. These inverted patterns are separated into elements that indicate the progression of the author's argument within an oral medium. One who is skeptical of an audience or "chiastic" method may approach this study as a form-critical or rhetorical analysis of 2 Cor 1:1—6:2 that structures the text based on patterns deduced by generic characteristics and, in particular, addresses the rhetorical effect of the final unit in 5:16—6:2 on the audience.

Audience Response to 2 Corinthians 1:1—5:15

The intention of the letter, according to the text, is to heal the tense relationship between author and audience. The arguments that the audience hears defend Paul's ministry, but that is not the only reason for writing. The second and equally important goal of the letter is to bring reconciliation between Paul and the Corinthian community (1:12—2:13; 3:1–6;

---

3. In particular, see Lambrecht ("Structure," 284) and Matera (2 *Corinthians*, 54).

4. See, e.g., Buss, "Study of Forms," 1–15, 45–54; Bailey and Vander Broek, *Literary Forms*, 49–54; Milinovich, "Form Criticism," 13–26.

4:1–6, 12–18; 5:11–15). The defense of his ministry is a necessary step toward that goal.

Paul's rhetorical arguments engage the audience to recognize the importance of their relationship with him as it pertains to their salvation. As he informs them in 1:12–14, the present letter is written to complete their understanding of him. This includes, in a particular way, his ministry (which Paul defends throughout 2:14—6:2, and beyond). Yet the consistent use of ambiguous first person plural pronouns ("we," "us," etc.),[5] the eschatological urgency, and the defense of his ministry tied directly to the spiritual benefits of salvation that are gained by the Corinthians from his gospel, serve to underscore the letter's main rhetorical focus, which is the renovation of the relationship between author and audience (see especially 1:12–14). This focus on the relationship culminates in Paul's call to be reconciled to God (5:20—6:2). In view of the letter's concerns throughout, the community's reconciliation with Paul is as much a concern in the text as their relationship with God and Christ (1:1–3, 8; 5:20). As presented in 1:1–11, the relationship between apostle and community is symbiotic in nature and reorients both parties in a new way toward salvation in Christ as God's own people.

Greeting and Blessing (1:1–7)

In the greeting (1:1–2) the members of the audience are reminded of their membership among God's sanctified people, the continuation of Israel. Their recent dispute with Paul is implicitly challenged when he reminds them that others in their area have accepted him as an authorized apostle of "our Lord Jesus Christ" by God's will (1:1c). The

---

5. The ambiguous plural pronouns are a noted problem in 2 Corinthians. This study takes the position that Paul employs the pronouns as a rhetorical strategy to draw in his audience. Three optional referents emerge for the pronouns: exclusive to Paul alone (literary plural); exclusive to Paul and his co-workers; or inclusive of Paul, the audience, and possibly all believers. From an audience-oriented perspective, Paul uses the pronouns in a consistent manner. When he is speaking of his apostolic responsibilities or hardships the pronouns are literary or exclusive to himself and his co-workers (1:3b–7, 9–20; 2:14—3:6; 4:1–5, 7–14; 5:11–15, 18b, 19b, 20; 6:1). But when Paul is speaking in terms of the spiritual benefits that all believers might gain from the gospel the pronouns are inclusive of the audience, that is, the audience hears themselves included in pronouns that concern benefits that all believers would presume to share (1:1–3a, 8, 21–22; 2:11; 3:12–18; 4:6, 16–18; 5:1–10, 16–18a, 21). This pattern seems consistent throughout 2 Cor 1:1—6:2.

greeting's structure underscores a theme that will remain prominent throughout the letter: the Corinthians' salvation and Paul's qualification as minister of the gospel are interrelated; the validity of Paul's call to be an apostle of Christ is necessary for them to have received an effective gospel and the Spirit of sanctification (1:2).

This symbiotic relationship between apostle and community is restated in a new way in the blessing (1:3–7). Although they had questioned his authority because of his afflictions, Paul argues that what he endures is for the audience's benefit. Consolation is given to the community from Christ through the agency of Paul (1:5). So his suffering does not limit Paul's authority but strengthens both his standing as an apostle and his bond with the Corinthians themselves.

Macrochiasm I (1:8—2:13)

Having reminded the audience of his authority to be an apostle of Christ by the will of God and presenting the relationship between them and him as symbiotic, such that it benefits both parties, in the first macrochiastic argument of the letter (1:8—2:13) Paul will defend his recent administrative decisions that the Corinthians have criticized. These incidents include his travel plan changes (1:15–17; 1:23—2:3), the painful visit (2:4–5), the offender (2:5–9), the tearful letter (2:4–9), and the new opponents (3:1–2; 4:1–4; 5:11–13). Paul argues that his sincerity and decisions are validated by God's own faithfulness (1:18–22) and his abounding love and concern for the spiritual well-being of the community (1:15–17; 1:23—2:13). The symbiotic relationship between him and the audience (first mentioned in 1:7) is recalled and built upon throughout the macro-structure.

In the A unit (1:8–11) of the first macrochiastic argument, the audience hears how they aid Paul in the recent affliction that has come upon him in Asia (1:8). In the central elements, this experience inspires Paul to trust in God who raises the dead, who has rescued him before, and who will rescue him again (1:9-10). The climactic conclusion of the unit returns to Paul's relationship with the audience since his rescue is related to their prayers on his behalf and their solidarity with him (1:11). As expressed in 1:3–7, this relationship is symbiotic with both sides benefiting from the spiritual fruits of the gospel.

The B unit (1:12–14) states Paul's reasons for writing, namely, to defend his ministry to the audience and emphasize the importance of their relationship with him. As the unit opens, Paul's boast is that he conducted himself in a godly and sincere manner to the audience, even more so than to others (1:12). The central elements defend his sincerity by reminding the audience that he only writes to them what they can read and understand. This sincere manner of communication, he hopes, will lead to their complete understanding of him and his ministry (1:13). At the conclusion, Paul explains that he hopes this complete understanding will result in both parties having a mutual boast in each other on the day of Christ's return (1:14). The status of their relationship (that is, how well they understand each other) will determine their recompense at the Parousia.

The C unit (1:15–17) addresses Paul's travel plans, the first contentious issue with the community. The audience is informed that Paul's first change in plans (to visit them twice on his trip from Macedonia to Ephesus rather than only once) was to give them a double favor (1:15). The conclusion asks rhetorically whether such a decision was made from vacillation or insecurity (1:17).

In the pivotal D unit (1:18–22) of Macrochiasm I, Paul defends his recent administrative decisions (1:15–17) by basing his own pastoral sincerity on the faithfulness of God. Paul and his co-workers proclaimed a message that is not both "yes" and "no" because in Christ it is always "yes" (1:19). That is, all of the promises of God, who is faithful, are "yes" in Christ (1:20). God, who affirms Paul's sincerity, established Paul and his co-workers with the community, put his seal upon and anointed all believers, and gave his Spirit in their hearts as a present experience of forthcoming glory (1:21–22). The sincerity of Paul's ministry, the solidarity of his relationship with the community, and the subsequent present experience of the Spirit that comes with their relationship in Christ, are all affirmed by God who is faithful and has completed in Christ his promises for the elect.

Within the progression of the macrochiastic argument, Paul's defense of his sincerity and administrative decisions begins to fold back on itself in the C′ unit (1:23—2:3). Just as the C unit (1:15–17) concerned Paul's change in travel plans prior to the painful visit, the C′ unit (1:23—2:3) deals with his travel changes afterward. The emphasis on the shared "joy" of Paul and the audience (1:24; 2:2–3) echoes the double "favor" of the C unit (1:15–17) that Paul intended to give them.[6] Both units emphasize how Paul and the audience share joy within their symbiotic relationship.

In the C´ unit (1:23—2:3), Paul testifies with God as his witness that all of his recent decisions were for the audience's benefit. Paul did not return to Corinth as he first planned (1:15) so that he might spare them and continue his work for their joy. As he points out, if he causes pain to the ones to whom he is entrusted as an apostle, how can the relationship benefit anyone (2:1–2)? Rather, Paul wrote the tearful letter to prepare for his future return to the audience to remove the pain from their tense relationship and so that his joy might be their joy as well (2:3).

The B´ unit (2:4–9) parallels the B unit (1:12–14) within the progression of the macrochiastic argument. That Paul wrote the tearful letter in order that the audience might know of his "overflowing" love for them (2:4) develops and affirms Paul's particular relationship with the community in the B unit (1:12–14) when he claimed he acted in godly holiness and the sincerity of God in an "overflowing" manner toward them. The intensity of Paul's love reinforces the sincerity of his ministry to the audience and underscores his concern for his relationship with them.

The opening of the B´ unit (2:4–9) informs the audience that Paul wrote the tearful letter with much anxiety not to cause them pain but to express his overflowing love for them (2:4). Paul demurs that if anyone was pained by the offender during the painful visit it was not him but the audience (2:5). Since the audience has punished the offender appropriately, the central elements explain, they are now encouraged to receive him back and solidify their relationship, lest he be overwhelmed by pain (2:6–7). The closing elements of the unit explain that Paul wrote the tearful letter to address the offender and evaluate the Corinthians' obedience (2:8–9).

Within the progression of the macrochiastic structure (1:8—2:13), the assertion that "we are not unaware" of Satan's schemes to cause division within the symbiotic relationship of the community and Paul in the A´ unit (2:10–13) underscores his earlier concern that the Corinthians "not be unaware" of his affliction in Asia in the A unit (1:8–11) since the audience's prayers for Paul and solidarity with him contribute to his

---

6. In Greek, both "joy" (χαρά) and "favor" (χάρις) have the same root.

rescue from death (1:11). In the same way, that Paul "has" no rest in his spirit as he awaits word from Titus in the A′ unit (2:10–13), just as he fears he "has" a death sentence in the A unit (1:8–11), underscores the anxiety that Paul feels as he awaits to hear how the community responded to his tearful letter. The status of their relationship and solidarity in light of 1:8–11, 14; 2:10–13 affects their standing at the Parousia.

In the A′ unit (2:10–13), Paul affirms his love for the audience. He reminds them that within their relationship anyone they forgive he also forgives; and what he forgives he does for the audience's sake in the presence of Christ (1:20). The center of the chiastic unit notes that this unity is counter to the schemes of Satan, who wishes to divide the holy ones and detain the elect from salvation (2:11; see also 1:14; 2:5). The unit addresses Paul's recent retreat from preaching the gospel because of illness. He left a successful ministry at Troas, the audience learns, because he had no rest in his spirit as he awaited word from Titus regarding the tearful letter (2:12–13).

In sum, in response to doubts and accusations regarding his sincerity and recent decisions, Paul begins the reparation of his relationship with the audience in this macrochiastic argument (1:8—2:13) by defending the most recent points of tension: his change in travel plans (1:15–17; 1:23—2:3), the painful visit, the offender, and the tearful letter (2:4–9). The pivotal unit of the argument (1:18–22) sets God's faithfulness in Christ and the present experience of the Spirit among the audience as proof of Paul's faithfulness as an apostle. This acts to counter the audience's concerns regarding Paul's change in plans (1:15–17; 1:23—2:3), which they learn were only for their benefit. Paul writes so that they may understand him completely (1:12–14), even when his letter is harsh (2:4–9), so that they may know of his overflowing love for them. This is the goal of the letter: to reaffirm their symbiotic relationship so that both apostle and audience may benefit at the return of their Lord Jesus Christ (1:8–11, 14; 2:10–13).

Macrochiasm II (2:14—4:14)

Having defended in the first macrochiastic argument (1:8—2:13) his faithfulness and sincerity as an apostle of Christ to the audience in order to heal the tension in their relationship, in the next macrochiastic argument (2:14—4:14) Paul will continue his reparation of the relationship by defending his ministry against the accusations of the opponents and the anti-Pauline contingent in Corinth.

In the opening A unit (2:14—3:6) of the second macrochiastic structure, Paul thanks God, who in Christ leads him in a triumphal procession, in which Paul and his co-workers are the aroma of Christ for God in their proclamation of the gospel to the elect (2:14–17). The central elements address the need for letters of recommendation and notify the audience that they themselves are Paul's letter, with the Spirit written on their hearts, to be read by all and act as recommendation for Paul and his ministry (3:1–3). The unit's conclusion states that, whereas others peddle the word of God, Paul is qualified by God to be a minister of a new covenant (3:4–6). This unit draws in the audience by giving their own spiritual experience in Christ as proof of Paul's qualification.

Having opened the defense of his ministry by giving the audience's experience as evidence of his qualification that has come from God to proclaim the new covenant, in the B unit (3:7–18) Paul will present his new ministry as superior to that of Moses. Moses' ministry brought condemnation and death, and his veil hid the fading glory of the old covenant and does so still in the audience's time (3:7–11, 14a). Yet the new ministry of Paul brings righteousness and life (3:8–9). The central elements of the unit state that those who receive the gospel and interpret the law through the lens of Christ have the veil lifted from their eyes and perceive the fading glory of the old covenant (3:14–16). The climactic conclusion of the unit focuses on the freedom that all believers share in Christ. All who receive the gospel (as the audience has from Paul) look with unveiled face on the glory of Christ and are transformed into the same glorious image (3:18). This unit then again points to the present spiritual experience of the audience as evidence for Paul's qualification as an apostle.

The audience experiences the pivot of the second macrochiastic argument in the C unit (4:1–6) as Paul turns to defend his ministry directly. In the opening element, Paul clarifies that he does not act with trickery or falsify God's words but with honest transparency commends himself before God (4:1–2). The central elements contend that Paul's gospel is not veiled, as others allege, except to those who are perishing because Satan has blinded them so that they do not see the glory of Christ, the image of God, who is apparent in the gospel (4:3–4; see also 3:14–18). The unit's conclusion again presents the audience as proof of his apostleship as he claims that God has set in the hearts of all believers the light of the knowledge of the glory of God as they look on the face of Christ (4:5–6; see also 3:18).

Having begun the defense of his ministry by first presenting the audience as evidence of his qualification, and thus countering the opponents' accusations, in the next unit the argument turns to defend Paul's own weakness. As above (in 1:8–11, 18–22; 2:14—3:18), Paul will point to the quality of the relationship with the audience that has brought them salvation as proof of his qualification and to disarm the opponents' accusations and criticism. The B′ unit (4:7–11) presents a chiastic progression from the B unit (3:7–18). The "surpassing" power of God that is manifest in Paul's suffering with Christ in the B′ unit (4:7) develops the glory of the new covenant that "surpasses" that of the old in the B unit (3:11). In both cases, only those who view Paul through the lens of Christ and his cross, the focus of Paul's gospel, will fully understand the message of salvation in Christ and the apostle who proclaims it.

The B′ unit (4:7–11) addresses directly Paul's physical weaknesses that had become an issue among the community and the opponents (1:3–11). The opening element contends that Paul's frame, though fragile, houses God's glory so that the power may be shown to be from God alone (4:7). The central elements present Paul as one who bends under the strain of his apostolic duties but does not break unto destruction (4:8–9). As the unit closes, Paul explains that his weaknesses only manifest further the resurrection life of Jesus and thus the power of the gospel. Paul, in his weakness, is a walking example of God's life-giving power (4:10–11). The opponents had insisted on signs and wonders as qualifications of apostleship, but Paul here counters that suffering in solidarity with Christ is what truly manifests God's glory. Whatever the Corinthians' concerns about Paul may be, they cannot deny that the gospel that came to them, by which they received the Spirit of God in their hearts (1:21–22; 3:1–3) and experience the glorious transformation in Christ (3:18) and illumination of the knowledge of God (4:6), came to them by a fragile, dying apostle—and thus the glory of God is made apparent not in spite of weakness but because of it. As seen throughout this letter, the argument here again points to the benefits of the relationship as evidence of Paul's sincerity and qualification.

In the final unit (4:12–14) of the second macrochiastic argument (2:14—4:14), the audience experiences an inversion that returns them to the opening unit (2:14—3:6). What is "written" in Scripture by God's will that encourages Paul to further proclaim the gospel in the A′ unit (4:12–14) underscores how Paul proclaimed this word of the gospel to the Corinthians in spite of his weaknesses so that the Spirit might be "written" on their hearts in the A unit (3:1-4). Furthermore, that Paul "speaks" with the same Spirit as the suffering psalmist in the A′ unit (4:12–14) explains how he can "speak" with sincerity in Christ before God in the A unit (2:14—3:6).

Paul returns to his relationship with the audience directly in the closing A′ unit (4:12–14) of this macrochiastic argument. The opening element claims that what works death in Paul works life in the audience since his dangerous apostolic lifestyle brings him near to destruction but brings the gospel of righteousness and life to his communities (4:12). The central elements claim that Paul speaks by the same Spirit of faith that inspired the suffering psalmist to hope in rescue from God (4:13). At the conclusion of the unit, and the macrostructure as a whole, Paul emphatically points to his relationship with the audience as proof of his qualification. Their relationship has brought them much, namely, the hope that God who raised Jesus will also raise all believers, uniting Paul forever with the audience (4:14).

In sum, in the second macrochiastic argument (2:14—4:14) Paul continues to point to the benefits the audience has gained from their relationship with him as proof that he is qualified as an apostle. These arguments inherently disarm the accusations of the opponents, who question both his sincerity as pastor and qualification as an apostle (3:1-3; 4:1-4). Even his weaknesses, Paul claims, are actually a benefit to the community because they manifest the surpassing glory of God (4:7-11). Even if he is a fragile jar of clay (4:7), yet he still carries the glorious new covenant and proclaims it so that those who receive it may look with unveiled face on the glory of Christ and be transformed into the same glory (3:18) as well as receive the Spirit and the light of the knowledge of God in their hearts (3:7—4:6). Who is qualified for such a ministry? The unfolding argument points out that such qualification can come only from God, whose glory has been made evident in the mortal body of Paul because of the present spiritual experience of transformation and illumination in the Corinthians themselves (3:1-3, 14-18; 4:5-6), the Spirit written on their hearts (3:1-3), and their hope in the future resurrection (4:12-14).

Macrochiasm III (4:15—6:2)

In the first macrochiastic argument (1:8—2:13), Paul defended the sincerity of his ministry and his recent administrative decisions by pointing to God's faithfulness and the fulfillment of his promises in Christ that the elect (and the Corinthians in particular) receive from Paul so that they may gain the present experience of salvation in the Spirit. In the second macrochiastic argument (2:14—4:14), Paul defended his qualification to be an apostle to the community (against the accusations of the opponents) by pointing to the spiritual benefits that the audience receive from his ministry, despite his lack of written credentials or weak demeanor and illness. Now, in the third macrochiastic argument (4:15—6:2), Paul continues to defend his ministry by focusing on the spiritual benefits that the audience and all the elect gain in Christ because of the gospel.

The A unit (4:15-18) opens by building on the image of life for the community from 4:11-14 and states that all things, including the suffering that Paul endures in his ministry and the content of his message, are for the audience's benefit (4:15a). Paul's ministry endures much so that the grace that overflows among his growing communities may increase their giving thanks to glorify God (4:15b). Building on the hope in the resurrection in 4:11-14 and the assurance of grace in 4:15, the central elements explain that believers are not discouraged because even though "our outer self" is continually decaying, yet "our inner self" is being renewed daily (4:16) by the indwelling Spirit (1:21-22; 3:1-3), the glorious transformation (3:18), and the light of the knowledge of God's glory (4:6). Yet these present experiences only prefigure the future eternal weight of glory, the resurrection body (4:17). This emphasis on the present internal experience and future glory encourages the audience to focus not on things seen but on things unseen (4:18). In this unit, Paul's use of the ambiguous plural in reference to the hope in the gospel's benefits for all believers draws in the audience and underscores his sincerity and qualification to serve the Corinthians in the same manner as all his growing communities.

Having begun to talk about the future glory of the resurrection in 4:12-18, he explains further in the B unit (5:1-5) the confidence of believers from 4:16 by stating that even if their earthly dwelling (body) is destroyed, God has prepared an eternal house for them in heaven

(5:1). The central elements contend that we groan while here in the temporary situation of life and desire to put on our heavenly residence in addition to our mortal body so that we will not be like the glory-less, Adam-like humanity, but will be clothed in the glorious resurrection body (5:2–4a). God, who in the opening element prepares a heavenly, eternal house for believers, now in the closing element conditions them for this future glory by giving them the present experience of the Spirit (5:5; see also 1:21–22; 3:1–3). As above, Paul again points to their spiritual experience and draws in the audience with shared points of faith.

Building on the preceding units, the C unit (5:6–10) begins by asserting that the courage of believers comes from their focus on their internal spiritual experience and faith in the future glory of the resurrection, not on things seen (5:6–7; 4:18). The central elements concede that we prefer to be with the Lord in heaven and away from the body, but this preference leads us to aspire to be acceptable to him, whether we are at home or away (5:8–9). The closing element of the unit, which involves the inevitable judgment of humanity before Christ (5:10), makes the believers' courage in life (5:6), desire to be with the Lord, and aspiration to be acceptable to him (5:8–9) all the more relevant and beneficial.

In the parallel C′ unit (5:11–13) the audience experiences the pivot within the third macrochiastic structure. Having laid a foundation for his sincerity and qualification in the previous complex arguments, and with hope in a shared present spiritual experience and future glory that extends to all believers from his gospel, Paul now turns again to defend himself and his ministry from the opponents' accusations. That Paul is "apparent" to God and should also be "apparent" to the audience in the C′ unit (5:11) is based on the power of his gospel, which he proclaims for their benefit, that they might have proper focus on things that are not seen, in order to aspire to be acceptable to the Lord to prepare them for when they "appear" before his judgment seat (in the C unit, 5:6–10). In the C′ unit (5:11–13) "whether" he preaches poorly or well, Paul's gospel is evident to the elect, who aspire in the C unit (5:6–10) to be with the Lord, "whether" at home or whether away, so that they may stand confidently before him when he judges their bodily actions, "whether" good or bad (5:9–10).

In the C′ unit (5:11–13) the audience hears that, in light of the inevitable future judgment (5:10), since Paul knows the fear of the Lord and preaches a gospel of Christ that he himself has accepted, he tries to persuade others in accordance with his charge to be an apostle of Christ. His selfless service and sincere proclamation of salvation make him apparent to God and all the more so to the audience, to whom he was sent to proclaim salvation in Christ (5:11; see 1:1–2). The central elements contend that Paul is not so much commending himself to them as he is giving them an opportunity to boast in him. That is, since his gospel of salvation has oriented them to look with faith and not by sight so that they might focus on the unseen things, they should have a boast in him and defend him against the accusations of the opponents who have a boast in external matters (5:12). Whatever criticism Paul has received regarding his method of persuasion, the closing element contends that if he speaks poorly, it is to glorify God; and if he speaks well, it is only for the audience's benefit (5:13).

The penultimate B′ unit (5:14–15) reprises the life/death contrast found in the B unit (5:1–5). That all may "live" as a consequence of Christ's "death" (5:15b) in the B′ unit, develops that we desire to be clothed in the resurrection body so that what is "mortal" may be swallowed up by "life" (5:4–5) in the B unit. Since one died for all and was raised, what is "mortal" will be swallowed up (5:4) for those who are raised with him in the resurrection "life" (5:15). Christ's death for those who now "live" (5:14) prefigures the future glory of "life" over what is "mortal" (5:5) and gives a model of selfless living for believers (5:15).

The B′ unit (5:14–15) centers around the newfound present life of believers (5:15b–c). Paul is compelled to preach the gospel because of Christ's sacrificial death that manifested his love for all and gave them a model of selfless living (5:14). For this reason, all those who live because of Christ's death also die to the self so that they may live for others and for the one who died for them and was raised (5:15d). Paul shows Christ's death as an expression of selfless love for all to be the impetus that drives his sincere and qualified ministry to proclaim the gospel to the elect so that they too may die to themselves and live for others (5:15). The unit is both a defense of Paul's ambition and an implied exhortation to the audience to recognize Christ's death as both a benefit for the elect and a model for a new way of life. The argument again points to their relationship: whatever life the audience experiences now in Christ came to them through the paradoxical life-giving ministry of the suffering

Paul who is compelled to mirror the paradoxical life-giving death of his Lord Jesus Christ, for whom he is an apostle to the elect.

Audience Response to 5:16—6:2

The section 5:16—6:2 acts as the final A´ unit of the third macrochiastic argument and thus recapitulates three important themes begun in the opening parallel A unit (4:15–18): renewal, grace, and time. Because of Paul's gospel, believers are "renewed" daily (4:16) and are made into a "new" creation in Christ; and so they are "new things" that mark the arrival of the messianic age (5:17). "Grace" arrives to the elect in Corinth by Paul's ministry (4:15), and this is "grace" that the audience should not receive in vain by rejecting the apostle who brought them the gospel (6:1). They should instead recognize with their new vision (5:7) and knowledge (5:16) the benefits that they have received in Christ from their relationship with Paul and be reconciled to God (5:20). Just as the "temporary" things seen (4:18) and the daily renewal of the believers are limited points of "time," so too is the close of the present age a limited time for the embattled elect to be reconciled to God (5:20; 6:1). Paul, who sincerely loves the audience and carries out his selfless, qualified ministry to proclaim life in Christ to them, concludes this third complex argument by acting as an ambassador for Christ, crying, "Behold, 'now' is the acceptable time; behold, 'now' is the day of salvation" to be reconciled to him and to God (6:2), so that they do not receive in vain the grace that came to them through his proclamation.

Having explained the effect of Christ's death on both his ministry and the new life of believers in the previous unit (5:14–15), the final A´ unit (5:16—6:2) opens by explaining what is so new about the believers' lives: they now know Christ in a new way, no longer according to the flesh (5:16), and this new way of knowing makes those in Christ a new creation. As such, the Corinthians themselves mark the passing of the present age and the entrance of the messianic era (5:17).

The central elements focus on the renewed relationship between humanity—especially the Corinthians—and God. Christ's death that brings life to all (5:14–15) is revealed to be the content of Paul's ministry (5:18). This renewed relationship with God comes from the remission of humanity's sins (5:19). In the central elements, Paul views both the death of Christ and his own ministry as part of God's reconciling activity (5:18–19). As an ambassador of Christ, Paul implores the audience to be reconciled to God (5:20).

The climactic conclusion to the unit and the macrochiastic argument as a whole supports and emphasizes the exhortation in 5:20. God made Christ to be sin so that the elect might become in him the righteousness of God (5:21). The inversion is paradoxical, as is the life/death comparison in the B and B′ units (5:1–5, 14–15); but such inversions parallel Paul's paradoxical ministry of a suffering apostle who brings life to his communities (4:7–14) and the ongoing contrast of boasting in things unseen rather than things seen (4:18; 5:7, 11–13). The cross is the light that shines on believers' hearts to illuminate them to "see" with faith the future glory of the resurrection (4:6; 5:5, 7); Paul's ministry is the lantern that carries that light to bring to the elect the proper way of seeing (4:18; 5:7) and knowing (5:16), thus allowing them to have the Spirit dwell within them and be gloriously transformed in Christ to become a new creation (1:21–22; 3:18; 5:17), renewing their relationship with God in righteousness and the remission of sins (3:6–8; 5:18–21).

This indicative of salvation (esp. 5:14–21) underscores the imperative for the audience to be reconciled to God (5:20; 6:1–2). Paul, as an ambassador of Christ, works in unison with God to complete the reconciliation of the elect (5:18—6:2). From this standpoint, there is no reason for the audience to remain ambivalent toward Paul and to receive God's grace in vain. Rather now, at the moment of hearing this letter of apologia and exhortation, the audience should look with their new focus and new knowledge to recognize and understand Paul in a new and complete way, through the lens of the paradoxical cross, and concede that whatever the apostle's faults may be, they gained from Paul's ministry the present experience of the Spirit (1:21–22; 5:5), new life in Christ (5:15), transformation to glory and righteousness (3:18; 5:21), new knowledge (5:16), and daily renewal (4:16). Their relationship with Paul brought about their renewed relationship in Christ with God (5:18–21). It is time to renew *now* their relationship with God's ambassador and no longer strain their status as God's elect.

In conclusion, having argued for his sincerity (1:8—2:13) and qualification (2:14—4:14) as an apostle in the first two macrochiastic arguments, Paul turns in the third argument (4:15—6:2) to address the hope in the resurrection and the courage that believers gain from faith, not sight. Paul will argue that true Christian faith orients believers to hope in things unseen (4:18; 5:7), prepares them for the resurrection (5:5), and remakes them as a new creation (5:17), so that they might be reconciled to him (5:18–19) and become in Christ the righteousness of God (5:21). Building his argument on the benefits that the audience has received from their relationship with him and his gospel, Paul calls on them to understand his compulsion to proclaim the gospel for their own benefit (4:12–15; 5:14) and accept him again as their rightful apostle. In so doing, the audience will allow the reconciliation in Christ with God to have its effect for their salvation.

Contributions of This Study to the Interpretation of 2 Corinthians 5:16—6:2

Second Corinthians 5:16—6:2 rests within one of the most magisterial and problematic sections in Paul's letters and has invited numerous careful studies. These studies have varied on how to delimit the section (5:11–21; 5:14–21; 5:11—6:2) and how to understand the call to reconciliation in 5:18–21 within Paul's theology and the message of the letter as a whole. For the most part, these have tried to grasp this latter concept from the perspective of the author Paul, often comparing 2 Cor 5:18–21 with other texts, such as Rom 5:1–10 (among others), or attempting to understand the origin of the concept within his theological matrix. This work represents the first audience-oriented study of 5:16—6:2, and as such contributes several new insights regarding this intriguing section.

(1) Whereas previous studies have delimited the text based on subjective understandings of theological content, this study demonstrates 5:16—6:2 to be a chiastic unit with an A (5:16–17), B (5:18), B´ (5:19–20), A´ (5:21—6:2) structure that is grounded objectively on grammatical and lexical criteria.

(2) Whereas previous studies have depended on Paul's other letters to explain the theological difficulties in 2 Cor 5:16—6:2, this study has focused on the authorial audience, and thus bases its primary analysis on the materials of which this audience would be aware (including the LXX, 1 Corinthians, events between 1 and 2 Corinthians, and matters pertinent to Second Temple Judaism and Greco-Roman culture). This study also evaluates how the authorial audience responds to 5:16—6:2 as the letter progresses in an aural performance (as it was intended),

rather than in a purely diachronic manner. Such a method serves to analyze the text as a document that was composed and performed for an ideal (i.e., "authorial") audience and to underscore the author's rhetorical argument at the time of writing rather than speculating on a trajectory of thought.

(3) Furthermore, this study demonstrates 5:16—6:2 to be the closing A′ unit to a six part macrochiastic unit in 4:15—6:2, and thus presents lexical parallels with the A unit (4:15–18). The themes that connect the A and A′ units of the macrochiastic argument include renewal (4:16; 5:17), grace (4:15; 6:1), and time (4:16, 18; 5:16; 6:1–2). The section is supported also by arguments found in the preceding units of the macrochiasm in 4:15—5:15, especially the antithetical properties of things seen/unseen (4:18) and the grace that the audience has received from God through Paul's ministry to have daily renewal (4:15–16; 5:17), new knowledge (5:17), and reconciliation with God in Christ (5:18–19).

(4) As a chiastic unit, 5:16—6:2 has paralleling elements that develop Paul's exhortation as it progresses through the unit's structure. The central B and B′ elements (5:18, 19–20) present reconciliation of humanity to God as the content of Paul's ministry (5:18) and his message (5:19). As an ambassador, Paul pleads for the Corinthians to be reconciled to God (5:20). The emphasis on reconciliation then serves as the pivot of the unit as a whole. The bordering A and A′ elements (5:16–17; 5:21—6:2) support the exhortation in the central elements (5:18–20) with exclamations (behold! 5:17; 6:2) and by explaining further benefits that the audience receives in Christ: new knowledge (5:16) and transformation to a new creation and the righteousness of God (5:17, 21). These benefits act as the climax to the indwelling of the Spirit (1:21–22; 3:3–6), glorious transformation (3:18), internal illumination (4:6), and daily renewal (4:16) that the audience are said to have received from Paul's ministry. The persuasive effect of the unit is punctuated by applying Scripture (Isa 43:19) to the present time of the letter's performance, stating that "now" is the very acceptable time and "now" is the day of salvation to accept Paul's plea for reconciliation to his ministry and to God (6:1–2).

(5) In addition to being the conclusion of the macrochiasm 4:15—6:2, the unit 5:16—6:2 is also shown to be the climactic exhortation of 2 Cor 1:1—6:2, which consists of three macrochiastic arguments (1:8—2:13; 2:14—4:14; 4:15—6:2). This unit punctuates and builds on

the rhetorical arguments in 2 Cor 1:1—5:15, especially the fulfillment of God's promises in Christ (1:18-22; 3:3-6, 18; 4:4-6; 5:16-17), the eschatological focus and urgency (1:14; 2:9-10; 3:3-6; 4:4; 5:10, 16-17; 6:1-2), and the seemingly dichotomous reality of God's glory being manifest by weak instruments (1:8-11; 4:7-11; 5:17, 20-21).

(6) Finally, this work shows Paul's call to reconciliation in 5:16—6:2 to be a climactic point of his argument throughout the letter, which consistently emphasizes the symbiotic relationship that Paul and the audience share in Christ. Following the painful visit and tearful letter, Paul had received news from Titus of some, albeit incomplete, relief in the community's relationship with him. The content of 2 Corinthians 1:1—6:2 presents Paul's attempt to fully heal this relationship. His rhetorical placement of renewal and reconciliation in 5:16—6:2 underscores for the audience his call to renewal and reconciliation with his ministry and, due to their conflict with the divinely appointed apostle, with God as well. Paul's argument is that renewal and reconciliation are necessary in the audience's lives and their relationship with him and God. Renewal comes through accepting his gospel of reconciliation with God in Christ—but more importantly, the time to accept this offer is "now."

Bibliography

Achtemeier, Paul. "*Omne verbum sonat*: The New Testament and the Oral Environment of Late Western Antiquity." *JBL* 109 (1990) 3–27.
Ahern, Barnabas. "The Fellowship of His Sufferings." In *A Companion to Paul: Readings in Pauline Theology*, edited by M. Taylor, 37–66. New York: Alba House, 1975.
Allo, E.-B. *Saint Paul: Seconde Épître aux Corinthiens*. Ebib. Paris: Gabalda, 1956.
Arnold, Clinton E. *Powers of Darkness: Principalities and Powers in Paul's Letters*. Downers Grove, IL: InterVarsity, 1992.
Assis, Elie. "Chiasmus in Biblical Narrative: Rhetoric of Characterization." *Prooftexts* 22 (2002) 273–305.
Aune, David. "Anthropological Duality in the Eschatology of 2 Corinthians 4:16—5:10." In *Paul beyond the Judaism/Hellenism Divide*, edited by T. Engberg-Pedersen, 215–40. Louisville: Westminster John Knox, 2001.
Bailey, James L., and Lyle D. Vander Broek. *Literary Forms in the New Testament: A Handbook*. Louisville: Westminster John Knox, 1992.
Barnett, Paul. *The Second Epistle to the Corinthians*. NICNT. Grand Rapids: Eerdmans, 1997.
———. *The Message of 2 Corinthians: Power in Weakness*. Downers Grove, IL: InterVarsity, 1988.
Barrett, C. K. *The First Epistle to the Corinthians*. HNTC. New York: Harper & Row, 1968.
———. *The Second Epistle to the Corinthians*. HNTC. New York: Harper & Row, 1973.
———. "HO ADIKĒSAS (2 Cor 7.12)." In *Essays on Paul*, 108–17. Louisville: Westminster, 1982.
———. "Paul's Opponents in II Corinthians." *NTS* 17 (1970–71) 233–54.
———. *Paul: An Introduction to His Thought*. Louisville: Westminster John Knox, 1994.
———. "Paul the Controversialist." Unpublished lecture, Ashland Theological Seminary, 1990.
Batey, Richard. "Paul's Interaction with the Corinthians." *JBL* 84 (1966) 139–46.
Baumgärtel, Friedrick. "καρδία." In *TDNT* 3:606–7.
Baur, Ferdinand Christian. *Paul, the Apostle of Jesus Christ: His Life and Works, His Epistles and Teachings*. 2 vols. in 1. Peabody, MA: Hendrickson, 2001.
Beale, G. K. "The Old Testament Background of Reconciliation in 2 Corinthians 5–7 and Its Bearing on the Literary Problem of 2 Corinthians 6,14—7,1." *NTS* 35 (1989) 550–81.

———. *We Become What We Worship: A Biblical Theology of Idolatry*. Downers Grove, IL: InterVarsity, 2008.

Behm, Johannes. "μεταμορφόω." In *TDNT* 4:755–59.

———. "ἔσω." In *TDNT* 2:698–99.

———. "νοῦς, νοέω." In *TDNT* 4:960–61.

Belleville, Linda L. "A Letter of Apologetic Self-Commendation: 2 Cor 1:8—7:16." *NovT* 31 (1989) 142–63.

———. *2 Corinthians*. INTCS 8. Downers Grove, IL: InterVarsity, 1996.

———. "Paul's Polemic and the Theology of the Spirit in Second Corinthians." *CBQ* 58 (1996) 281–304.

———. *Reflections of Glory: Paul's Polemical Use of the Moses-Doxa Tradition in 2 Corinthians 3.1–18*. JSNTSup 52. Sheffield: Sheffield Academic, 1991.

Best, Ernest. *Second Corinthians*. Interpretation. Louisville: Westminster John Knox, 1997.

Betz, Hans D. "Corinthians, Second Epistle to." In *ABD* 1:1148–54.

———. "2 Cor 6:14—7:1: An Anti-Pauline Fragment?" *JBL* 92 (1973) 88–108.

———. "The Concept of the 'Inner Human Being' (ὁ ἔσω ἄνθρωπος) in the Anthropology of Paul." *NTS* 46 (2000) 315–41.

Bieringer, R. "2 Kor 5,19a und die Versöhnung der Welt." In *Studies on 2 Corinthians*, edited by R. Bieringer and J. Lambrecht, 429–59. BETL 112. Leuven: Leuven University Press, 1994.

Boadt, Lawrence. "The A:B:B:A Chiasm of Identical Roots in Ezekiel." *VT* 25 (1975) 693–99.

Boers, Hendrick. "2 Cor 5:14—6:2: A Fragment of Pauline Christology." *CBQ* 64 (2002) 527–47.

Bornkamm, Günther. *Die Vorgeschichte des sogenannten zweiten Korintherbriefes*. Sitzungsberichte der Heidelberger Akademie der Wissenschaften, Philosophisch-Historische Klasse. Heidelberg: C. Winter Universitätsverlag, 1961.

Blomberg, Craig. "The Structure of 2 Corinthians 1–7." *CTR* 4 (1989) 4–8.

Breck, John. "Biblical Chiasmus: Exploring Structure for Meaning." *BTB* 17 (1984) 70–74.

Bultmann, Rudolph. *Second Epistle to the Corinthians*. Translated by H. Attridge. Minneapolis: Fortress, 1985.

———. "ἔλεος, ἐλεέω." In *TDNT* 2:477–87.

———. "νέκρωσις." In *TDNT* 4:895.

Buss, Martin. "The Study of Forms." In *Old Testament Form Criticism*, edited by J. Hayes, 1–56. San Antonio: Trinity University Press, 1977.

Byrne, Brendan. *Romans*. SP 6. Collegeville, MN: Liturgical, 1996.

Carter, Warren, and John Paul Heil. *Matthew's Parables: Audience-Oriented Perspectives*. CBQMS 30. Washington, DC: Catholic Biblical Association, 1998.

Collange, Jean-François. *Énigmes de la deuxième épître de Paul aux Corinthiens: Étude Éxégétique de 2 Cor. 2:14—7:4*. SNTSMS 18. Cambridge: Cambridge University Press, 1972.

Collins, John J. "Chiasmus, the 'ABA' Pattern and the Text of Paul." In *Studiorum Paulinorum Internationalis Catholicus 1961*, 2:575–83. AnBib 18. Rome: Pontifical Biblical Institute, 1963.

Collins, Raymond F. *First Corinthians*. SP 7. Collegeville, MN: Liturgical, 1990.

Conzelmann, Hans. *1 Corinthians*. Hermeneia. Minneapolis: Fortress, 1970.

Cousar, Charles B. *A Theology of the Cross: The Death of Jesus in the Pauline Letters*. OBT. Minneapolis: Fortress, 1990.

———. "II Corinthians 5:17–21." *Int* 35 (1981) 180–83.
Danker, Frederick. "Paul's Debt to the *De Corona* of Demosthenes: A Study of Rhetorical Techniques in Second Corinthians." In *Persuasive Artistry: Studies in New Testament Rhetoric in Honor of George A. Kennedy*, edited by Duane F. Watson, 262–80. JSNTSup 50. Sheffield: Sheffield Academic, 1991.
Davis, Stephan K. *The Antithesis of the Ages: Paul's Reconfiguration of Torah.* CBQMS 33. Washington, DC: Catholic Biblical Association, 2002.
Davis, William. "Structural Secrets: Shakespeare's Complex Chiasmus." *Literary Style* 39 (2005) 237–58.
De Waard, Jan. "The Chiastic Structure of Amos V 1–17." *VT* 27 (1977) 170–77.
Delling, Gerhard. "θριαμβεύω." In *TDNT* 3:159–60.
Denney, James. *The Death of Christ*, edited by R. V. G. Tasker. London: Tyndale, 1951.
Douglas, Mary. *Thinking in Circles: An Essay on Ring Composition.* Terry Lecture Series. New Haven, CT: Yale University Press, 2007.
Duff, Paul. "2 Corinthians 1–7: Sidestepping the Division Hypothesis Dilemma." *BTB* 24 (1985) 16–25.
———. "Metaphor, Motif, and Meaning: The Rhetorical Strategy behind the Image 'Led in Triumph' in 2 Corinthians 2:14." *CBQ* 53 (1991) 79–92.
———. "Glory in the Ministry of Death: Gentile Condemnation and Letters of Recommendation in 2 Cor. 3:6–18." *NovT* 46 (2004) 313–37.
Dunn, James D. G. *Theology of Paul the Apostle.* Grand Rapids: Eerdmans, 1998.
———. "2 Corinthians III. 17—'The Lord Is the Spirit.'" *JTS* 21 (1970) 309–20.
———. *Romans 1–8.* WBC 38A. Waco: Word, 1988.
Du Toit, Andrie. "Vilification as a Pragmatic Device in Early Christian Epistolography." *Bib* (1994) 403–12.
Ellis, E. Earle. *Paul's Use of the Old Testament.* Grand Rapids: Baker, 1957. Reprint; Eugene, OR: Wipf and Stock, 2003.
Ellis, Peter. *Seven Pauline Letters.* Collegeville, MN: Liturgical, 1982.
Fee, Gordon. *The First Epistle to the Corinthians.* NICNT. Grand Rapids: Eerdmans, 1987.
———. "ΧΑΡΙΣ in II Corinthians I. 15: Apostolic Parousia and Paul-Corinth Chronology." *NTS* 24 (1977–78) 533–38.
———. *God's Empowering Presence: The Holy Spirit in the Letters of Paul.* Peabody, MA: Hendrickson, 1994.
———. *Pauline Christology: An Exegetical-Theological Study.* Peabody, MA: Hendrickson, 2007.
Fitzgerald, John. "Paul and Paradigm Shifts: Reconciliation and Its Linkage Group." In *Paul beyond the Hellenism/Judaism Divide*, edited by T. Engberg-Pedersen, 241–62. Louisville: Westminster John Knox, 2001.
Fitzmyer, Joseph A. "Reconciliation in Pauline Theology." In *To Advance the Gospel: New Testament Studies*, 162–85. New York: Crossroad, 1981.
———. *Essays on the Semitic Background of the New Testament.* SBLSBS 5. Missoula, MT: Scholars, 1975.
———. "Glory Reflected on the Face of Christ (2 Cor 3:7–4:6) and a Palestinian Jewish Motif." In *According to Paul: Studies in the Theology of the Apostle*, 64–79. New York: Paulist, 1993.
———. "Paul and the Law." In *A Companion to Paul: Readings in Pauline Theology*, edited by M. Taylor, 73–88. New York: Alba House, 1975.
———. *Pauline Theology: A Brief Sketch.* London: Prentice-Hall, 1967.
———. *First Corinthians.* AB 32. New Haven, CT: Yale University Press, 2008.

Fredericks, Daniel. "Chiasm and Parallel Structure in Qoheleth 5:9–6:9." *JBL* 108 (1989) 17–35.
Friedrich, Gerhard. "Die Gegner des Paulus im 2. Korintherbrief." In *Abraham unser Vater: Juden und Christen im Gespräch über die Bibel*, edited by O. Betz and M. Hengel, 181–215. AGSU 5. Leiden: Brill, 1963.
Fulton, Sidney. "A Rhetorical Analysis of Second Corinthians with a View to the Unity Question." PhD diss., Southern Baptist Theological Seminary, 1999.
Furnish, Victor Paul. *II Corinthians*. AB 32A. New York: Doubleday, 1984.
———. *Theology and Ethics in Paul*. Nashville: Abingdon, 1968.
Georgi, Dieter. "Corinthians, Second Letter to the." In *IDB* Supplemental Volume, 182–86. Nashville: Abingdon, 1976.
———. *The Opponents of Paul in Second Corinthians: A Study in Religious Propaganda in Late Antiquity*. Philadelphia: Fortress, 1986.
Gignilliat, Mark. "2 Corinthians 6:2: Paul's Eschatological 'Now' and Hermeneutical Invitation." *WTJ* 67 (2005) 147–61.
Gillman, John. "A Thematic Comparison: 1 Cor 15:50–57 and 2 Cor 5:1–5." *JBL* 107 (1988) 439–54.
Gloer, W. Hulitt. "2 Corinthians 5:14–21." *RevExp* 86 (1989) 397–405.
Grabner-Haider, Anton. "The Pauline Meaning of 'Resurrection' and 'Glorification.'" In *A Companion to Paul: Readings in Pauline Theology*, edited by M. Taylor, 23–36. New York: Alba House, 1975.
Grundmann, Walter. "The Teacher of Righteousness of Qumran and the Question of Justification by Faith in the Theology of the Apostle Paul." In *Paul and the Dead Sea Scrolls*, edited by J. Murphy-O'Connor and J. H. Charlesworth, 85–114. Christian Origins Library. New York: Crossroad, 1990.
Gunther, John J. *St. Paul's Opponents and Their Background: A Study of Apocalyptic and Jewish Sectarian Teachings*. NovTSup 35. Leiden: Brill, 1973.
Hafemann, Scott J. *Suffering and Ministry in the Spirit: Paul's Defense of His Ministry in II Corinthians 2:14—3:3*. Grand Rapids: Eerdmans, 1990.
———. *Paul, Moses, and the History of Israel*. Peabody, MA: Hendrickson, 1996.
Hall, David R. *The Unity of the Corinthian Correspondence*. JSNTSup 251. London: T. & T. Clark, 2003.
Harris, Murray J. *The Second Epistle to the Corinthians*. NIGTC. Grand Rapids: Eerdmans, 2005.
———. "A Watershed in Paul's Eschatology: 2 Cor 5:1–10." *TynBul* 22 (1971) 35–57.
———. "2 Corinthians." In *The Expositor's Biblical Commentary*, edited by Frank E. Gaebelein et al., 10:299–406. Grand Rapids: Zondervan, 1976–92.
Harvey, A. E. *Renewal through Suffering: A Study of 2 Corinthians*. Edinburgh: T. & T. Clark, 1989.
Harvey, John D. *Listening to the Text: Oral Patterning in Paul's Letters*. ETS Studies 1. Grand Rapids: Baker, 1998.
Hausrath, Adolf. *Der Vier-Capitelbrief des Paulus an die Korinther*. Heidelberg: Bassermann, 1870.
Hays, Richard B. *Echoes of Scripture in the Letters of Paul*. New Haven, CT: Yale University Press, 1993.
Heil, John Paul. *The Rhetorical Role of Scripture in 1 Corinthians*. SBLStBl 15. Atlanta: SBL, 2005.
———. *Ephesians: Empowerment to Walk in Love for the Unity of All in Christ*. SBLStBl 13. Atlanta: Society of Biblical Literature, 2007.

———. "The Chiastic Structure and Meaning of Paul's Letter to Philemon." *Bib* 82 (2001) 179–206.
Héring, Jean. *The Second Epistle of Saint Paul to the Corinthians*. Translated by A. W. Heathcote and P. J. Allcock. London: Epworth, 1967.
Hickling, C. J. A. "The Sequence of Thought in II Corinthians, Chapter Three." *NTS* 21 (1974–75) 380–95.
———. "Paul's Use of Exodus in the Corinthian Correspondence." In *The Corinthian Correspondence*, edited by R. Bieringer, 367–76. BETL 125. Leuven: Leuven University Press, 1996.
Holladay, William. "Chiasmus, the Key to Hosea XII 3–6." *VT* 16 (1966) 53–64.
Holmgren, Frederick. "Chiastic Structure in Isaiah LI 1–11." *VT* 19 (1969) 196–201.
Hock, Andreas. "Christ Is the Parade: A Comparative Study of the Triumphal Procession in 2 Cor 2,14 and Col 2,15." *Bib* 88 (2003) 110–19.
Hooker, Morna D. "Interchange and Atonement." In *From Adam to Christ: Essays on Paul*, 26–41. Cambridge: Cambridge University Press, 1990.
———. "On Becoming the Righteousness of God: Another Look at 2 Cor 5:21." *NovT* 50 (2008) 358–75.
Hubbard, Moyer V. "Was Paul out of His Mind? Re-reading 2 Cor 5:13." *JSNT* 70 (1998) 39–64.
———. *New Creation in Paul's Letters and Thought*. SNTSMS 119. Cambridge: Cambridge University Press, 2002.
Hughes, Frank. "The Rhetoric of Reconciliation: 2 Corinthians 1.1–2.13 and 7.5–8.24." In *Persuasive Artistry: Studies in New Testament Rhetoric in Honor of George A. Kennedy*, edited by Duane F. Watson, 246–61. JSNTSup 50. Sheffield: Sheffield Academic, 1991.
Hughes, Philip Edgcumbe. *Paul's Second Epistle to the Corinthians*. NICNT. Grand Rapids: Eerdmans, 1962.
Iser, Wolfgang. "Indeterminacy and the Reader's Response in Prose Fiction." In *Aspects of Narrative: Selected Papers from the English Institute*, edited by J. H. Miller, 1–45. New York: Columbia University Press, 1971.
Jackson, Peter. "Retracing the Path: Gesture, Memory, and the Exegesis of Tradition." *History of Religions* 45 (2005) 1–28.
Jeremias, Joachim. "Chiasmus in den Paulusbriefen." *ZNW* 49 (1958) 145–56.
———. "ἄνθρωπος." In *TDNT* 1:364–66.
Jewett, Robert. *Paul's Anthropological Terms: A Study of Their Use in Conflict Settings*. AGSU 10. Leiden: Brill, 1971.
Kaisch, Wilhelm. "ῥύομαι." In *TDNT* 6:998–1003.
Käsemann, Ernst. "The Righteousness of God in Paul." In *New Testament Questions of Today*, translated by W. Montague, 168–82. Philadelphia: Fortress, 1969.
Kennedy, James Houghton. *The Second and Third Epistles of St. Paul to the Corinthians: With Some Proofs of Their Independence and Mutual Relation*. London: Meuthen, 1900.
Kertelge, Karl. "Letter and Spirit in 2 Corinthians 3." In *Paul and the Mosaic Law*, edited by J. D. G. Dunn, 117–30. WUNT 89. Grand Rapids: Eerdmans, 1996.
Kim, Seon. "2 Cor 5:11–21 and the Origin of Reconciliation in Paul's Theology." *NovT* 39 (1997) 360–84.
Kittel, Gottlob. "εἰκών." In *TDNT* 2:392–97.
Klaus, Nathan. *Pivot Patterns in the Former Prophets*. JSOTSup 247. Sheffield: Sheffield Academic, 2007.

Koester, Helmut. "Suffering Servant and Royal Messiah." In *Paul & His World: Interpreting the New Testament in Its Context*, 93–117. Minneapolis: Fortress, 2007.
Kreitzer, L. Joseph. *2 Corinthians*. NTG. Sheffield: Sheffield Academic, 1996.
Kruse, Colin G. *The Second Epistle of Paul to the Corinthians*. TNTC. Grand Rapids: Eerdmans, 1987.
———. "The Offender and the Offense in 2 Cor 2:5 and 7:12." *EvQ* 60 (1988) 129–39.
———. "Paul, the Law, and the Spirit." In *Paul and His Theology*, edited by S. E. Porter, 109–30. Pauline Studies 3. Leiden: Brill, 2006.
Kurz, William. "2 Corinthians: Implied Readers and Canonical Implications." *JSNT* 62 (1996) 43–63.
Kwon, Yon-Gyong. "'Αρραβών as Pledge in Second Corinthians." *NTS* 54 (2008) 525–41.
Ladd, Eldon. *A Theology of the New Testament*. Rev. ed., edited by D. A. Hagner. Grand Rapids: Eerdmans, 1993.
Lambrecht, Jan. "'Reconcile Yourselves . . .:' A Reading of 2 Cor 5,11–21." *Benedictina* 10 (1989) 161–209.
———. "The Favorable Time: A Study of 2 Corinthians 6,2a in its Context." In *Studies in 2 Corinthians*, edited by R. Bieringer and J. Lambrecht, 515–29. BETL 112. Leuven: Leuven University Press, 1994.
———. "Structure and Line of Thought in 1 Cor 15:23–28." *NovT* 32 (1990) 143–51.
———. "Structure and Line of Thought in 2 Cor 2,14—4,6." *Bib* 64 (1983) 344–80.
———. "The Eschatological Outlook in 2 Corinthians 4,7–15." In *Studies in 2 Corinthians*, edited by R. Bieringer and J. Lambrecht, 335–49. BETL 112. Leuven: Leuven University Press, 1995.
———. "Transformation in 2 Corinthians 3,18." *Bib* 64 (1983) 243–54.
———. *Second Corinthians*. SP 8. Collegeville, MN: Liturgical, 1999.
———. "Paul's Understanding of Diakonia in 2 Corinthians 5,18." In *Studies in 2 Corinthians*, edited by R. Bieringer and J. Lambrecht, 413–28. BETL 112. Leuven: Leuven University Press, 1994.
Long, Frederick J. *Ancient Rhetoric and Paul's Apology: The Compositional Unity of 2 Corinthians*. SNTSMS 131. Cambridge: Cambridge University Press, 2004.
Lüdemann, Gerd. *Opposition to Paul in Jewish Christianity*. Translated by M. E. Boring. Minneapolis: Fortress, 1989.
Lund, Nils Wilhelm. "The Presence of Chiasmus in the New Testament." *Journal of Religion* 10 (1930) 74–93.
———. *Chiasmus in the New Testament: A Study in the Form and Function of Chiastic Structures*. Peabody, MA: Hendrickson, 1992.
Luter, A. Boyd, and Michelle Lee. "Philippians as Chiasmus: Key to the Structure, Unity, and Theme Questions." *NTS* 41 (1995) 89–101.
Lütgert, Wilhelm. *Freiheitspredigt und Schwarmgeister in Korinth*. Gütersloh: Bertelsmann, 1908.
Martin, Ralph. *2 Corinthians*. WBC 40. Waco, TX: Word, 1986.
———. "The Opponents of Paul in 2 Corinthians: An Old Issue Revisited." In *Tradition and Interpretation in the New Testament: Essays in Honor of E. Earle Ellis*, edited by G. F. Hawthorne and O. Betz, 279–87. Grand Rapids: Eerdmans, 1987.
———. *Reconciliation: A Study of Paul's Theology*. Louisville: Westminster John Knox, 1981.
Martin, Troy. "Scythian Perspective or Elusive Chiasm: A Reply to Douglas A. Campbell." *NovT* 41 (1999) 256–65.

Martyn, J. Louis. "Epistemology at the Turn of the Ages: 2 Corinthians 5:16." In *Theological Issues in the Letters of Paul*, 89–110. Edinburgh: T. & T. Clark, 1997.
Matera, Frank J. *II Corinthians*. NTL. Louisville: Westminster John Knox, 2003.
———. *New Testament Theology: Exploring Diversity and Unity*. Louisville: Westminster John Knox, 2007.
———. "Paul and the Renewal of the Ministerial Priesthood: A Reflection on 2 Cor 2:14–7:4." *LS* 30 (2005) 49–69.
McCant, Jerry W. *2 Corinthians*. Readings. Sheffield: Sheffield Academic, 1999.
McDermott, J. M. "II Cor. 3: The Old and New Covenants." *Greg* 87 (2006) 25–63.
Mead, Richard. "An Exegesis of 2 Cor 5:14–21." In *Interpreting 2 Corinthians 5:11–21: An Exercise in Hermeneutics*, edited by J. P. Lewis, 143–62. SBEC 17. Lewiston, NY: E. Mellen, 1989.
Meeks, Wayne. *The First Urban Christians: The Social World of the Apostle Paul*. New Haven, CT: Yale University Press, 1980.
Milinovich, Timothy. "Form Criticism and the *Rib* in Isaiah 41:21—42:4." *Biblische Notizen* 136 (2008) 45–62.
Moffatt, James. *An Introduction to the Literature of the New Testament*. International Theological Library. Edinburgh: T. & T. Clark, 1918.
Moloney, Francis J. *Belief in the Word: Reading John 1–4*. Minneapolis: Fortress, 1991.
Moule, C. H. B. *The Second Epistle to the Corinthians*. London: Pickering & Inglis, 1962.
Muilenburg, James. "Form Criticism and Beyond." *JBL* 88 (1969) 1–18.
Murphy-O'Connor, Jerome. *The Theology of the Second Letter to the Corinthians*. NTT. Cambridge: Cambridge University Press, 1991.
———. "Faith and Resurrection in 2 Cor 4:13–14." *RB* 95 (1988) 543–50.
Myers, Charles. "Chiastic Inversion in the Argument of Romans 3–8." *NovT* 35 (1993) 30–47.
Nimis, Stephen. "Cycles and Sequence in Longus' *Daphne and Chloe*." In *Speaking Volumes: Orality and Literacy in the Greco-Roman World*, edited by J. Watson, 51–80. Leiden: Brill, 2001.
Osborne, Grant. "Hermeneutics." In *DPL* 388–97.
Parunak, H. Van Dyke. "Transitional Techniques in the Bible." *JBL* 102 (1983) 525–48.
Pate, C. Marvin. *Adam Christology as the Exegetical and Theological Substructure of 2 Corinthians 4:7—5:21*. Lanham, MD: University Press of America, 1991.
Plummer, Alfred. *A Critical and Exegetical Commentary on the Second Epistle of St. Paul to the Corinthians*. Edinburgh: T. & T. Clark, 1915.
Polhill, John. "Reconciliation at Corinth: 2 Corinthians 4–7." *RevExp* 86 (1989) 325–45.
Porter, Stanley E. "Paul's Concept of Reconciliation, Twice More." In *Paul and His Theology*, edited by S. E. Porter, 131–52. Pauline Studies 3. Leiden: Brill, 2006.
———. "Reconciliation and 2 Cor 5:18–21." In *The Corinthian Correspondence*, edited by R. Bieringer, 515–29. BETL 125. Leuven: Leuven University Press, 1994.
Porter, Stanley and Jeffery Reed. "Philippians as a Macro-chiasm and Its Exegetical Significance." *NTS* 44 (1998) 213–21.
Provence, Thomas. "'Who Is Sufficient for These Things?' An Exegesis of 2 Corinthians ii 15—iii 18." *NovT* 24 (1982) 54–81.
Quast, Kevin. *Reading the Corinthian Correspondence: An Introduction*. New York: Paulist, 1994.
Rabinowitz, Paul. "Whirl without End: Audience-Oriented Criticism." In *Contemporary Literary Theory*, edited by G. D, Atkins and L. Morro, 81–99. Amherst: University of Massachusetts Press, 1989.

Räisänen, Heikki. *Paul and the Law*. Philadelphia: Fortress, 1983.
Ramsay, William. "Historical Commentary on the Epistles to the Corinthians." *ExpTim* 3 (1901) 343–60.
Ridderbos, Herman N. *Paul: An Outline of His Theology*. Translated by J. R. de Witt. Grand Rapids: Eerdmans, 1975.
Sanders, E. P. *Paul and Palestinian Judaism: A Comparison of Patterns of Religion*. Philadelphia: Fortress, 1977.
Savage, Timothy B. *Power through Weakness: Paul's Understanding of the Christian Ministry in 2 Corinthians*. SNTSMS 86. Cambridge: Cambridge University Press, 1996.
Schmithals, Walter. "Die Korintherbriefe als Briefsammlung." *ZNW* 64 (1973) 263–88.
———. *Paul and the Gnostics*. Translated by J. E. Steely. Nashville: Abingdon, 1972.
———. *Die Gnosis in Korinth: Eine Untersuchung zu den Korintherbriefen*. FRLANT 66. Göttingen: Vandenhoeck & Ruprecht, 1965.
Schnelle, Udo. *The History and Theology of the New Testament Writings*. Translated by M. E. Boring. Minneapolis: Fortress, 1994.
———. *Apostle Paul: His Life and Theology*. Translated by M. E. Boring. Grand Rapids: Baker Academic, 2005.
Schniewind, Julius, and Gerhard Friedrich. "ἐπαγγέλλω." In *TDNT* 2:576–86.
Schreiner, Thomas R. *Paul, Apostle of God's Glory in Christ: A Pauline Theology*. Downers Grove, IL: InterVarsity, 2001.
Schrenk, Gottlob. "εὐδοκία." In *TDNT* 2:742–43.
Scroggs, Robin. *The Last Adam: A Study in Pauline Anthropology*. Philadelphia: Fortress, 1966.
Semler, Joh. Salomo. *Paraphrasis II Epistolae ad Corinthios*. Halle: C. H. Hemmerde, 1776.
Shea, William. "Chiasmus and the Structure of David's Lament." *JBL* 105 (1986) 13–25.
Soards, Marion. "The Righteousness of God in the Writings of the Apostle Paul." *BTB* 15 (2004) 104–9.
Stambaugh, John E., and David L. Balch. *The New Testament in Its Social Environment*. LEC 2. Philadelphia: Westminster, 1986.
Stanley, David. "Christ, the Last Adam." In *A Companion to Paul: Readings in Pauline Theology*, edited by M. Taylor, 13–22. New York: Alba House, 1975.
Stegman, Thomas. "Ἐπίστευσα, διὸ ἐλάλησα (2 Corinthians 4:13): Paul's Christological Reading of Psalm 115:1a LXX." *CBQ* 69 (2007) 725–45.
Stock, Augustine. "Chiastic Awareness and Antiquity." *BTB* 14 (1984) 22–28.
Stockhausen, Carol Kern. *Moses' Veil and the Glory of the New Covenant: The Exegetical Substructure of II Cor. 3,1—4,6*. AnBib 116. Rome: Pontifical Biblical Institute, 1989.
Talbert, Charles H. *Reading Corinthians: A Literary and Theological Commentary on 1 and 2 Corinthians*. New York: Crossroad, 1987.
Theissen, Gerd. *The Social Setting of Pauline Christianity: Essays on Corinth*. Philadelphia: Fortress, 1982.
Thiselton, Anthony C. *The First Epistle to the Corinthians*. NIGTC. Grand Rapids: Eerdmans, 2000.
Thurston, Bonnie. "2 Corinthians 2:14–16a: Christ's Incense." *ResQ* 29 (1987) 65–69.
Thrall, Margaret Eleanor. *A Critical and Exegetical Commentary on the Second Epistle to the Corinthians*. 2 vols. ICC. London: T. & T. Clark, 1994–2000.

———. "The Offender and the Offence: A Problem of Detection in 2 Corinthians." In *Scripture: Meaning and Method: Essays Presented to Anthony Tyrell Hanson for His Seventieth Birthday*, edited by B. P. Thompson, 65–78. Hull: Hull University Press, 1987.

———. "Super-Apostles, Servants of Christ, and Servants of Satan." *JSNT* 6 (1980) 42–57.

———. "Salvation Proclaimed V: 2 Corinthians 5:18–21: Reconciliation with God." *ExpTim* 93 (1981–82) 227–32.

Turner, David. "Paul and the Ministry of Reconciliation in 2 Cor 5:11–6:2." *CTR* 4 (1989) 77–95.

Ullen, Magnus. "Reading with the 'Eye of Faith': The Structural Principle of Hawthorne's Romances." *Texas Studies in Literature and Language* 48 (2006) 1–36.

Rad, Gerhard von. "εἰκών." In *TDNT* 2:290–92.

Wallace, Daniel B. *Greek Grammar beyond the Basics: An Exegetical Syntax of the New Testament*. Grand Rapids: Zondervan, 1997.

Wan, Sze-kar. *Power in Weakness: Conflict and Rhetoric in Paul's Second Letter to the Corinthians*. NTC. Harrisburg, PA: Trinity, 2000.

Watson, Francis. "2 Cor. x–xiii and Paul's Painful Visit to the Corinthians." *JTS* 35 (1984) 324–46.

Welch, John W. "Chiasmus in the New Testament." In *Chiasmus in Antiquity: Structures, Analyses, Exegesis*, edited by J. W. Welch, 211–50. Provo, UT: Research Press, 1999.

Westerholm, Stephen. *Israel's Law and the Church's Faith: Paul and His Recent Interpreters*. Grand Rapids: Eerdmans, 1988.

Willis, John. "The Juxtaposition of Synonymous and Chiastic Parallelism in Tricola in Old Testament Hebrew Psalm Poetry." *VT* 29 (1979) 465–80.

Windisch, Hans. "καπηλεύω." In *TDNT* 3:603–5.

Witherington, Ben. *Conflict and Community in Corinth: A Socio-Rhetorical Commentary on 1 and 2 Corinthians*. Grand Rapids: Eerdmans, 1995.

Woodcock, Eldon. "The Seal of the Holy Spirit." *BSac* 155 (1998) 139–63.

Wong, Emily. "The Lord Is the Spirit (2 Cor 3,17a)." *ETL* 61 (1985) 48–72.

Wright, N. T. "On Becoming the Righteousness of God: 2 Corinthians 5:21." In *Pauline Theology*, edited by D. Hay, 2:200–208. SBLSymS. Minneapolis: Fortress, 1991–97.

———. *What Saint Paul Really Said: Was Paul of Tarsus the Real Founder of Christianity?* Grand Rapids: Eerdmans, 1997.

Wuellner, Wilhelm. "Arrangement." In *Handbook on Classical Rhetoric in the Hellenistic Period, 330 B.C.–A.D. 400*, edited by S. E. Porter, 51–88. Leiden: Brill, 1997.

Young, Frances M., and David F. Ford. *Meaning and Truth in 2 Corinthians*. Grand Rapids: Eerdmans, 1987.

Yudkowsky, Rachel. "Chaos or Chiasm? The Structure of Abraham's Life." *JBQ* 35 (2007) 109–14.

www.ingramcontent.com/pod-product-compliance
Lightning Source LLC
Chambersburg PA
CBHW062047220426
43662CB00010B/1686